What Your Colleagues Are Saying . . .

"This book is a 'must-go-to' for classroom teachers as well as for coaches and leaders who support teachers in implementation of the Common Core Mathematics Standards. Connecting both the content standards and the practice standards with the effective teaching practices (Principles to Actions, NCTM, 2014), Linda Gojak and Ruth Harbin Miles provide the practical resources to enhance teachers' understanding of the mathematics in the standards in ways that will bring them alive for all students. This is a book that will be the cornerstone of our professional development."

—Cathy Martin, **Director of PreK–12 Mathematics Denver Public Schools, Denver, CO**

"The Common Core Companion series for ELA became a runaway bestseller because it made instructional planning to address the standards manageable—and meaningful. Jim Burke and his co-authors put best practices first, equipping teachers with the 'what-it-looks-like' teaching ideas for each and every standard. Teachers have been clamoring for a math version for more than a year, and now it's here! Linda Gojak and Ruth Harbin Miles do an amazing job demystifying the standards for grades 3–5. The authors have created a format and design that will have teachers dog-earing this book as they plan for instruction!"

—Leslie Blauman, **Author of *The Common Core Companion, Grades 3–5***

"This companion supports implementation of the Common Core Mathematics Standards with attention to the instructional shifts: focus, coherence, and rigor. The standard-by-standard examples provide an image of what the standards looks like in the classroom for both teachers and students. The attention to students' conceptions helps teachers plan with student thinking in mind and contributes to the collaborative work of grade-level teams."

—Nicole Rigelman, **Associate Professor Portland State University, Portland, OR**

"This practical, exemplary resource supports teachers in their understanding and learning of the Common Core Mathematics Standards. The book does an excellent job of unpacking what the standards mean and makes explicit connections both to the Standards for Mathematical Practice and common student misconceptions. It is an ideal choice for a book study at either the grade or school level."

—Jeffrey Shih, **Associate Professor**

gas

D1292541

The Common Core Companion at a Glance

Suggested Materials for This Domain: Provides teachers with a list of materials that will be helpful in introducing the concepts in this domain. "Reproducible" indicates that there is a handout that you can use to make multiple copies in the Resources section in the back of this book.

Operations and Algebraic Thinking

Domain Overview

GRADE 3

The major work of this domain in Grade 3 is to develop students' conceptual understanding of multiplication and division by using concrete materials to model multiplication and then relate their understanding of multiplication to division. Multiplication problem situations provide a context for understanding multiplication as finding the total number of items given a number of equal groups and the number of items in each group. Division problem situations develop the meaning of division and how it is related to multiplication. When you know the total number of items and the number of groups, you can determine how many items in a group, or, when you know the total number of items and the number of items in a group, you can find the number of groups. All of these activities culminate in the expectation that students will demonstrate fluency with multiplication and division within 100 using single-digit factors.

GRADE 4

Students in Grade 4 continue to solve problems using the four operations with whole numbers. New to this grade level are problem situations that involve multiplicative comparisons. Students become familiar with factors and multiples and how they relate to prime and composite numbers. They work in a variety of contexts to generate and analyze patterns.

GRADE 5

In preparation for the Expressions and Equations domain in grades 6–8, fifth graders begin to explore, interpret, and evaluate numerical expressions. Work with patterns that began in Grade 4 extends to generating patterns, forming ordered pairs, graphing on a coordinate plane, and then analyzing the graphical representations.

SUGGESTED MATERIALS FOR THIS DOMAIN

3	4	5	
✓	✓	✓	Hundreds chart (Reproducible 1)
✓	✓	✓	Chips, counters
✓	✓	✓	Cups, containers, other objects to represent "groups"
✓	✓	✓	Place value chart to hundreds (Reproducible 2)
✓	✓	✓	Square tiles
✓	✓	✓	Grid paper (Reproducible 3)
✓	✓	✓	Pattern blocks
✓	✓	✓	Number cards (such as a deck of playing cards)

KEY VOCABULARY

3	4	5	
✓	✓	✓	**add** to combine or join together related words: *add, and, plus, join, put together, (+)*
✓	✓	✓	**addend** any of the numbers added to find a sum
✓	✓	✓	**area model** a concrete model for multiplication or division made up of a rectangle. The length and width represent the factors and the area represents the product. 3×5 5×3
✓	✓	✓	**array model** a concrete model for multiplication in which items are arranged in rows and columns. Each row (or column) represents the number of groups and each column (or row) represents the number of items in a group. $5 \times 4 = 20$ 5 rows of 4 = 20
✓	✓	✓	*** associative property of multiplication** an extension of the commutative property; to change the order and group two factors to find convenient products (such as 10) in order to make the multiplication easier. Students may begin to use parentheses at this level. $7 \times 8 \times 5 = 7 \times (8 \times 5) = 7 \times 40 = 280$
✓	✓	✓	*** commutative property of multiplication** reversing the order of the factors does not change the product $8 \times 5 = 40$ and $5 \times 8 = 40$ therefore the product of $8 \times 5 = 5 \times 8$

Domain Overview: Gives a brief description of the big ideas, allowing you to see how the mathematical ideas develop across grade levels.

Key Vocabulary: Vocabulary included in the domain with grade levels at which that term is used. This terminology can be used for building a word wall in the classroom. Students should be able to use these terms in talking about mathematics in discussions unless otherwise noted. Standard for Mathematical Practice 6: Attend to Precision calls for students to use mathematical terminology appropriately.

Domain: General mathematical topic for this group of Standards.

Cluster: Statements that summarize groups of related Standards. Note that Standards from different clusters may sometimes be closely related, because mathematics is a connected subject.

Identifying number for this cluster: Grade, domain, cluster

Grade, domain, cluster

Domain

Each cluster begins with a brief description of the mathematics in that cluster.

Operations and Algebraic Thinking
3.OA.A.*

Cluster A

Represent and solve problems involving multiplication and division.

STANDARD 1   **3.OA.A.1:** Interpret products of whole numbers, e.g., interpret 5×7 as the total number of objects in 5 groups of 7 objects each. *For example, describe a context in which a total number of objects can be expressed as 5×7.*

STANDARD 2   **3.OA.A.2:** Interpret whole-number quotients of whole numbers, e.g., interpret $56 \div 8$ as the number of objects in each share when 56 objects are partitioned equally into 8 shares, or as a number of shares when 56 objects are partitioned into equal shares of 8 objects each. *For example, describe a context in which a number of shares or a number of groups can be expressed as $56 \div 8$.*

STANDARD 3   **3.OA.A.3:** Use multiplication and division within 100 to solve word problems in situations involving equal groups, arrays, and measurement quantities, e.g., by using drawings and equations with a symbol for the unknown number to represent the problem.[1]

[1] See Table 2 in the Resources, page 256.

STANDARD 4   **3.OA.A.4:** Determine the unknown whole number in a multiplication or division equation relating three whole numbers. *For example, determine the unknown number that makes the equation true in each of the equations $8 \times ? = 48, 5 = \_ \div 3, 6 \times 6 = ?$*

*Major cluster

Operations and Algebraic Thinking   3.OA.A

Cluster A: Represent and solve problems involving multiplication and division.
Grade 3 Overview

Third grade students explore the meaning of multiplication as finding the total number of objects (product) when they know the number of groups (factor) and the number of items in each group (factor). The relationship between multiplication and division helps students understand that when dividing, they are finding the number of groups (missing factor) when they know the total count (product) and the number of items in a group (factor), or finding the number of items in a group (missing factor) when they know the number of groups (factor) and the total count (product). Problem solving situations and activities that include a variety of representations showing equal-sized groups, arrays, and area models lay the foundation for multiplication and division of whole numbers.

Note that these Standards are not linear. It is important for students to understand the meaning of multiplication and division (3.OA.1, 3.OA.2) through the use of problem situations (3.OA.3). As students demonstrate understanding they begin to relate models to symbolic notation (3.OA.4). The use of symbols for easier facts and relating the symbols to fact families should be happening as students continue to use models to solve problems with the more difficult facts.

Standards for Mathematical Practice
SFMP 1. Make sense of problems and persevere in solving them.
SFMP 2. Use quantitative reasoning.
SFMP 3. Construct viable arguments and critique the reasoning of others.
SFMP 4. Model with mathematics.
SFMP 5. Use appropriate tools strategically.
SFMP 6. Attend to precision.
SFMP 7. Look for and make use of structure.
SFMP 8. Look for and express regularity in repeated reasoning.

Related Content Standards
2.OA.C.3   2.OA.C.4   4.OA.A.1   4.OA.A.2

Standards: Mathematical statements that define what students should understand and be able to do.

Related Content Standards: Provides a list of Standards connected to this topic in other grade levels as well as Standards in this grade level related to this topic that are in other domains. We recommend you look at the related Standards as you plan your instruction for this cluster.

Standards for Mathematical Practice: Although it is likely you will use a variety of Standards for Mathematical Practice in teaching each cluster, this section gives examples of how you might incorporate some of the practices into your instruction on this topic.

You will find the following components for each Standard in the cluster:

Standard: The Standard as written in the Common Core followed by an explanation of the meaning of the mathematics in that Standard, including examples.

Notes: We have included space beneath each Standard for you to take notes as you study its mathematical content. This might include vocabulary, materials, resources you want to use, or an explanation of the Standard in your own words.

What the TEACHER does: An overview of actions the teacher might take in introducing and teaching the Standard. This is not meant to be all-inclusive, but rather to give you an idea of what classroom instruction might look like. We included illustrations of how to use materials to teach a concept when using models and representations is called for in the Standard.

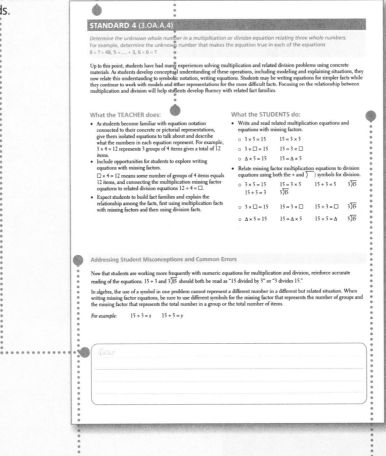

Addressing Student Misconceptions and Common Errors: Each Standard concludes with a description of possible student misconceptions or common student errors around the Standard and suggested actions to address those misconceptions or errors.

What the STUDENTS do: Some examples of what the students might be doing as they explore and begin to understand the Standard. Again, this is not intended to be directive but rather to frame what student actions might look like.

Sample Planning Page: We have provided one complete sample planning page for one Standard at the end of each cluster in each grade level. Although it may not be the final lesson plan, it does provide the areas you should consider while planning your lessons.

Goal: What is the purpose of this activity and how does it connect to previous (and future) ideas?

Standards for Mathematical Practice: What mathematical practices can you emphasize in this activity?

Planning Page: A planning template is provided at the end of each cluster. This template is provided for your use as you consider instructional actions around a particular Standard. You might want to make copies of this page and use them for each Standard within the cluster. This is not intended to be an all-inclusive lesson plan. Rather, it gives you a place to record your thoughts about teaching a mathematical topic as you read the Standard.

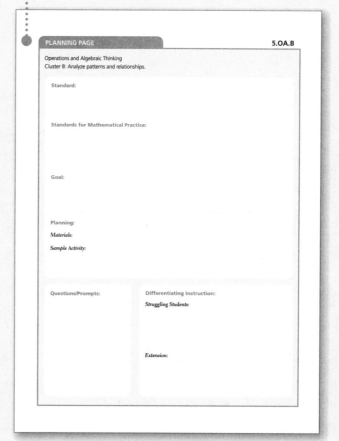

Sample PLANNING PAGE   5.OA.A

Operations and Algebraic Thinking
Cluster A: Write and interpret numerical expressions.

Standard: 5.OA.A.1. *Use parentheses, brackets, or braces in numerical expressions, and evaluate expressions with these symbols.*

Standards for Mathematical Practice:
SFMP 6. Attend to precision.
Students apply previous work with order of operations and pay close attention to the use of parentheses and the order of operations.

Goal:
Students will practice using order of operations to play a game in which they need to write expressions to make a given number.

Planning:

Materials: Dice or spinner with numbers 1 through 9, teacher-made cards with numbers from 15 to 30.

Sample Activity:
Students play in groups of four. Each person spins the spinner or rolls a die. They record the four numbers for that round. The teacher draws a card and gives the target number. Groups work together to make expressions using their four numbers following order of operations, including using parentheses, that will make the target number. They may use two, three, or all four of the numbers.

Students share their expressions and explain how they make the target using order of operations.

Sample: Playing numbers 2, 3, 3, 5 Target 16

$3 + 3 + (2 \times 5)$ or $3 + 3 + 2 \times 5$

Questions/Prompts:

As students share their expressions, you may find that as they explain what they did, it does not match how they wrote the equation. Ask questions to clarify student thinking, such as, "What did you do first? How did you write that in your equation?" You may also want to have them clarify why.

$3 + 3 + 2 \times 5$ is not equal to 40.

Differentiating Instruction:

Struggling Students: Work with a smaller range of numbers or use three numbers to make the target number.

Although parentheses may not be needed, students may find it easier to include parentheses in their expressions.

Extension: Students who easily find expressions should be encouraged to find more expressions. They can also write their expressions in different ways. For example, $3 + 3 + (2 \times 5)$ could also be written as

$2 \times 5 + 3 + 3$.

These students also work on being precise in their explanations of how their expressions are accurate.

PLANNING PAGE   5.OA.B

Operations and Algebraic Thinking
Cluster B: Analyze patterns and relationships.

Standard:

Standards for Mathematical Practice:

Goal:

Planning:

Materials:

Sample Activity:

Questions/Prompts:

Differentiating Instruction:

Struggling Students:

Extension:

Planning: What materials will you use to teach this Standard?

Sample Activity: An example of an activity that addresses this standard is provided.

Questions/Prompts: It is important to anticipate student thinking throughout the activity. Think about the questions or prompts you might give to help build student understanding and encourage student thinking so you do not find yourself telling students what to do.

Differentiating Instruction: How can you tweak the activity to address the needs of students who are struggling? How can you extend the activity for students who demonstrate understanding of the mathematics?

Resources: In the Resources section at the end of the book you will find an overview of each practice for teachers of grades 3–5 to consider and implement: Table 1, Addition and Subtraction Situations, Grades 3–5, which explains problem solving situations for addition and subtraction, and Table 2, Multiplication and Division Situations, Grades 3–5, which explains problem solving situations for multiplication and division and provides strategic competencies for students. Other resources include Table 3, which offers an overview of the Standards for Mathematical Practice and what each practice Standard means for students in grades 3–5; Table 4, the effective teaching practices from NCTM's *Principles to Actions;* and reproducibles for some of the materials recommended for each grade level.

An example of a problem that exemplifies the situation.

Equation(s) that represent the situation.

Table 1   Addition and Subtraction Situations, Grades 3–5

Situation	Problem	Equation(s)
Add to—result unknown	Frank had 235 pennies. Mark gave him 156 more. How many pennies does Frank have?	$235 + 156 = p$
Add to—change unknown	Frank had 235 pennies. Mark gave him some more. Now Frank has 391 pennies. How many pennies did Mark give to Frank?	$235 + p = 391$
Add—start unknown	Frank had some pennies in his piggy bank. Mark gave him 156 more. Now Frank has 391 pennies. How many pennies did Frank have at the beginning?	$p + 156 = 391$
Take from—result unknown	Frank had 45 pennies. He spent 29 pennies on a package of jawbreakers. How many pennies does he have left?	$45 - 29 = p$
Take from—change unknown	Frank had 45 pennies. He spent some pennies on a pack of jawbreakers. Now Frank has 16 pennies. How much did he spend on the jawbreaker?	$45 - p = 16$
Take from—start unknown	Frank had some pennies in his bank. He spent 29 pennies on a package of jawbreakers. Now he has 16 pennies. How many pennies did Frank have in his bank?	$p - 29 = 16$
Put together take apart—total unknown	Anna has been saving coins. She has 348 pennies and 267 nickels. How many coins does she have?	$348 + 267 = p$
Put together take apart—addend unknown	Anna 615 coins in her piggy bank. She has 348 pennies and the rest are nickels. How many coins are nickels?	$615 = 348 + p$
Put together take apart—addends unknown	Anna has 11 coins. Some are pennies and some are nickels. How many pennies and how many nickels could Anna have?	$1 + 10 = 11$ $2 + 9 = 11$ $3 + 8 = 11$ $4 + 7 = 11$ $5 + 6 = 11$ $6 + 5 = 11$ $7 + 4 = 11$ $8 + 3 = 11$ $9 + 2 = 11$ $10 + 1 = 11$

Various problem situations for addition and subtraction.

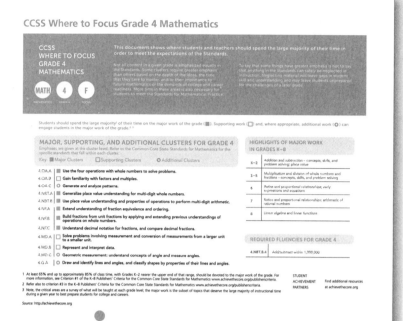

CCSS Where to Focus Grade 4 Mathematics

CCSS Where to Focus Mathematics: The major content focus for each grade level is identified on the grade-level focus charts included in the Resources.

Reproducibles: A variety of reproducibles can be duplicated and used by students in the classroom when working with concrete materials.

Reproducible 1. Hundreds Chart

1	2	3	4	5	6	7	8	9	10
11	12	13	14	15	16	17	18	19	20
21	22	23	24	25	26	27	28	29	30
31	32	33	34	35	36	37	38	39	40
41	42	43	44	45	46	47	48	49	50
51	52	53	54	55	56	57	58	59	60
61	62	63	64	65	66	67	68	69	70
71	72	73	74	75	76	77	78	79	80
81	82	83	84	85	86	87	88	89	90
91	92	93	94	95	96	97	98	99	100

Quick Reference Guide

GRADE 3

A. Represent and solve problems involving multiplication and division.

1. Interpret products of whole numbers, e.g., interpret 5×7 as the total number of objects in 5 groups of 7 objects each. *For example, describe a context in which a total number of objects can be expressed as 5×7.*

2. Interpret whole-number quotients of whole numbers, e.g., interpret $56 \div 8$ as the number of objects in each share when 56 objects are partitioned equally into 8 shares, or as a number of shares when 56 objects are partitioned into equal shares of 8 objects each. *For example, describe a context in which a number of shares or a number of groups can be expressed as $56 \div 8$.*

3. Use multiplication and division within 100 to solve word problems in situations involving equal groups, arrays, and measurement quantities, e.g., by using drawings and equations with a symbol for the unknown number to represent the problem.[1]

4. Determine the unknown whole number in a multiplication or division equation relating three whole numbers. *For example, determine the unknown number that makes the equation true in each of the equations $8 \times ? = 48$, $5 = \_ \div 3$, $6 \times 6 = ?$.*

B. Understand properties of multiplication and the relationship between multiplication and division.

5. Apply properties of operations as strategies to multiply and divide.[2] *Examples: If $6 \times 4 = 24$ is known, then $4 \times 6 = 24$ is also known. (Commutative property of multiplication.) $3 \times 5 \times 2$ can be found by $3 \times 5 = 15$, then $15 \times 2 = 30$, or by $5 \times 2 = 10$, then $3 \times 10 = 30$. (Associative property of multiplication.) Knowing that $8 \times 5 = 40$ and $8 \times 2 = 16$, one can find 8×7 as $8 \times (5 + 2) = (8 \times 5) + (8 \times 2) = 40 + 16 = 56$. (Distributive property.)*

6. Understand division as an unknown-factor problem. *For example, find $32 \div 8$ by finding the number that makes 32 when multiplied by 8.*

C. Multiply and divide within 100.

7. Fluently multiply and divide within 100, using strategies such as the relationship between multiplication and division (e.g., knowing that $8 \times 5 = 40$, one knows $40 \div 5 = 8$) or properties of operations. By the end of Grade 3, know from memory all products of two one-digit numbers.

D. Solve problems involving the four operations, and identify and explain patterns in arithmetic.

8. Solve two-step word problems using the four operations. Represent these problems using equations with a letter standing for the unknown quantity. Assess the reasonableness of answers using mental computation and estimation strategies including rounding.[3]

9. Identify arithmetic patterns (including patterns in the addition table or multiplication table), and explain them using properties of operations. *For example, observe that 4 times a number is always even, and explain why 4 times a number can be decomposed into two equal addends.*

1. See Table 2 in the Resources, page 256.

2. Students need not use formal terms for these properties.

3. This Standard is limited to problems posed with whole numbers and having whole-number answers; students should know how to perform operations in the conventional order when there are no parentheses to specify a particular order (Order of Operations).

A. Use place value understanding and properties of operations to perform multi-digit arithmetic.[1]

1. Use place value understanding to round whole numbers to the nearest 10 or 100.

2. Fluently add and subtract within 1000 using strategies and algorithms based on place value, properties of operations, and/or the relationship between addition and subtraction.

3. Multiply one-digit whole numbers by multiples of 10 in the range 10–90 (e.g., 9×80, 5×60) using strategies based on place value and properties of operations.

1. A range of algorithms may be used.

A. Develop understanding of fractions as numbers.

1. Understand a fraction $\frac{1}{b}$ as the quantity formed by 1 part when a whole is partitioned into b equal parts; understand a fraction $\frac{a}{b}$ as the quantity formed by a parts of size $\frac{1}{b}$.

2. Understand a fraction as a number on the number line; represent fractions on a number line diagram.

   a. Represent a fraction $\frac{1}{b}$ on a number line diagram by defining the interval from 0 to 1 as the whole and partitioning it into b equal parts. Recognize that each

---

Note: More detail and examples from individual Standards can be found in the complete Standards document available at www.corestandards.org.

part has size $\frac{1}{b}$ and that the endpoint of the part based at 0 locates the number $\frac{1}{b}$ on the number line.

b. Represent a fraction $\frac{a}{b}$ on a number line diagram by marking off a lengths $\frac{1}{b}$ from 0. Recognize that the resulting interval has size $\frac{a}{b}$ and that its endpoint locates the number $\frac{a}{b}$ on the number line.

3. Explain equivalence of fractions in special cases, and compare fractions by reasoning about their size.

a. Understand two fractions as equivalent (equal) if they are the same size, or the same point on a number line.

b. Recognize and generate simple equivalent fractions, e.g., $\frac{1}{2} = \frac{2}{4}$, $\frac{4}{6} = \frac{2}{3}$. Explain why the fractions are equivalent, e.g., by using a visual fraction model.

c. Express whole numbers as fractions, and recognize fractions that are equivalent to whole numbers. *Examples: Express 3 in the form $3 = \frac{3}{1}$; recognize that $\frac{6}{1} = 6$; locate $\frac{4}{4}$ and 1 at the same point of a number line diagram.*

d. Compare two fractions with the same numerator or the same denominator by reasoning about their size. Recognize that comparisons are valid only when the two fractions refer to the same whole. Record the results of comparisons with the symbols >, =, or <, and justify the conclusions, e.g., by using a visual fraction model.

1. Grade 3 expectations in this domain are limited to fractions with denominators 2, 3, 4, 6, and 8.

Measurement and Data   3.MD

A. Solve problems involving measurement and estimation of intervals of time, liquid volumes, and masses of objects.

1. Tell and write time to the nearest minute and measure time intervals in minutes. Solve word problems involving addition and subtraction of time intervals in minutes, e.g., by representing the problem on a number line diagram.

2. Measure and estimate liquid volumes and masses of objects using standard units of grams (g), kilograms (kg), and liters (l).[1] Add, subtract, multiply, or divide to solve one-step word problems involving masses or volumes that are given in the same units, e.g., by using drawings (such as a beaker with a measurement scale) to represent the problem.[2]

B. Represent and interpret data.

3. Draw a scaled picture graph and a scaled bar graph to represent a data set with several categories. Solve one- and two-step "how many more" and "how many less" problems using information presented in scaled bar graphs. *For example, draw a bar graph in which each square in the bar graph might represent 5 pets.*

4. Generate measurement data by measuring lengths using rulers marked with halves and fourths of an inch. Show the data by making a line plot, where the horizontal scale is marked off in appropriate units—whole numbers, halves, or quarters.

C. Geometric measurement: Understand concepts of area and relate area to multiplication and to addition.

5. Recognize area as an attribute of plane figures and understand concepts of area measurement.

a. A square with side length 1 unit, called "a unit square," is said to have "one square unit" of area, and can be used to measure area.

b. A plane figure which can be covered without gaps or overlaps by n unit squares is said to have an area of n square units.

6. Measure areas by counting unit squares (square cm, square m, square in, square ft, and improvised units).

7. Relate area to the operations of multiplication and addition.

a. Find the area of a rectangle with whole-number side lengths by tiling it, and show that the area is the same as would be found by multiplying the side lengths.

b. Multiply side lengths to find areas of rectangles with whole-number side lengths in the context of solving real world and mathematical problems, and represent whole-number products as rectangular areas in mathematical reasoning.

c. Use tiling to show in a concrete case that the area of a rectangle with whole-number side lengths a and $b + c$ is the sum of $a \times b$ and $a \times c$. Use area models to represent the distributive property in mathematical reasoning.

d. Recognize area as additive. Find areas of rectilinear figures by decomposing them into non-overlapping rectangles and adding the areas of the non-overlapping parts, applying this technique to solve real world problems.

D. Geometric measurement: Recognize perimeter as an attribute of plane figures and distinguish between linear and area measures.

8. Solve real world and mathematical problems involving perimeters of polygons, including finding the perimeter given the side lengths, finding an unknown side length, and exhibiting rectangles with the same perimeter and different areas or with the same area and different perimeters.

1. Excludes compound units such as cm^3 and finding the geometric volume of a container.

2. Excludes multiplicative comparison problems (problems involving notions of "times as much"; see Table 2 in the Resources, page 256).

A. Reason with shapes and their attributes.

1. Understand that shapes in different categories (e.g., rhombuses, rectangles, and others) may share attributes (e.g., having four sides), and that the shared attributes can define a larger category (e.g., quadrilaterals). Recognize rhombuses, rectangles, and squares as examples of quadrilaterals, and draw examples of quadrilaterals that do not belong to any of these subcategories.

2. Partition shapes into parts with equal areas. Express the area of each part as a unit fraction of the whole. *For example, partition a shape into 4 parts with equal area, and describe the area of each part as $\frac{1}{4}$ of the area of the shape.*

GRADE 4

A. Use the four operations with whole numbers to solve problems.

1. Interpret a multiplication equation as a comparison, e.g., interpret $35 = 5 \times 7$ as a statement that 35 is 5 times as many as 7 and 7 times as many as 5. Represent verbal statements of multiplicative comparisons as multiplication equations.

2. Multiply or divide to solve word problems involving multiplicative comparison, e.g., by using drawings and equations with a symbol for the unknown number to represent the problem, distinguishing multiplicative comparison from additive comparison.[1]

3. Solve multistep word problems posed with whole numbers and having whole-number answers using the four operations, including problems in which remainders must be interpreted. Represent these problems using equations with a letter standing for the unknown quantity. Assess the reasonableness of answers using mental computation and estimation strategies including rounding.

B. Gain familiarity with factors and multiples.

4. Find all factor pairs for a whole number in the range 1–100. Recognize that a whole number is a multiple of each of its factors. Determine whether a given whole number in the range 1–100 is a multiple of a given one-digit number. Determine whether a given whole number in the range 1–100 is prime or composite.

C. Generate and analyze patterns.

5. Generate a number or shape pattern that follows a given rule. Identify apparent features of the pattern that were not explicit in the rule itself. *For example, given the rule "Add 3" and the starting number 1, generate terms in the resulting sequence and observe that the terms appear to alternate between odd and even numbers. Explain informally why the numbers will continue to alternate in this way.*

1. See Table 2 in the Resources, page 256.

A. Generalize place value understanding for multi-digit whole numbers.

1. Recognize that in a multi-digit whole number, a digit in one place represents ten times what it represents in the place to its right. *For example, recognize that $700 \div 70 = 10$ by applying concepts of place value and division.*

2. Read and write multi-digit whole numbers using base-ten numerals, number names, and expanded form. Compare two multi-digit numbers based on meanings of the digits in each place, using >, =, and < symbols to record the results of comparisons.

3. Use place value understanding to round multi-digit whole numbers to any place.

B. Use place value understanding and properties of operations to perform multi-digit arithmetic.

4. Fluently add and subtract multi-digit whole numbers using the standard algorithm.

5. Multiply a whole number of up to four digits by a one-digit whole number, and multiply two two-digit numbers, using strategies based on place value and the properties of operations. Illustrate and explain the calculation by using equations, rectangular arrays, and/or area models.

6. Find whole-number quotients and remainders with up to four-digit dividends and one-digit divisors, using strategies based on place value, the properties of operations, and/or the relationship between multiplication and division. Illustrate and explain the calculation by using equations, rectangular arrays, and/or area models.

1. Grade 4 expectations in this domain are limited to whole numbers less than or equal to 1,000,000.

A. Extend understanding of fraction equivalence and ordering.

1. Explain why a fraction $\frac{a}{b}$ is equivalent to a fraction $\frac{(n \times a)}{(n \times b)}$ by using visual fraction models, with attention to how the number and size of the parts differ even though the two fractions themselves are the same size. Use this principle to recognize and generate equivalent fractions.

2. Compare two fractions with different numerators and different denominators, e.g., by creating common denominators or numerators, or by comparing to a benchmark fraction such as $\frac{1}{2}$. Recognize that comparisons are valid only when the two fractions refer to the same whole. Record the results of comparisons with symbols >, =, or <, and justify the conclusions, e.g., by using a visual fraction model.

B. Build fractions from unit fractions by applying and extending previous understandings of operations on whole numbers.

3. Understand a fraction $\frac{a}{b}$ with $a > 1$ as a sum of fractions $\frac{1}{b}$.

   a. Understand addition and subtraction of fractions as joining and separating parts referring to the same whole.

   b. Decompose a fraction into a sum of fractions with the same denominator in more than one way, recording each decomposition by an equation. Justify decompositions, e.g., by using a visual fraction model. *Examples:* $\frac{3}{8} = \frac{1}{8} + \frac{1}{8} + \frac{1}{8}$; $\frac{3}{8} = \frac{1}{8} + \frac{2}{8}$; $2\frac{1}{8} = 1 + 1 + \frac{1}{8} = \frac{8}{8} + \frac{8}{8} + \frac{1}{8}$.

   c. Add and subtract mixed numbers with like denominators, e.g., by replacing each mixed number with an equivalent fraction, and/or by using properties of operations and the relationship between addition and subtraction.

   d. Solve word problems involving addition and subtraction of fractions referring to the same whole and having like denominators, e.g., by using visual fraction models and equations to represent the problem.

4. Apply and extend previous understandings of multiplication to multiply a fraction by a whole number.

   a. Understand a fraction $\frac{a}{b}$ as a multiple of $\frac{1}{b}$. *For example, use a visual fraction model to represent $\frac{5}{4}$ as the product $5 \times \frac{1}{4}$, recording the conclusion by the equation $\frac{5}{4} = 5 \times \frac{1}{4}$.*

   b. Understand a multiple of $\frac{a}{b}$ as a multiple of $\frac{1}{b}$, and use this understanding to multiply a fraction by a whole number. *For example, use a visual fraction model to express $3 \times \frac{2}{5}$ as $6 \times \frac{1}{5}$, recognizing this product as $\frac{6}{5}$. (In general, $n \times \frac{a}{b} = \frac{(n \times a)}{b}$.)*

   c. Solve word problems involving multiplication of a fraction by a whole number, e.g., by using visual fraction models and equations to represent the problem. *For example, if each person at a party will eat $\frac{3}{8}$ of a pound of roast beef, and there will be 5 people at the party, how many pounds of roast beef will be needed? Between what two whole numbers does your answer lie?*

C. Understand decimal notation for fractions, and compare decimal fractions.

5. Express a fraction with denominator 10 as an equivalent fraction with denominator 100, and use this technique to add two fractions with respective denominators 10 and 100.[2] *For example, express $\frac{3}{10}$ as $\frac{30}{100}$, and add $\frac{3}{10} + \frac{4}{100} = \frac{34}{100}$.*

6. Use decimal notation for fractions with denominators 10 or 100. *For example, rewrite 0.62 as $\frac{62}{100}$; describe a length as 0.62 meters; locate 0.62 on a number line diagram.*

7. Compare two decimals to hundredths by reasoning about their size. Recognize that comparisons are valid only when the two decimals refer to the same whole. Record the results of comparisons with the symbols >, =, or <, and justify the conclusions, e.g., by using a visual model.

1. Grade 4 expectations in this domain are limited to fractions with denominators 2, 3, 4, 5, 6, 8, 10, 12, and 100.

2. Students who can generate equivalent fractions can develop strategies for adding fractions with unlike denominators in general. But addition and subtraction with unlike denominators in general is not a requirement at this grade.

Measurement and Data   4.MD

A. Solve problems involving measurement and conversion of measurements from a larger unit to a smaller unit.

1. Know relative sizes of measurement units within one system of units including km, m, cm; kg, g; lb, oz.; l, ml; hr, min, sec. Within a single system of measurement, express measurements in a larger unit in terms of a smaller unit. Record measurement equivalents in a two-column table. *For example, know that 1 ft is 12 times as long as 1 in. Express the length of a 4 ft snake as 48 in. Generate a conversion table for feet and inches listing the number pairs (1, 12), (2, 24), (3, 36), . . .*

2. Use the four operations to solve word problems involving distances, intervals of time, liquid volumes, masses of objects, and money, including problems involving simple fractions or decimals, and problems that require expressing measurements given in a larger unit in terms of a smaller unit. Represent measurement quantities using diagrams such as number line diagrams that feature a measurement scale.

3. Apply the area and perimeter formulas for rectangles in real world and mathematical problems. *For example, find the width of a rectangular room given the area of the flooring and the length, by viewing the area formula as a multiplication equation with an unknown factor.*

B. Represent and interpret data.

4. Make a line plot to display a data set of measurements in fractions of a unit ($\frac{1}{2}, \frac{1}{4}, \frac{1}{8}$). Solve problems involving addition and subtraction of fractions by using information presented in line plots. *For example, from a line plot find and interpret the difference in length between the longest and shortest specimens in an insect collection.*

C. Geometric measurement: Understand concepts of angle and measure angles.

5. Recognize angles as geometric shapes that are formed wherever two rays share a common endpoint, and understand concepts of angle measurement:

   a. An angle is measured with reference to a circle with its center at the common endpoint of the rays, by considering the fraction of the circular arc between the points where the two rays intersect the circle. An angle that turns through $\frac{1}{360}$ of a circle is called a "one-degree angle," and can be used to measure angles.

   b. An angle that turns through n one-degree angles is said to have an angle measure of n degrees.

6. Measure angles in whole-number degrees using a protractor. Sketch angles of specified measure.

7. Recognize angle measure as additive. When an angle is decomposed into non-overlapping parts, the angle measure of the whole is the sum of the angle measures of the parts. Solve addition and subtraction problems to find unknown angles on a diagram in real world and mathematical problems, e.g., by using an equation with a symbol for the unknown angle measure.

Geometry   4.G

A. Draw and identify lines and angles, and classify shapes by properties of their lines and angles.

1. Draw points, lines, line segments, rays, angles (right, acute, obtuse), and perpendicular and parallel lines. Identify these in two-dimensional figures.

2. Classify two-dimensional figures based on the presence or absence of parallel or perpendicular lines, or the presence or absence of angles of a specified size. Recognize right triangles as a category, and identify right triangles.

3. Recognize a line of symmetry for a two-dimensional figure as a line across the figure such that the figure can be folded along the line into matching parts. Identify line-symmetric figures and draw lines of symmetry.

GRADE 5

Operations and Algebraic Thinking   5.OA

A. Write and interpret numerical expressions.

1. Use parentheses, brackets, or braces in numerical expressions, and evaluate expressions with these symbols.

2. Write simple expressions that record calculations with numbers, and interpret numerical expressions without evaluating them. *For example, express the calculation "add 8 and 7, then multiply by 2" as $2 \times (8 + 7)$. Recognize that $3 \times (18932 + 921)$ is three times as large as $18932 + 921$, without having to calculate the indicated sum or product.*

B. Analyze patterns and relationships.

3. Generate two numerical patterns using two given rules. Identify apparent relationships between corresponding terms. Form ordered pairs consisting of corresponding terms from the two patterns, and graph the ordered pairs on a coordinate plane. *For example, given the rule "Add 3" and the starting number 0, and given the rule "Add 6" and the starting number 0, generate terms in the resulting sequences, and observe that the terms in one sequence are twice the corresponding terms in the other sequence. Explain informally why this is so.*

Number and Operations in Base Ten   5.NBT

A. Understand the place value system.

1. Recognize that in a multi-digit number, a digit in one place represents 10 times as much as it represents in the place to its right and $\frac{1}{10}$ of what it represents in the place to its left.

2. Explain patterns in the number of zeros of the product when multiplying a number by powers of 10, and explain patterns in the placement of the decimal point when a decimal is multiplied or divided by a power of 10. Use whole-number exponents to denote powers of 10.

3. Read, write, and compare decimals to thousandths.

   a. Read and write decimals to thousandths using base-ten numerals, number names, and expanded form, e.g., $347.392 = 3 \times 100 + 4 \times 10 + 7 \times 1 + 3 \times \frac{1}{10} + 9 \times \frac{1}{100} + 2 \times \frac{1}{1000}$.

   b. Compare two decimals to thousandths based on meanings of the digits in each place, using >, =, and < symbols to record the results of comparisons.

4. Use place value understanding to round decimals to any place.

B. Perform operations with multi-digit whole numbers and with decimals to hundredths.

5. Fluently multiply multi-digit whole numbers using the standard algorithm.

6. Find whole-number quotients of whole numbers with up to four-digit dividends and two-digit divisors, using strategies based on place value, the properties of operations, and/or the relationship between multiplication and division. Illustrate and explain the calculation by using equations, rectangular arrays, and/or area models.

7. Add, subtract, multiply, and divide decimals to hundredths, using concrete models or drawings and strategies based on place value, properties of operations, and/or the relationship between addition and subtraction; relate the strategy to a written method and explain the reasoning used.

A. Use equivalent fractions as a strategy to add and subtract fractions.

1. Add and subtract fractions with unlike denominators (including mixed numbers) by replacing given fractions with equivalent fractions in such a way as to produce an equivalent sum or difference of fractions with like denominators. *For example,* $\frac{2}{3} + \frac{5}{4} = \frac{8}{12} + \frac{15}{12} = \frac{23}{12}$.

   (In general, $\frac{a}{b} + \frac{c}{d} = \frac{(ad+bc)}{(bd)}$.)

2. Solve word problems involving addition and subtraction of fractions referring to the same whole, including cases of unlike denominators, e.g., by using visual fraction models or equations to represent the problem. Use benchmark fractions and number sense of fractions to estimate mentally and assess the reasonableness of answers. *For example, recognize an incorrect result* $\frac{2}{5} + \frac{1}{2} = \frac{3}{7}$, *by observing that* $\frac{3}{7} < \frac{1}{2}$.

B. Apply and extend previous understandings of multiplication and division to multiply and divide fractions.

3. Interpret a fraction as division of the numerator by the denominator ($\frac{a}{b} = a \div b$). Solve word problems involving division of whole numbers leading to answers in the form of fractions or mixed numbers, e.g., by using visual fraction models or equations to represent the problem. *For example, interpret* $\frac{3}{4}$ *as the result of dividing 3 by 4, noting that* $\frac{3}{4}$ *multiplied by 4 equals 3, and that when 3 wholes are shared equally among 4 people each person has a share of size* $\frac{3}{4}$. *If 9 people want to share a 50-pound sack of rice equally by weight, how many pounds of rice should each person get? Between what two whole numbers does your answer lie?*

4. Apply and extend previous understandings of multiplication to multiply a fraction or whole number by a fraction.

   a. Interpret the product $\frac{a}{b} \times q$ as a parts of a partition of q into b equal parts; equivalently, as the result of a sequence of operations $a \times q \div b$. *For example, use a visual fraction model to show* $\frac{2}{3} \times 4 = \frac{8}{3}$, *and create a story context for this equation. Do the same with* $\frac{2}{3} \times \frac{4}{5} = \frac{8}{15}$. *(In general,* $\frac{a}{b} \times \frac{c}{d} = \frac{ac}{bd}$.)

   b. Find the area of a rectangle with fractional side lengths by tiling it with unit squares of the appropriate unit fraction side lengths, and show that the area is the same as would be found by multiplying the side lengths. Multiply fractional side lengths to find areas of rectangles, and represent fraction products as rectangular areas.

5. Interpret multiplication as scaling (resizing), by:

   a. Comparing the size of a product to the size of one factor on the basis of the size of the other factor, without performing the indicated multiplication.

   b. Explaining why multiplying a given number by a fraction greater than 1 results in a product greater than the given number (recognizing multiplication by whole numbers greater than 1 as a familiar case); explaining why multiplying a given number by a fraction less than 1 results in a product smaller than the given number; and relating the principle of fraction equivalence $\frac{a}{b} = \frac{(n \times a)}{(n \times b)}$ to the effect of multiplying $\frac{a}{b}$ by 1.

6. Solve real world problems involving multiplication of fractions and mixed numbers, e.g., by using visual fraction models or equations to represent the problem.

7. Apply and extend previous understandings of division to divide unit fractions by whole numbers and whole numbers by unit fractions.[1]

   a. Interpret division of a unit fraction by a non-zero whole number, and compute such quotients. *For example, create a story context for* $\frac{1}{3} \div 4$, *and use a visual fraction model to show the quotient. Use the relationship between multiplication and division to explain that* $\frac{1}{3} \div 4 = \frac{1}{12}$ *because* $\frac{1}{12} \times 4 = \frac{1}{3}$.

   b. Interpret division of a whole number by a unit fraction, and compute such quotients. *For example, create a story context for* $4 \div \frac{1}{5}$, *and use a visual fraction model to show the quotient. Use the relationship between multiplication and division to explain that* $4 \div \frac{1}{5} = 20$ *because* $20 \times \frac{1}{5} = 4$.

   c. Solve real world problems involving division of unit fractions by non-zero whole numbers and division of whole numbers by unit fractions, e.g., by using visual fraction models and equations to represent the problem. *For example, how much chocolate will each person get if 3 people share* $\frac{1}{2}$ *lb of chocolate equally? How many* $\frac{1}{3}$-cup servings are in 2 cups of raisins?*

1. Students able to multiply fractions in general can develop strategies to divide fractions in general, by reasoning about the relationship between multiplication and division. But division of a fraction by a fraction is not a requirement at this grade.

Measurement and Data   5.MD

A. Convert like measurement units within a given measurement system.

1. Convert among different-sized standard measurement units within a given measurement system (e.g., convert 5 cm to 0.05 m), and use these conversions in solving multi-step, real world problems.

B. Represent and interpret data.

2. Make a line plot to display a data set of measurements in fractions of a unit ($\frac{1}{2}$, $\frac{1}{4}$, $\frac{1}{8}$). Use operations on fractions for this grade to solve problems involving information presented in line plots. *For example, given different measurements of liquid in identical beakers, find the amount of liquid each beaker would contain if the total amount in all the beakers were redistributed equally.*

C. Geometric measurement: Understand concepts of volume and relate volume to multiplication and to addition.

3. Recognize volume as an attribute of solid figures and understand concepts of volume measurement.

   a. A cube with side length 1 unit, called a "unit cube," is said to have "one cubic unit" of volume, and can be used to measure volume.

   b. A solid figure which can be packed without gaps or overlaps using n unit cubes is said to have a volume of n cubic units.

4. Measure volumes by counting unit cubes, using cubic cm, cubic in, cubic ft, and improvised units.

5. Relate volume to the operations of multiplication and addition and solve real world and mathematical problems involving volume.

   a. Find the volume of a right rectangular prism with whole-number side lengths by packing it with unit cubes, and show that the volume is the same as would be found by multiplying the edge lengths, equivalently by multiplying the height by the area of the base. Represent threefold whole-number products as volumes, e.g., to represent the associative property of multiplication.

   b. Apply the formulas $V = l \times w \times h$ and $V = b \times h$ for rectangular prisms to find volumes of right rectangular prisms with whole-number edge lengths in the context of solving real world and mathematical problems.

   c. Recognize volume as additive. Find volumes of solid figures composed of two non-overlapping right rectangular prisms by adding the volumes of the non-overlapping parts, applying this technique to solve real world problems.

Geometry	5.G

A. Graph points on the coordinate plane to solve real-world and mathematical problems.

1. Use a pair of perpendicular number lines, called axes, to define a coordinate system, with the intersection of the lines (the origin) arranged to coincide with the 0 on each line and a given point in the plane located by using an ordered pair of numbers, called its coordinates. Understand that the first number indicates how far to travel from the origin in the direction of one axis, and the second number indicates how far to travel in the direction of the second axis, with the convention that the names of the two axes and the coordinates correspond (e.g., x-axis and x-coordinate, y-axis and y-coordinate).

2. Represent real world and mathematical problems by graphing points in the first quadrant of the coordinate plane, and interpret coordinate values of points in the context of the situation.

B. Classify two-dimensional figures into categories based on their properties.

3. Understand that attributes belonging to a category of two-dimensional figures also belong to all subcategories of that category. *For example, all rectangles have four right angles and squares are rectangles, so all squares have four right angles.*

4. Classify two-dimensional figures in a hierarchy based on properties.

Standards for Mathematical Practice (3–5)

1. Make sense of problems and persevere in solving them.

2. Reason abstractly and quantitatively.

3. Construct viable arguments and critique the reasoning of others.

4. Model with mathematics.

5. Use appropriate tools strategically.

6. Attend to precision.

7. Look for and make use of structure.

8. Look for and express regularity in repeated reasoning.

The Common Core Mathematics Companion: The Standards Decoded, Grades 3–5

What They Say, What They Mean, How to Teach Them

Linda M. Gojak

Ruth Harbin Miles

Series Creator: Jim Burke

Name: _____

Department: _____

Learning Team: _____

A JOINT PUBLICATION OF

A SAGE Company

FOR INFORMATION:

Corwin

A SAGE Company

2455 Teller Road

Thousand Oaks, California 91320

(800) 233-9936

www.corwin.com

SAGE Publications Ltd.

1 Oliver's Yard

55 City Road

London EC1Y 1SP

United Kingdom

SAGE Publications India Pvt. Ltd.

B 1/I 1 Mohan Cooperative Industrial Area

Mathura Road, New Delhi 110 044

India

SAGE Publications Asia-Pacific Pte. Ltd.

3 Church Street

#10-04 Samsung Hub

Singapore 049483

Printed in the United States of America

ISBN: 978-1-4833-8160-2

Series Creator: Jim Burke

Acquisitions Editor: Erin Null

Senior Associate Editor: Desirée A. Bartlett

Editorial Assistant: Andrew Olson

Production Editor: Melanie Birdsall

Copy Editor: Pam Suwinsky

Typesetter: C&M Digitals (P) Ltd.

Proofreader: Theresa Kay

Cover and Interior Designer: Scott Van Atta

Director of Marketing Strategy: Maura Sullivan

This book is printed on acid-free paper.

SUSTAINABLE FORESTRY INITIATIVE

Certified Chain of Custody
Promoting Sustainable Forestry
www.sfiprogram.org
SFI-01268

SFI label applies to text stock

15 16 17 18 19 10 9 8 7 6 5 4 3 2

Contents

Acknowledgments

Thank you to all who have influenced my work as a K–8 mathematics teacher: the vision of Dr. James Heddens, my graduate advisor; Dr. Johnny Hill, who always pushed my thinking; Kay Gilliland, my mentor and friend; the many colleagues with whom I have worked and learned throughout my teaching career. Finally, thank you to all of my students who, through their work and questions, helped me to think more deeply about my own understanding of mathematics and to realize how lucky I am to have spent my time doing something I love!

—Linda M. Gojak

A very special thanks is due to the best teacher I have ever known, my incredible father, Dr. Calvin E. Harbin, who taught me to value my education and at the age of 99 is still modeling lifelong learning. Acknowledgment and thanks must also be given to my extraordinary mentors, Dr. Ramona Anshutz and Dr. Shirley A. Hill, who both inspired me to become a mathematics education leader. Their influence and guidance completely changed my life's work. Words could never express the thanks and credit I owe to my dear colleagues, Dr. Ted H. Hull and Dr. Don S. Balka, who are simply the best partners and team I have had the privilege to work with. Most important, I thank my loving husband, Sam Miles, for *always* being there for me.

—Ruth Harbin Miles

Letter to Grades 3–5 Teachers

Dear Teachers of Grades 3–5,

The Common Core Mathematics Companion: The Standards Decoded, Grades 3–5: What They Say, What They Mean, How to Teach Them is designed to support you as you help your students learn the mathematics they need to know and be able to do. This book includes critical mathematical ideas for each grade and is intended to be your guide to both the Content Standards and the Mathematical Practices. A brief overview for each Standard, along with effective teaching practices, mathematics vocabulary, suggested models, manipulatives, representations, and ideas for each Standard are included. The book is intended to help you make sense of the Content Standards and Mathematical Practices.

The Common Core State Standards for Mathematics (CCSSM) were developed to promote student achievement and have the potential for changing traditional classroom instruction across the United States. This is significant, because the Content Standards will help ensure students deeply understand the mathematics they are expected to learn. The Content Standards lay a foundation for the development of a rigorous, relevant, and coherent mathematics curriculum for every student and will help ensure all students are ready for their futures, including college and the workforce.

The CCSSM promote conceptual understanding and reasoning as well as skill proficiency. Included in the Common Core Mathematics document are five domains, clusters, and standards. The domains for 3–5 mathematics include the topics of Operations and Algebraic Thinking, Number and Operations in Base Ten, Number and Operations—Fractions, Measurement and Data, and Geometry. The Standards under each domain include developing conceptual understanding, skills based on that understanding, and application of key ideas. Clusters are groups of related Standards for each domain. Also included in the CCSSM are eight Standards for Mathematical Practice. These Standards describe the mathematical habits of mind that mathematically proficient students demonstrate in doing mathematics with understanding. The Practice Standards are

1. Make sense of problems and persevere in solving them.

2. Reason abstractly and quantitatively.

3. Construct viable arguments and critique the reasoning of others.

4. Model with mathematics.

5. Use appropriate tools strategically.

6. Attend to precision.

7. Look for and make use of structure.

8. Look for and express regularity in repeated reasoning.

When students are actively involved in using the Practice Standards, they are learning meaningful, high-quality mathematics.

We suggest you work with your grade-level colleagues and use this book when you are studying the Standards, as you decide on the sequencing and clustering of the Standards, as well as the selection of appropriate instructional resources. Be sure to examine the content for the grade before and after the one you teach so you will understand what students should have learned and what they will be learning the next year. Keep in mind that implementation of the Standards and Practices is a process and may take time to do well. Your devotion to teaching the Standards will make a difference for students who will be learning to think, reason, and apply the mathematics you have taught them.

We hope you will find this book a helpful resource and a valuable companion as you work to help your students become successful mathematics learners.

Sincerely,

Linda M. Gojak

Ruth Harbin Miles

Letter to Elementary School Principals

Dear Elementary School Principal,

An instructional leader must clearly explain and help teachers understand that student success and achievement are the goals for implementing the Common Core Mathematics Standards and the Standards for Mathematical Practice. The role of the leader is not only to promote the Standards but also to ensure the Content Standards are taught and the Standards for Mathematical Practice are achieved in every classroom. As an instructional leader, a principal must help teachers engage in professional learning to study both the Content and the Practice Standards they will be teaching. Teachers will need guidance to understand the depth and the sequencing of each Standard as well as the content before and after their grade levels. Leaders must help teachers understand that the Common Core Mathematics Standards have the prospect of ensuring equity and access to high-quality mathematics for every student.

The Common Core Standards for Mathematics define what students should understand and be able to do in grades 3–5. Implemented properly, these Standards lay the foundation for the concepts and skills students will be expected to know in grades 6–12. Included in the Common Core Standards for Mathematics document are domains, clusters, and standards. The domains for 3–5 mathematics include five broad topics: Operations and Algebraic Thinking, Number and Operations in Base Ten, Number and Operations—Fractions, Measurement and Data, and Geometry. The Standards under each domain stress conceptual understanding, skills, and applications of key mathematical ideas. Clusters are groups of related Standards for each domain.

Also included in the Common Core Standards document are eight Standards for Mathematical Practice. These Standards describe the mathematical habits of mind that mathematically proficient students demonstrate in doing mathematics with understanding. The Practice Standards are

1. Make sense of problems and persevere in solving them.

2. Reason abstractly and quantitatively.

3. Construct viable arguments and critique the reasoning of others.

4. Model with mathematics.

5. Use appropriate tools strategically.

6. Attend to precision.

7. Look for and make use of structure.

8. Look for and express regularity in repeated reasoning.

When students are actively involved in using the Practice Standards, they are learning meaningful, high-quality mathematics.

The Common Core Mathematics Companion: The Standards Decoded, Grades 3–5: What They Say, What They Mean, How to Teach Them is designed to support teachers in their learning and implementation of the Common Core Mathematics Standards. The book focuses on the critical ideas of 3–5 mathematics, including a meaningful explanation of each Standard along with effective teaching practices and learning activities. Mathematics vocabulary and suggested teaching materials are highlighted for each Standard. The book is not only a reference but a guide to helping teachers more deeply understand all aspects of the Standards.

Elementary schools, professional learning communities, individual classroom and special education teachers will all have different knowledge, various skills, and distinct ideas about using *The Common Core Mathematics Companion: The Standards Decoded, Grades 3–5: What They Say, What They Mean, How to Teach Them.* You may wish to supply every teacher with a personal copy of the book for use as a school-wide initiative or book study. Such a study will help improve both content knowledge and understanding of the mathematics teachers are expected to teach. Providing the opportunity for teachers to engage and use the book in grade-level planning with colleagues will allow teachers to dig deeply into the Standards. Use of this resource will add cohesiveness and consistency, ensuring all grades 3–5 students will benefit from similar instruction. Be sure to invite teachers to bring this resource to all planning and professional development work. You may even want teachers to start or end a meeting with a lesson they've planned based upon the suggestions and strategies found in this reference guide. As a result of the book study, *The Common Core Mathematics Companion: The Standards Decoded, Grades 3–5: What They Say, What They Mean, How to Teach Them* will influence professional practice at both the classroom and school levels and will help transform instruction.

Sincerely,

Linda M. Gojak

Ruth Harbin Miles

Introduction

A Brief History of the Common Core

Contrary to popular belief, academic standards are not new. In fact they have been around for more than 25 years. The first set of curriculum specific standards, *The Curriculum and Evaluation Standards for School Mathematics*, was released by the National Council of Teachers of Mathematics in 1989, followed by an updated set of standards, *Principles and Standards for School Mathematics*, in 2000. Both of these documents provided a vision for K–12 mathematics by grade-level band. They also formed the foundation for most states' grade-level standards.

In April 2009 the National Governor's Association and the Council of Chief State School Officers met to discuss the creation of the Common Core State Standards Initiative. The purpose of such an initiative was to develop a set of common standards across states in order to balance the quality of mathematics instruction and learning. Following that meeting, the process of writing the Common Core Standards began. The Standards Development team, led by William McCallum, Phil Daro, and Jason Zimba, included mathematicians, mathematics educators, mathematics education researchers, and classroom teachers. The process included an open invitation for feedback, not only from mathematics educators and associations, including the National Council of Teachers of Mathematics, but also from the general public. This feedback was considered and much of it was incorporated into the final document released in June 2010. Following the release of the Standards, individual states went through their own processes for reviewing, adopting, and, if necessary, ratifying the adoption of the Common Core State Standards.

The Common Core State Standards for Mathematics

"The Common Core State Standards are a clear set of shared goals and expectations for the knowledge and skills students need in English language arts and mathematics at each grade level so they can be prepared to succeed in college, career, and life" (www.corestandards.org/about-the-standards/frequently-asked-questions/#faq-2303).

The Common Core State Standards for Mathematics (CCSSM) include two critical components of learning mathematics. The Content Standards explicitly outline the mathematics we want students to know and be able to do at each grade level. The Content Standards of the Common Core are fewer in number than most previous state standards. At the same time, the expectation is that students will develop deeper understanding of that content so less time is spent on reteaching from year to year. Additionally, the Standards were carefully constructed to show connections among ideas at a grade level as well as vertical progressions across grades. For example, you will find that the Standards in Grade 3 develop from the mathematical work that students have completed in previous grades. Similarly, the Standards in Grade 4 develop from work completed in grades K–3. Thus it is important for teachers to be knowledgeable of the Standards not only at the level they are teaching but also at the preceding grade level and the following grade level.

The second group of Standards, the Standards for Mathematical Practice, describes the habits of mind that students should develop as they do mathematics. These eight Standards are the same across all grade levels, K–12. As teachers plan mathematics lessons, they should consider how students will use the Practices in learning and doing mathematics.

The Common Core Standards *are not* a curriculum. Decisions about mathematics programs, textbooks and materials, sequencing topics and units, and instructional frameworks are left for local districts to make. They do not tell teachers how to teach. It is important to remember the Standards describe what students need to know and be able to do. Schools and teachers know best how to help students reach both the Content and the Practice Standards.

The Common Core Standards *do not* dictate specific assessments. Some states will be using assessments developed by PARCC (Partnership for Assessment of Readiness for College and Careers) or SBAC (Smarter Balanced Assessment Consortium). Others will develop and use their own assessments. Other facts and information can be found at http://www.corestandards.org.

Instructional Shifts

While the Standards do not call for a particular instructional model or philosophy, they are based on the best of existing standards. What is different is that they call for specific instructional shifts: *focus*, *coherence*, and *rigor*.

Focus: The Content Standards call for greater focus on fewer topics. An examination of the mathematics standards of high-performing countries indicate that fewer, more focused topics at a grade level allow students to deepen their understanding of the mathematics and gain a stronger foundation for ongoing study of mathematics. Within the Standards, the major mathematical work of each grade level has been identified (www.corestandards.org). That means that not all of the content within a grade is emphasized equally among the Content Standards. The list of Content Standards for a grade is not linear, nor is it a checklist. Some clusters require greater emphasis than others. They take more time for students to master with depth of understanding. The major work of grades 3–5 includes multiplication and division of whole numbers and foundational understanding of fractions, leading to work in all operations with fractional numbers. This includes developing concepts, skills, and problem solving. This means the majority of instructional time in grades 3–5 (65% to 85%) should be spent on these mathematical topics. This does not mean that other Standards should be skipped. Rather, the supporting Standards should be taught to connect mathematical ideas among the essential Standards. The additional Standards provide students with experiences that will be foundational to work in future grades. Neglecting material will leave gaps in student skill and understanding (see the tables on pages 264–266).

Coherence: Many of us learned mathematics as a set of disconnected topics, with much of our skill based on tricks ("Ours is not to reason why, just invert and multiply!") or mnemonic devices ("Please Excuse My Dear Aunt Sally"). In reality, mathematics is a coherent body of knowledge made up of topics that are connected and build on each other. The call for coherence in the Content Standards ensures that there are carefully constructed progressions from grade to grade so students build new understandings on the foundations built in previous years. Each Standard is not a new topic, but an extension of previous learning. In addition to the progressions across grade levels, the Standards incorporate specific connections within a grade level. For example, as students develop conceptual understanding of multiplication and division, the relationship of these operations to each other is consistently reinforced through building conceptual understanding, procedural skills, and applying these understanding and skills to various contexts.

Rigor: The final instructional shift, rigor, refers to how we support students in developing deep understanding of each Standard. Understanding does not develop by assigning more worksheets or more difficult examples and problems. Rather, it calls for instructional practice that balances conceptual understanding, procedural skills, and applying mathematical ideas to a variety of contexts.
    The following descriptions of each component of rigor come from www.corestandards.org.

Conceptual understanding: The Standards call for conceptual understanding of key concepts such as multiplication and division. Students must be able to access concepts from a number of perspectives in order to see mathematics as more than a set of rules or procedures.

Procedural skills and fluency: The Standards call for speed and accuracy in calculation. Students must practice core skills, such as basic facts and multiplication and division computation, in order to have access to more complex concepts and procedures. Fluency is built upon conceptual understanding and, with elementary children, through the development of ideas through representations using concrete materials, pictures, numbers, and words.

Application: The Standards call for students to use mathematics in situations that require mathematical knowledge. Correctly applying mathematical knowledge depends on students having a solid conceptual understanding and procedural fluency.

Major Work of Grades 3–5

To help drive the focus of the Standards, at least 65% and as much as 85% of instructional time should focus on the major work for each grade level. Areas of major work include:

Grade 3: Represent and solve problems involving multiplication and division; understand properties of multiplication and the relationship between multiplication and division; multiply and divide within 100; solve problems involving the four operations, and identify and explain patterns in arithmetic; develop understanding of fractions as numbers; solve problems involving measurement and estimation of intervals of time, liquid volumes, and masses of objects; geometric measurement: understand concepts of area and relate area to multiplication and to addition.

Grade 4: Use the four operations with whole numbers to solve problems; generalize place value understanding for multi-digit whole numbers; use place value understanding and properties of operations to perform multi-digit arithmetic; extend understanding of fraction equivalence and ordering; build fractions from unit fractions by applying and extending previous understandings of operations on whole numbers; understand decimal notation for fractions, and compare decimal fractions.

Grade 5: Understand the place value system; perform operations with multi-digit whole numbers and with decimals to hundredths; use equivalent fractions as a strategy to add and subtract fractions; apply and extend previous understandings of multiplication and division to multiply and divide fractions; geometric measurement: understand concepts of volume and relate volume to multiplication and to addition.

Additional information on the focus for each grade level can be found in the Resources at the end of this book.

Common Core Word Wall

The language of the Common Core differs from traditional standards. Familiarity with section names and their functions will help you to make the best use of the Common Core Standards.

Standards define what students should understand and be able to do.

Clusters summarize groups of related Standards. Note that Standards from different clusters may sometimes be closely related, because mathematics is a connected subject.

Domains are larger groups of related Standards. Standards from different domains may sometimes be closely related.

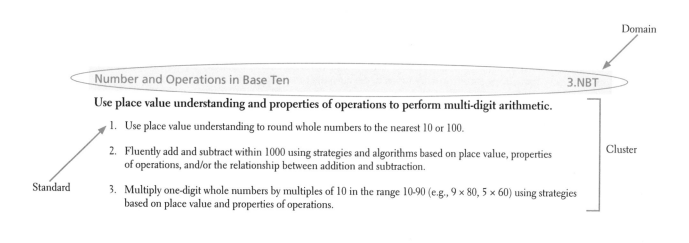

Source: Common Core State Standards for Mathematics (www.corestandards.org)

As districts develop units of study for a grade level, careful consideration should be given to the order and connection among topics and Standards. For example, as third graders develop an understanding of the meaning of multiplication (3.OA.A.1), they use area models for multiplication to solve problems (3.OA.A.3), extend this understanding to multiply by multiples of 10 (3.NBT.A.3), and use area models to explore finding area of rectangular figures (3.MD.C.5,6,7).

The Common Core Standards for Mathematical Practice

The Common Core Standards for Mathematical Practice describe eight habits of mind teachers must incorporate into classroom instruction to help students develop depth of understanding of critical mathematical concepts. The mathematical Practices are not intended to be taught in isolation but should be integrated into daily lessons. Some lessons may focus on developing one or two of these Standards, and others may incorporate seven or all eight Standards. Note that you do not "teach" these Standards. Rather, they are the type of mathematical thinking and doing that we want students to practice as they are developing mathematical understanding.

Throughout the following chapters, we have included examples of mathematical practice that can be used in each cluster. These are not meant to limit lessons to using only those Practices. They are examples of key practices that should be included in lessons around that particular cluster. It is likely that you will use all of the Practices throughout the cluster and domain.

These eight Practices, briefly explained on the following page, are essential for student success. If students are actively engaged in using the eight Practices, they are learning rigorous, meaningful mathematics.

SFMP 1. Make sense of problems and persevere in solving them.

Students work to understand the information given in a problem and the question that is asked. They plan a solution path by choosing a strategy they can use to find a solution, and check to make sure their answer makes sense. As students in grades 3–5 work to make sense out of multiplication and division of whole numbers and fractions in these grades, using materials to solve problems helps them to develop conceptual understanding that leads to procedural fluency.

SFMP 2. Reason abstractly and quantitatively.

Students make sense of quantities and their relationships in problem situations. They develop operational sense by associating contexts to numbers (thinking about 4×7 in a context of 4 baskets with 7 eggs in each basket) and associate mathematical meaning to given contexts (having 4 baskets of 7 eggs can be expressed as 4×7). Modeling problem situations with concrete materials will help students to understand the meaning of multiplication and division and build a foundation for work with fractions.

SFMP 3. Construct viable arguments and critique the reasoning of others.

Students in grades 3–5 should have many opportunities to explain their thinking and justify and communicate their conclusions both orally and in writing. Listening to others and finding how their strategies are similar may take prompting questions from the teacher such as "Why do you think that works?" or "How is your method the same as . . . ?" Mathematical discussions should be a common expectation in mathematics lessons. It will take time for students to become comfortable explaining their thinking, but this will develop over time. Explaining one's thinking helps to develop deeper conceptual understanding.

SFMP 4. Model with mathematics.

Students use various representations, models, and symbols to connect conceptual understanding to skills and applications. As students work with the big ideas of grades 3–5, they should represent mathematics situations using objects, pictures, numbers, and words. Problem solving strategies such as draw a picture, make a list, find a pattern, and write an equation have explicit connections to representations and models and can be developed at the same time.

SFMP 5. Use appropriate tools strategically.

Students consider the available tools when solving a mathematics problem. Representations such as making equal groups, arrays, and area models will help students to see the connections between multiplication and division as well as the importance of place value in understanding these operations. Bar models, area models, and the number line will help students to understand fraction number concepts. A variety of concrete materials such as cubes, tiles, straws and rubber bands, fraction bars, and physical number lines will support students in these representations.

SFMP 6. Attend to precision.

Students communicate precisely with others. Students in grades 3–5 explain their thinking using appropriate mathematical vocabulary. Students expand their knowledge of mathematical symbols that should explicitly connect to vocabulary development.

SFMP 7. Look for and make use of structure.

Students look closely to find patterns and structure in their mathematics work. For example, students begin their work with fractions using unit fractions, which helps them to better understand the meaning of the numerator and the denominator. They extend their understanding of unit fractions to other common fractions as they develop a sense of equivalence and addition and subtraction of all fractions including mixed numbers. The relationship between multiplication and division of whole numbers extends to work with fractions.

SFMP 8. Look for and express regularity in repeated reasoning.

Students notice when calculations are repeated and begin to make generalizations. By recognizing what happens when multiplying or dividing tens or hundreds, students extend that understanding to more difficult problems. Although this Standard mentions shortcuts, it should be noted that shortcuts are only appropriate when students discover them through making generalizations and understand why they work.

Effective Teaching Practices

Quality mathematics teaching is a critical key for student success. In *Principles to Actions* (2014), the National Council of Teachers of Mathematics outlines eight valuable teaching practices every teacher should incorporate to guarantee student achievement. These eight research-informed practices briefly explained below provide a foundation for effective common core mathematics teaching and student learning.

1. Establish mathematics goals to focus learning.

Establishing learning goals sets the stage and helps to guide instructional decisions. Teachers must keep in mind what is to be learned, why the goal is important, where students need to go (the trajectory), as well as how learning can be extended. Students must clearly understand the purpose of each lesson beyond simply repeating the Standard.

2. Implement tasks that promote reasoning and problem solving.

Implementing tasks that promote reasoning and problem solving provides opportunities for students to engage in exploration and encourages students to use procedures in ways that are connected to conceptual understanding. The tasks teachers choose should be built on current student understandings and have various entry points with multiple ways for the problems to be solved.

3. Use and connect mathematical representations.

Using and connecting representations leads students to deeper understanding. Different representations, including concrete models, pictures, words, and numbers, should be introduced, discussed, and connected to support students in explaining their thinking and reasoning.

4. Facilitate meaningful mathematical discourse.

Facilitating meaningful student mathematical conversations provides students with opportunities to share ideas, clarify their understanding, and develop convincing arguments. Talking and sharing aloud can advance the mathematical thinking of the whole class.

5. Pose purposeful questions.

Posing purposeful questions reveals students' current understanding of a concept and encourages students to explain, elaborate, and clarify thinking. Asking good questions makes the learning of mathematics more visible and accessible for student examination.

6. Build procedural fluency from conceptual understanding.

Building procedural fluency from conceptual understanding based on experiences with concrete representations allows students to flexibly choose from a variety of methods to solve problems.

7. Support productive struggle in learning mathematics.

Supporting productive struggle in learning mathematics is significant and essential to learning mathematics with understanding. Productive struggle allows students to grapple with ideas and relationships. Giving young students ample time to work with and make sense out of new ideas is critical to their learning with understanding.

8. Elicit and use evidence of student thinking.

Eliciting and using evidence of student thinking helps teachers access learning progress and can be used to make instructional decisions during the lessons as well as help to prepare what will occur in the next lesson. Formative assessment through student written and oral ideas are excellent artifacts to assess student thinking and understanding.

How to Use This Book

The purpose of this book is to help teachers more deeply understand the mathematical meaning of each cluster and Standard within the five domains of grades 3–5. We want this book to be your toolkit for teaching the mathematics Standards, and we have left ample space for you to take notes and add ideas and other resources you have found to be helpful.

You will find each part of this book includes one domain and begins with an overview of how the domain progresses across third, fourth, and fifth grades. A list of helpful materials, reproducibles, and key vocabulary from the domain is included in the overview as well.

We track each domain across third, fourth, and fifth grades with a page for each cluster and the Standards within that cluster. A description of the cluster and how the Standards for Mathematical Practice can be incorporated into your teaching of the cluster concepts follows. Because the Standards are intentionally designed to connect within and across domains and grade levels, a list of related Standards is included in the cluster overview. We suggest that as you prepare work on a cluster you look at these Standards to have a better idea of the mathematics students learned in previous grades and where they are going in future grades. A list of all of the Standards is found in the Quick Reference Guide at the beginning of the book.

Each Standard within a cluster is explained with an example of *What the TEACHER does* to work with that Standard in the classroom followed by a description of *What the STUDENTS do*. It is important to note that most Standards will take several days, and you should be connecting conceptual understanding across Standards and domains as you teach for understanding.

Addressing student misconceptions and common errors in developing student understanding of a concept concludes the contents for each Standard.

Each cluster ends with a template for planning instruction for that cluster. At the end of each domain you will find a sample planning page based on one Standard for that domain. Also included are planning page templates for each cluster within the domain for you to duplicate and use in your planning.

In the Resources section, you will find tables that are fundamental to the Operations and Algebraic Thinking and Number and Operations in Base Ten domains. You will also find reproducibles for key materials. These are designed to be samples, and we encourage you to use them or redesign them to best meet the needs of your students. A list of our favorite resource books and high-quality online resources that are particularly useful to developing mathematical ideas in grades 3–5 are also included.

We believe that this can become your common core bible! Read it and mark it with questions, comments, and ideas. We hope that it will help you to use these Standards and good teaching practice to lay the essential foundation that will ensure your students success not only in your grade, but in all of their future study of mathematics.

Reflection Questions

1. How are the three instructional shifts called for by the Common Core similar to your current instructional practice? What is conceptual understanding? How is it different from procedural skills? What do you need to consider to teach for conceptual understanding? How can you connect conceptual understanding to help students develop procedural skills? How does the information in Table 1, page 254, on problem situations support the development of conceptual understanding?

2. The Standards for Mathematical Practice describe the habits of mind that students need for thinking about and doing mathematics. While not every Standard will be in every lesson, select one Standard at your grade level and consider some ways you can incorporate these Practices in a lesson for that Standard. How will these Practices provide you with information about student understanding? How will this help you to better assess students? How will this information help you in planning lessons?

3. The Effective Teaching Practices describe specific actions that teachers must consider in planning and implementing lessons and assessing student performance. How are these Practices connected? Work with colleagues to plan a lesson that employs all of these Practices. What needs to be considered as you consider goals for the lesson? How can you modify a traditional task so that it promotes reasoning and problem solving? What representations will help students more deeply understand the concept? What questions will you ask students? How will you connect the conceptual understanding to build procedural fluency? What questions will support students who are working to make sense of a new idea? What kind of information will you look for to help inform you instruction? (For more information on the Effective Teaching Practices, go to www.nctm.org.)

Part 1

Operations and Algebraic Thinking

Operations and Algebraic Thinking

Domain Overview

GRADE 3

The major work of this domain in Grade 3 is to develop students' conceptual understanding of multiplication and division by using concrete materials to model multiplication and then relate their understanding of multiplication to division. Multiplication problem situations provide a context for understanding multiplication as finding the total number of items given a number of equal groups and the number of items in each group. Division problem situations develop the meaning of division and how it is related to multiplication. When you know the total number of items and the number of groups, you can determine how many items in a group, or, when you know the total number of items and the number of items in a group, you can find the number of groups. All of these activities culminate in the expectation that students will demonstrate fluency with multiplication and division within 100 using single-digit factors.

GRADE 4

Students in Grade 4 continue to solve problems using the four operations with whole numbers. New to this grade level are problem situations that involve multiplicative comparisons. Students become familiar with factors and multiples and how they relate to prime and composite numbers. They work in a variety of contexts to generate and analyze patterns.

GRADE 5

In preparation for the Expressions and Equations domain in grades 6–8, fifth graders begin to explore, interpret, and evaluate numerical expressions. Work with patterns that began in Grade 4 extends to generating patterns, forming ordered pairs, graphing on a coordinate plane, and then analyzing the graphical representations.

SUGGESTED MATERIALS FOR THIS DOMAIN

3	4	5	
✓	✓	✓	Hundreds chart (Reproducible 1)
✓	✓	✓	Chips, counters
✓	✓	✓	Cups, containers, other objects to represent "groups"
✓	✓	✓	Place value chart to hundreds (Reproducible 2)
✓	✓	✓	Square tiles
✓	✓	✓	Grid paper (Reproducible 3)
✓	✓	✓	Pattern blocks
✓	✓	✓	Number cards (such as a deck of playing cards)

KEY VOCABULARY

3	4	5	
✓	✓	✓	**add** to combine or join together related words: *add, and, plus, join, put together, (+)*
✓	✓	✓	**addend** any of the numbers added to find a sum
✓	✓	✓	**area model** a concrete model for multiplication or division made up of a rectangle. The length and width represent the factors and the area represents the product.

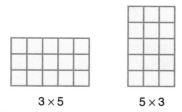

3×5 5×3

3	4	5	
✓	✓	✓	**array model** a concrete model for multiplication in which items are arranged in rows and columns. Each row (or column) represents the number of groups and each column (or row) represents the number of items in a group.

$5 \times 4 = 20$ 5 rows of $4 = 20$

3	4	5	
✓	✓	✓	*** associative property of multiplication** an extension of the commutative property; to change the order and group two factors to find convenient products (such as 10) in order to make the multiplication easier. Students may begin to use parentheses at this level. $7 \times 8 \times 5 = 7 \times (8 \times 5) = 7 \times 40 = 280$
✓	✓	✓	*** commutative property of multiplication** reversing the order of the factors does not change the product $8 \times 5 = 40$ and $5 \times 8 = 40$ therefore the product of $8 \times 5 = 5 \times 8$

(Continued)

(Continued)

3   4   5

	✓	✓	**comparison model** a multiplication or division situation in which one number is a multiple of the other *Example:* Maya has 5 marbles. Alexa has 3 times as many. How many marbles does Alexa have?
	✓	✓	**compose** put a number together using other numbers 1 + 9, 2 + 8, 3 + 7, 4 + 6, 5 + 5, 1 + 2 + 3 + 4 are ways to compose 10
	✓	✓	**composite number** a number that has more than two factors
		✓	**coordinate plane** a plane determined by a horizontal number line, called the *x*-axis, and a vertical number line, called the *y*-axis, intersecting at a point called the origin. Each point in the coordinate plane can be specified by an ordered pair of numbers.

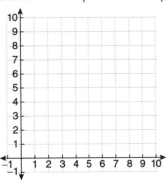

✓	✓	✓	**decompose** separate a number into parts using other numbers 8 can be decomposed into 4 + 4, 3 + 5, 2 + 2 + 2 + 2
✓	✓	✓	*** distributive property** multiplying a sum by a given number is the same as multiplying each addend by the number and then adding the products 6 × 9 = 54 6 × (5 + 4) = (6 × 5) + (6 × 4) = 30 + 24 = 54 The distributive property says that if a, b, and c are real numbers, then: a × (b + c) = (a × b) + (a × c)
✓	✓	✓	**division** sharing a number into equal groups and finding the number of groups or the number of items in each group
✓	✓	✓	**equal groups model (measurement division)** a division model in which the total number of items and the number of items in each group is known and the number of groups that can be made is the unknown. *Example:* I have 48 peanuts. I want to put 8 peanuts in a cup. How many cups will I need?
✓	✓	✓	**equation** a mathematical sentence in which one part is the same or equal to the other part 3 + 5 = 8 12 − 7 = 5 11 = 8 + 3 6 = 9 − 3
✓	✓	✓	**estimate** to make an approximation or calculate using closer or easier numbers
	✓	✓	**evaluate** find the numerical value of mathematical expression
✓	✓	✓	**expression** one or more mathematical symbols that represent a number or quantity examples of expressions 3 × 6 4 + 7 × 3 8
✓	✓	✓	**fact family** a set of related mathematics facts, such as 3 × 5 = 15 15 = 5 × 3 15 ÷ 3 = 5 3 = 15 ÷ 5
✓	✓	✓	**factor** one of the numbers multiplied to find a product

3	4	5	
	✓	✓	**factor pair** a pair of numbers that when multiplied give a product; for example, 1 and 15, 3 and 5 are factor pairs for 15
✓	✓	✓	**fair share model (partitive division)** a division model in which the total number and the number of groups is known and the number of items in each group is unknown
			Example: I have 48 peanuts and want to put them into 6 cups. If I put the same number of peanuts into each cup, how many peanuts will be in each cup?
✓	✓	✓	*** identity property of multiplication** any number multiplied by 1 equals the number
			$3 \times 1 = 3$ $1 \times 3 = 3$
✓	✓	✓	**measurement division (equal groups model)** a division model in which the total number of items and the number of items in each group is known and the number of groups that can be made is the unknown
			Example: I have 48 peanuts. I want to put 8 peanuts in a cup. How many cups will I need?
✓	✓	✓	**missing factor** the unknown factor when a product and one factor are known
			$4 \times \square = 32$ The missing factor is 8.
	✓	✓	**multiple** the result of multiplying a whole number by other whole numbers
			multiples of 5 are 0, 5, 10, 15, 20, 25, 30
✓	✓	✓	**multiplication** a mathematical operation in which a number is added to itself a specific number of times; one factor tells the number of groups or sets, the other factor tells the number of items in a group or set and the result, or product, tells the total number of items
			$3 \times 5 = 15$ 3 groups with 5 in each group would give a total of 15
✓	✓	✓	**number line** a line used to show the position of a number in relation to zero and other numbers
		✓	**ordered pair** a pair of numbers that gives a location on a coordinate plane. The first number is the x coordinate and the second number is the y coordinate.
✓	✓	✓	**partitive division (fair share model)** a division model in which the total number and the number of groups is known and the number of items in each group is unknown
			Example: I have 48 peanuts and want to put them into 6 cups. If I put the same number of peanuts into each cup, how many peanuts will be in each cup?
✓	✓	✓	**pattern** set of numbers or objects that can be described by a specific rule
	✓	✓	**prime number** a number that has exactly two factors
✓	✓	✓	**product** the result when two numbers are multiplied
✓	✓	✓	**quotient** the result when two numbers are divided; the missing factor
✓	✓	✓	**remainder** amount left when two numbers are divided
✓	✓	✓	**round** to change a number to a less exact number that is more convenient for computation
✓	✓	✓	**strategy** a plan to find an answer or solve a problem that makes sense
✓	✓	✓	**sum** the result when two numbers are added
✓	✓	✓	**unknown** the quantity you are finding in a mathematics problem
✓	✓	✓	*** zero property of multiplication** any number multiplied by 0 equals 0
			$8 \times 0 = 0$ (8 groups of 0 is 0) $0 \times 8 = 0$ (0 groups of 8 is 0)

*Students are not responsible for these vocabulary words; however, they should understand the mathematical concept.

Operations and Algebraic Thinking
3.OA.A.*

Represent and solve problems involving multiplication and division.

STANDARD 1 | **3.OA.A.1:** Interpret products of whole numbers, e.g., interpret 5 × 7 as the total number of objects in 5 groups of 7 objects each. *For example, describe a context in which a total number of objects can be expressed as 5 × 7.*

STANDARD 2 | **3.OA.A.2:** Interpret whole-number quotients of whole numbers, e.g., interpret 56 ÷ 8 as the number of objects in each share when 56 objects are partitioned equally into 8 shares, or as a number of shares when 56 objects are partitioned into equal shares of 8 objects each. *For example, describe a context in which a number of shares or a number of groups can be expressed as 56 ÷ 8.*

STANDARD 3 | **3.OA.A.3:** Use multiplication and division within 100 to solve word problems in situations involving equal groups, arrays, and measurement quantities, e.g., by using drawings and equations with a symbol for the unknown number to represent the problem.[1]

[1] See Table 2 in the Resources, page 256.

STANDARD 4 | **3.OA.A.4:** Determine the unknown whole number in a multiplication or division equation relating three whole numbers. *For example, determine the unknown number that makes the equation true in each of the equations 8 × ? = 48, 5 = _ ÷ 3, 6 × 6 = ?*

*Major cluster

Operations and Algebraic Thinking   3.OA.A

Cluster A: Represent and solve problems involving multiplication and division.
Grade 3 Overview

Third grade students explore the meaning of multiplication as finding the total number of objects (product) when they know the number of groups (factor) and the number of items in each group (factor). The relationship between multiplication and division helps students understand that when dividing, they are finding the number of groups (missing factor) when they know the total count (product) and the number of items in a group (factor), or finding the number of items in a group (missing factor) when they know the number of groups (factor) and the total count (product). Problem solving situations and activities that include a variety of representations showing equal-sized groups, arrays, and area models lay the foundation for multiplication and division of whole numbers.

Note that these Standards are not linear. It is important for students to understand the meaning of multiplication and division (3.OA.A1, 3.OA.A.2) through the use of problem situations (3.OA.A.3). As students demonstrate understanding they begin to relate models to symbolic notation (3.OA.A.4). The use of symbols for easier facts and relating the symbols to fact families should be happening as students continue to use models to solve problems with the more difficult facts.

Standards for Mathematical Practice
SFMP 1. Make sense of problems and persevere in solving them.
SFMP 2. Use quantitative reasoning.
SFMP 3. Construct viable arguments and critique the reasoning of others.
SFMP 4. Model with mathematics.
SFMP 5. Use appropriate tools strategically.
SFMP 6. Attend to precision.
SFMP 7. Look for and make use of structure.
SFMP 8. Look for and express regularity in repeated reasoning.

Students solve a variety of problems as contexts for learning what it means to multiply or divide. They use quantitative reasoning to determine what is happening when they multiply (given the number of groups and the number of items in a group, they find the total number of items) and divide (given the total number of items and the number of groups, they find the number of items in a group *or* given the total number of items and the number of items in a group, they find the number of groups). Constructing mathematical arguments to justify their reasoning and comparing their strategies with those of classmates helps students to make connections among ideas and between concrete models and numerical notations (expressions and equations). They use a variety of tools to model multiplication and division including sets, arrays, area models, and the number line to represent what is happening when they multiply or divide. Developing the mathematical vocabulary of multiplication and division (factor × factor = product and product ÷ factor = missing factor) helps students to explain their thinking not only about the individual operations but also how they are related to each other. The commutative, associative, and distributive properties lay the foundation for fluency with basic facts through looking at the structure of multiplication and division and provide students with strategies for solving problems. Students use patterns and repeated reasoning (multiplication by 0, 1, 5, and 10) to help them identify patterns and become fluent with basic facts.

Related Content Standards

2.OA.C.3   2.OA.C.4   4.OA.A.1   4.OA.A.2

Notes

Interpret products of whole numbers, e.g., interpret 5 × 7 as the total number of objects in 5 groups of 7 objects each. For example, describe a context in which a total number of objects can be expressed as 5 × 7.

Students develop an initial understanding of multiplication of whole numbers by modeling situations in which there are a specific number of groups with the same number of items in each group. Unlike addition, in which each addend represents a certain number of items, in multiplication one factor represents the number of groups and the other factor represents the number of items in each group. The product represents the total number of items in all of the groups. Problem situations provide students contexts for using concrete materials.

New vocabulary includes *factor, equal groups, product.* The symbol × means groups of (or times) and 3 × 5 can initially be read as "3 groups of 5."

Example:

Mrs. Flack has 4 packages of pencils for the class. Each package contains 6 pencils. How many pencils does Mrs. Flack have?

This can be expressed as 4 × 6 or 4 groups of 6.

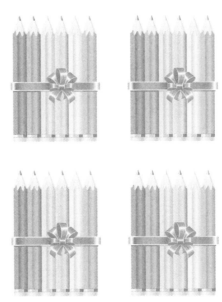

What the TEACHER does:

- Provide students with a variety of multiplication situations to model using concrete materials such as chips, counters, straws to represent the items, and cups, egg carton, paper to represent groups.
- Ask students to identify the number of groups and the number of items in each group and then the total number of items.

  There are 3 seats in the van and each seat can hold 4 people. How many people can ride in the van?

  3 groups of 4 people

  3 × 4 = 12

- Introduce multiplication terminology and symbols as students are ready. Add these terms and symbols to the class multiplication and division word wall.

  o factors, product, groups, times

  o ×

- Introduce students to numerical representations by writing equations that represent their work.

  3 × 4 = 12

- As students show understanding and can identify the number of groups, the number of items in a group, and connect that to the symbolic representation, progress to situations with pictures, numbers, and words.

What the STUDENTS do:

- Use concrete materials to model various multiplication situations.
- Identify the number of groups and the number of items in each group.
- Explain how they determined the total number of items.
- Connect representations to numeric expressions.
- Use pictorial representations for multiplication situations.
- Use appropriate vocabulary (*factor, product, times, groups of*) to describe their work.
- Write expressions and equations for their models and drawings.

Addressing Student Misconceptions and Common Errors

In previous work with addition, both addends represented the count or number of items that are joined for a total count. For example, 6 markers and 3 more markers give a total of 9 markers. In multiplication, one factor represents the number of groups, sets, or collections, and the other factor represents the number of items in each group, set, or collection. Students need multiple experiences identifying which factor represents the number of groups and which factor represents the number of items in each group. Early experiences with concrete models and pictures and explicit connections to the symbolic notation will not only help students to identify multiplication situations but will also support student understanding of division.

Notes

Interpret whole-number quotients of whole numbers, e.g., interpret 56 ÷ 8 as the number of objects in each share when 56 objects are partitioned equally into 8 shares, or as a number of shares when 56 objects are partitioned into equal shares of 8 objects each. For example, describe a context in which a number of shares or a number of groups can be expressed as 56 ÷ 8.

Once students understand the meaning of multiplication in terms of finding the total number of items given the number of groups and the number of items in a group, division can be understood by thinking in terms of finding a missing factor (either the number of groups or the number of items in a group).

There are two distinct meanings of division. The first is the partitive (or fair share) meaning.

Example 1:

John has 32 crayons and 4 bags. If he wants to put the same number of crayons in each bag, how many crayons will he put in each bag?

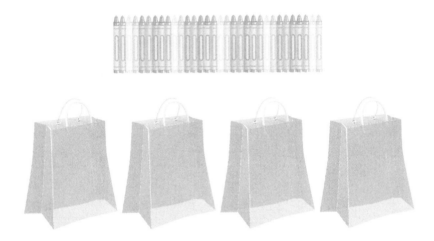

In this case, John knows the total number of items (product) and the number of bags or groups (factor) and he is looking for the number of items to put in each bag (missing factor). This can be written as 4 × _____ = 32 or as the division expression 32 ÷ 4 = _____.

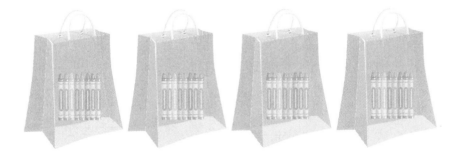

The other meaning of division is the measurement (or repeated subtraction) meaning.

Example 2:

John has 32 crayons. He wants to give 8 crayons to each person in his group. How many people are in John's group?

In this case, John knows the total number of items (product) and the number of items for each person (factor). He wants to find the number of people or groups of 8 he can make (missing factor). This can be written as ____ × 8 = 32 or as the division expression $32 \div 8 =$ ____.

It is not necessary for students to know the names of each division meaning; however, they should be able to identify the unknown in a given situation.

Type of Division	Number of Groups	Number of Items in a Group	Total Number of Items
Partitive	known	unknown	known
Measurement	unknown	known	known

What the TEACHER does:

- Provide a variety of division situations for students to model using concrete materials.
- Ask questions that support students in identifying information in the problem and connecting it to the division models. What do you know? (For example, the number of groups) What do you want to find out? (For example, how many in a group?)
- Present opportunities for students to explain their reasoning.
- Introduce division symbols and terminology. Add these terms to the class multiplication and division word wall.

  o $\div$, $\overline{)}$

  o factor, missing factor, product, divisor, dividend, quotient

- Introduce students to numerical representations by writing equations that represent their work.

  o $15 \div 5 = 3$

  o $3\overline{)15}$

- As students show understanding and can identify the given information (number of groups or number of items in a in a group) and connect it to the symbolic representation, progress to situations with pictures, numbers, and words.

What the STUDENTS do:

- Use concrete materials to model various division situations.
- Identify the information given in the problem as well as the missing information.

  o **There are 18 marbles and each player needs 6 marbles. How many people can play?**

    o I know each player (group) has 6 marbles and there are 18 marbles. I want to find how many people (groups) can play. $18 \div 6 = 3$

  o **There are 20 candies in a package. I have 4 candy cups. If I need to put the same number of candies in each cup, how many cups can I fill?**

    o I know there are 20 candies and I have 4 cups (groups). I want to find out how many candies I can put in each cup. $20 \div 4 = 5$

- Explain how they determined the missing factor.
- Use pictorial representations for division situations.
- Connect representations to numeric expressions.

Addressing Student Misconceptions and Common Errors

Because multiplication is commutative ($3 \times 7 = 7 \times 3$), some students think that $21 \div 3$ and $3 \div 21$ mean the same thing. This is especially true the equations are written two different ways.

$21 \div 3$ and $3\overline{)21}$

Connecting concrete and pictorial models to both forms of division equations is essential to eliminating this misconception.

Students read $3\overline{)21}$ as 3 "goes into" 21. Although these words are commonly used, they do not reinforce the meaning of division. Getting students to read this as "3 divides 21" or "21 divided by 3" or "How many groups of 3 are in 21?" is a habit that should be developed early in division instruction.

The sharing model (How many in a group?) is often easier for students to recognize as division. The measurement model is more difficult. Students need to work with many problem situations for each type of division using concrete materials and drawing pictures.

Use multiplication and division within 100 to solve word problems in situations involving equal groups, arrays, and measurement quantities, e.g., by using drawings and equations with a symbol for the unknown number to represent the problem.[1]

[1] See Table 2 in the Resources, page 256.

Table 2 (page 256) provides problem situations for multiplication and division. These contexts provide important links to developing conceptual understanding of the meaning of multiplication and division. Begin with modeling equal group situations and progress to array and area situations. Note that comparison situations do not need to be introduced until Grade 4.

It is important for students to have many opportunities to use concrete materials to model the situations and identify the number of groups and the number of items in a group. Only after evidence of students' understanding using concrete models should they begin to draw pictures and use the number line as representations of multiplication.

Once students demonstrate understanding with multiplication situations, use connected division examples in which students identify the total number of objects and explain whether they know the number of groups or the number of items. Later, provide array and area situations with multiplication examples in which students find the total number of items, and make connections to division examples in which students need to find the missing factor (number of columns or number of rows).

What the TEACHER does:

- Provide students with a variety of equal group multiplication situations and have them model each situation to solve the problem.

  o Students identify the factor that represents the groups and the factor that represents the total number in a group.

  o Give students opportunities to discuss their representations and explain their thinking.

Example:

There are 5 bags of apples. Each bag contains 3 apples. How many apples are there?

- Provide students with related partitive (fair share) division situations in which they identify the given information (total number of items, number of groups) and find the number of items in each group.

Example:

I have 15 apples and 5 bags. I want to put the same number of apples in each bag. How many apples are in each bag?

- Provide students with related measurement division situations in which they identify the given information (total number of items and number of items in each group) and find the number of groups.

(continued)

What the TEACHER does (continued):

Example:

I have 15 apples and I want to put 3 apples in each bag. How many bags do I need?

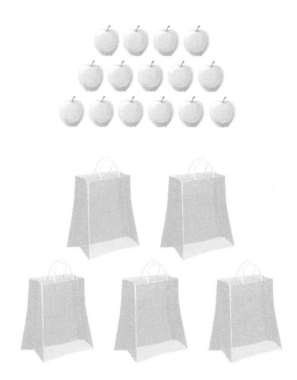

- After a variety of experiences representing equal group problems with concrete materials and pictorial representations, make connections to the written symbols for multiplication and division, including missing factor notation.

  ○ 5 groups of 3 is 15 $5 \times 3 = 15$

  ○ $5 \times \square = 15$ $15 \div 5 = \square$ $5)\overline{15}^{\,3}$

  ○ $\square \times 3 = 15$ $15 \div 3 = \square$ $3)\overline{15}^{\,5}$

  ○ Continue with similar situations using array representations and following the procedure as described for equal group situations (see Table 2, page 256).

What the STUDENTS do:

- Work collaboratively using concrete materials to represent multiplication problems.
- Identify the information given in the problem and explain their thinking using multiplication vocabulary (*groups, total, factor,* and *product*).
- Use mathematical symbols to represent the problem situation.
- Work collaboratively to model related division problems.
- Identify the information given in the problem and explain their thinking using division vocabulary (*factor—number of groups, number of items in a group,* and *product—total number of items*).
- Use mathematical symbols to represent the problem situation using either multiplication notation with a missing factor or division notation.
- Explain their reasoning for each problem situation.

Addressing Student Misconceptions and Common Errors

Students who have trouble identifying information in a problem situation (which number represents the total, the number of groups and/or the number of items in a group) need more experience making explicit connections between their representations (concrete models or pictures) and determining the number of groups **or** the number of items in a group.

Determine the unknown whole number in a multiplication or division equation relating three whole numbers. For example, determine the unknown number that makes the equation true in each of the equations $8 \times ? = 48$, $5 = \_\_ \div 3$, $6 \times 6 = ?$

Up to this point, students have had many experiences solving multiplication and related division problems using concrete materials. As students develop conceptual understanding of these operations, including modeling and explaining situations, they now relate this understanding to symbolic notation, writing equations. Students may be writing equations for simpler facts while they continue to work with models and other representations for the more difficult facts. Focusing on the relationship between multiplication and division will help students develop fluency with related fact families.

What the TEACHER does:

- As students become familiar with equation notation connected to their concrete or pictorial representations, give them isolated equations to talk about and describe what the numbers in each equation represent. For example, $3 \times 4 = 12$ represents 3 groups of 4 items gives a total of 12 items.
- Include opportunities for students to explore writing equations with missing factors.

  $\square \times 4 = 12$ means some number of groups of 4 items equals 12 items, and connecting the multiplication missing factor equations to related division equations $12 \div 4 = \square$.

- Expect students to build fact families and explain the relationship among the facts, first using multiplication facts with missing factors and then using division facts.

What the STUDENTS do:

- Write and read related multiplication equations and equations with missing factors.

  - $3 \times 5 = 15$ $15 = 3 \times 5$
  - $3 \times \square = 15$ $15 = 3 \times \square$
  - $\triangle \times 5 = 15$ $15 = \triangle \times 5$

- Relate missing factor multiplication equations to division equations using both the $\div$ and $\overline{)}$) symbols for division.

  - $3 \times 5 = 15$ $15 = 3 \times 5$ $15 \div 3 = 5$ $3\overline{)15}$
    $15 \div 5 = 3$ $5\overline{)15}$

  - $3 \times \square = 15$ $15 = 3 \times \square$ $15 \div 3 = \square$ $3\overline{)15}$

  - $\triangle \times 5 = 15$ $15 = \triangle \times 5$ $15 \div 5 = \triangle$ $5\overline{)15}$

Addressing Student Misconceptions and Common Errors

Now that students are working more frequently with numeric equations for multiplication and division, reinforce accurate reading of the equations. $15 \div 3$ and $3\overline{)15}$ should both be read as "15 divided by 3" or "3 divides 15."

In algebra, the use of a symbol in one problem cannot represent a different number in a different but related situation. When writing missing factor equations, be sure to use different symbols for the missing factor that represents the number of groups and the missing factor that represents the total number in a group or the total number of items.

For example: $15 \div 3 = x$ $15 \div 5 = y$

Notes

Operations and Algebraic Thinking
3.OA.B*

Understand properties of multiplication and the relationship between multiplication and division.

STANDARD 5

3.OA.B.5: Apply properties of operations as strategies to multiply and divide.[2] *Examples: If 6 × 4 = 24 is known, then 4 × 6 = 24 is also known. (Commutative property of multiplication.) 3 × 5 × 2 can be found by 3 × 5 = 15, then 15 × 2 = 30, or by 5 × 2 = 10, then 3 × 10 = 30. (Associative property of multiplication.) Knowing that 8 × 5 = 40 and 8 × 2 = 16, one can find 8 × 7 as 8 × (5 + 2) = (8 × 5) + (8 × 2) = 40 + 16 = 56. (Distributive property.)*

[2] Students need not use formal terms for these properties.

STANDARD 6

3.OA.B.6: Understand division as an unknown-factor problem. *For example, find 32 ÷ 8 by finding the number that makes 32 when multiplied by 8.*

*Major cluster

Operations and Algebraic Thinking   3.OA.B

Cluster B: Understand properties of multiplication and the relationship between multiplication and division.
Grade 3 Overview

As students have a variety of experiences solving problems and modeling multiplication and division situations with one-digit factors, they explore the properties of multiplication, develop strategies based on these properties, and use the properties to build their understanding of the relationship between multiplication and division. Properties include the commutative and associative properties, the identity element for multiplication, and the zero property. These properties can be connected to earlier work with addition. The distributive property will help students to develop efficient strategies for multiplication—not only for basic facts but also for more complex multiplication examples. It is also a foundational property for future work with algebra.

Standards for Mathematical Practice
SFMP 3. Construct viable arguments and critique the reasoning of others.
SFMP 4. Model with mathematics and SFMP 5. Use appropriate tools strategically.
SFMP 6. Attend to precision.
SFMP 7. Look for and make use of structure.
SFMP 8. Look for and express regularity in repeated reasoning.

Students use concrete models, pictures, words, and numbers to justify their ideas showing the patterns they find in multiplication and division. Developing the precise language of multiplication and division helps students to explain their thinking not only about the individual operations but how they are related to each other. The commutative, associative, and distributive properties lay the foundation for fluency with basic facts through looking at the structure of multiplication and division and providing students with strategies for solving problems. Students look for and describe patterns they notice as they work with multiplication and division facts.

Related Content Standards
4.NBT.B.5   4.NBT.B.6   5.NBT.B.6 5   NBT.B.8

Apply properties of operations as strategies to multiply and divide.[2] Examples: If 6 × 4 = 24 is known, then 4 × 6 = 24 is also known. (Commutative property of multiplication.) 3 × 5 × 2 can be found by 3 × 5 = 15, then 15 × 2 = 30, or by 5 × 2 = 10, then 3 × 10 = 30. (Associative property of multiplication.) Knowing that 8 × 5 = 40 and 8 × 2 = 16, one can find 8 × 7 as 8 × (5 + 2) = (8 × 5) + (8 × 2) = 40 + 16 = 56. (Distributive property.)

[2] Students need not use formal terms for these properties.

As third graders explore and develop conceptual understanding of multiplication and division, they recognize the structure of multiplication by noticing patterns and making generalizations about multiplication and division applying a variety of properties. These properties are not taught in isolation, but rather should be developed and discussed as a part of carefully related student experiences. Note that instruction does not stop to "teach" the properties. Incorporate opportunities for students to use the properties to develop strategies and patterns to simplify what is happening when they multiply two numbers.

Providing students with multiple experiences to multiply with a factor of 1 will lead to a discussion of 1 as the identity element for multiplication. Multiplying a number by 1 does not change the number.

$$\square \times 1 = \square \qquad 1 \times \square = \square \qquad 1 \times 7 = 7 \qquad 7 \times 1 = 7$$

$$\square = \square \times 1 \qquad \square = 1 \times \square \qquad 7 = 1 \times 7 \qquad 7 = 7 \times 1$$

The zero property of multiplication states that if one of the factors is zero (I have zero groups or zero items in a group) the product is zero.

$$\square \times 0 = 0 \qquad 0 \times \square = 0 \qquad 3 \times 0 = 0 \qquad 0 \times 3 = 0$$

$$0 = \square \times 0 \qquad 0 = 0 \times \square \qquad 0 = 3 \times 0 \qquad 0 = 0 \times 3$$

Although students worked with the commutative property of addition in earlier grades, the commutative structure of multiplication is different because factors represent two different quantities—one being the number of groups and the other being the number of items in each group. So, although the product for 6 × 3 and 3 × 6 is the same, the actual multiplication situations are not the same. One represents 6 groups of 3 and the other represents 3 groups of 6.

$a \times b = c$ and $b \times a = c$

3 × 5 = 15   and   5 × 3 = 15

The associative property of multiplication shows that when multiplying three or more numbers, the product is always the same regardless of their grouping. That is, $(a \times b) \times c = a \times (b \times c)$. This property is particularly helpful in developing strategies for mental computation and decomposing factors to help students learn more difficult multiplication facts.

$$(a \times b) \times c = a \times (b \times c) \qquad (7 \times 2) \times 5 = 70 \qquad 7 \times (2 \times 5) = 70$$

The distributive property should be explored in the context of composing and decomposing factors. Although the use of this property becomes much more formal in algebraic contexts, third graders who understand the distributive property can use it to help learn more difficult basic facts. Using concrete representations will help students to conceptually understand the distributive property rather than to learn it as a rule or formal procedure.

Example:

When multiplying 6 × 7, I can think of this as 6 groups of 7—or I can also decompose the 7 to think about it as 5 + 2 so I can show 6 groups of 5, which is 30, and 6 groups of 2, which is 12. Adding 30 and 12 is 42, so 6 × 7 = 42.

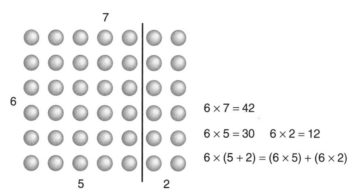

$6 \times 7 = 42$

$6 \times 5 = 30$ $6 \times 2 = 12$

$6 \times (5 + 2) = (6 \times 5) + (6 \times 2)$

What the TEACHER does:

- Present students with a variety of multiplication examples using concrete representations including equal group and array models. Ask students questions that lead them to conclude that the order of the factors does not affect the product. For example:

Hank has 4 bags with 3 marbles in each bag.

Denise has 3 bags with 4 marbles in each bag.

- ○ What is similar in these two situations?
- ○ What is different in these two situations?
- ○ What do you notice about the factors in these two problems?
- ○ What does each factor represent for Hank?
- ○ What does each factor represent for Denise?
- ○ What do you notice about the total number of marbles each person has?
- ○ Try this with two different factors. What do you notice about the product of these factors?
- ○ Do you think this will always be true?

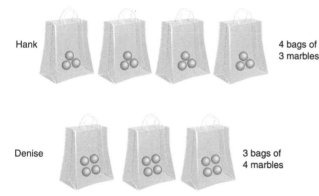

- Provide students with opportunities to explore the identity element for multiplication. (*Note:* They do not need to know that 1 is the identity element; rather, they recognize that when I multiply a number times 1, the product is the number.) Have students investigate a variety of situations for multiplication by one and generalize the identity element.

Karen has 1 package with 6 cupcakes. How many cupcakes in all?

Marianne has 6 packages with 1 cupcake. How many cupcakes in all?

- Continue similar experiences with multiplication by zero.

Cathy is paid $4 an hour for mowing the lawn. It rains so she cannot mow today. How much will she get paid? $0 \times 4 = 0$

Cathy volunteers to mow the lawn for her grandmother. It takes her 4 hours to mow the lawn. She does not ask for any money. How much will she get paid? $4 \times 0 = 0$

(Although these situations may seem trivial, they do provide an example of context that demonstrates that when multiplying with 0 the product will be 0.)

- Provide examples for students to explore that model the associative property to help them discover strategies for making multiplication of several factors easier.

- ○ Find the product of 3 × 8 × 5.
- ○ Find the product of 3 × (8 × 5), or multiply 8 × 5 and then multiply that product by 3.
- ○ What do you notice about these two problems?
- ○ What do you notice about the products?
- ○ Which is easier to do? Why?

- Introduce the distributive property by having students build a multiplication array for 6 × 7 using square tiles. Write the equation for this array. Ask them to divide the array into 2 pieces along a horizontal or vertical line, as shown below.

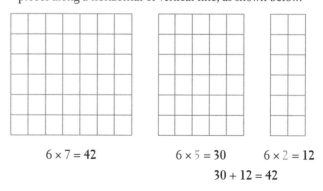

$6 \times 7 = 42$ $6 \times 5 = 30$ $6 \times 2 = 12$

$30 + 12 = 42$

(continued)

What the TEACHER does (continued):

- Collect the models and equations from the various ways students divided the array. Record the equations on the board. Facilitate a discussion that helps students to understand the relationship between the two figures. Ask
  - What are the factors in the first array?
  - How many tiles are in the first array?
  - How are the factors in the new arrays similar to the factors in the first array?
  - What do you notice about the total number of tiles in the new arrays?

- Provide students with a variety of opportunities similar to that above. Give students many opportunities to explore the distributive property and then connect it to the symbolic notation.

$$6 \times 7 = 42 \qquad 6 \times (5 + 2) = 42 \qquad 6 \times 5 + 6 \times 2 = 42$$

- Encourage students to use models of the distributive property to help them find the product of facts with which they struggle.

What the STUDENTS do:

- Use concrete materials to model specific multiplication situations.
- Discuss patterns they notice from their models.
- Describe properties of multiplication they find in their models.
  - The order of the factors does not change the product.
  - When I multiply a number by 1, I get that number.
  - When I add zero to a number, I get the number I started with.
  - When I multiply a number times 0, the product is 0.
  - When I have 3 or more factors, I can change the order and grouping of the factors to make the problem easier to solve.
  - I can decompose one factor into 2 parts and multiply each part by the other factor and find the sum of those parts to help me find the product.

- Explain their reasoning to others.
- Write equations for the examples they have modeled.
- Solve problems that use these properties.

Addressing Student Misconceptions and Common Errors

Students often confuse multiplying by zero with adding to zero. Although this property seems obvious, providing students with problems and using models will help to reinforce the correct understanding.

The distributive property forms the foundation for all future work with multiplying whole numbers. However, in Grade 3, students should use this valuable property to help learn more difficult basic facts through array models. Introduce and continue work with this property using models throughout early work with multiplication. Students need opportunities to use and describe this property in order to make sense of it.

Notes

STANDARD 6 (3.OA.B.6)

Understand division as an unknown-factor problem. For example, find 32 ÷ 8 by finding the number that makes 32 when multiplied by 8.

This Standard is an extension of previous work relating multiplication and division (3.OA.A.3 and 3.OA.A.4). It also supports the problem situations in Table 2 (page 256), as students solve problems that involve looking for missing factors they relate that work to multiplication. Thinking about division in terms of multiplication will help students to use the multiplication facts they know to become fluent with division facts. This Standard supports the use of fact families to reinforce the relationship between multiplication and division.

$$6 \times 4 = 24 \qquad 4 \times 6 = 24 \qquad 24 \div 6 = 4 \qquad 24 \div 4 = 6 \qquad 6)\overline{24}^{\,4}$$

$$24 = 6 \times 4 \qquad 24 = 4 \times 6 \qquad 4 = 24 \div 6 \qquad 6 = 24 \div 4 \qquad 4)\overline{24}^{\,6}$$

What the TEACHER does:

- Provide problem situations that involve finding a missing factor for students to model and solve. (See Table 2, page 256.)
- Make explicit connections between the model, the written multiplication equation, and the related division equation.
- Include class activities that relate division to thinking about a missing factor.

What the STUDENTS do:

- Describe information in problem situations and relate that information to written multiplication and division equations.
- Practice using missing factors to find the solution to the division problem.

  ○ To solve 42 ÷ 6, think what number multiplied by 6 equals 42.
  ○ Describe their thinking using words and numbers.

Addressing Student Misconceptions and Common Errors

Students often consider multiplication and division as discrete operations and do not understand the importance of the relationship between them as they learn basic facts or solve problems. It is important for students to understand division in terms of finding a missing factor and relate this work to writing division expressions and equations. Students need much experience identifying what information is known and what they are looking for using concrete materials and drawing pictures as well as asking themselves the right question, such as "How many groups of 7 can I make from 28?" Relating work with models to written missing factor multiplication equations and division equations is essential for students to develop this understanding.

Notes

Operations and Algebraic Thinking
3.OA.C*

Multiply and divide within 100.

STANDARD 7   **3.OA.C.7:** Fluently multiply and divide within 100, using strategies such as the relationship between multiplication and division (e.g., knowing that 8 × 5 = 40, one knows 40 ÷ 5 = 8) or properties of operations. By the end of Grade 3, know from memory all products of two one-digit numbers.

*Major cluster

Operations and Algebraic Thinking   3.OA.C

Cluster C: Multiply and divide within 100.
Grade 3 Overview

Thinking about this cluster in terms of rigor, students build conceptual understanding of multiplication and division by modeling a variety of problem situations and using properties to develop reasoning strategies. From these experiences, fluency with facts becomes a natural progression that is much more effective than solely drilling multiplication and division tables. Although some students will need more practice than others, drilling facts should happen only after students have had substantive experiences building conceptual understanding through modeling and solving problems that reinforce the meaning of multiplication and division.

Standards for Mathematical Practice
SFMP 1. Make sense of problems and persevere in solving them.
SFMP 2. Use quantitative reasoning.
SFMP 3. Construct viable arguments and critique the reasoning of others.
SFMP 4. Model with mathematics.
SFMP 5. Use appropriate tools strategically.
SFMP 6. Attend to precision.
SFMP 7. Look for and make use of structure.
SFMP 8. Look for and express regularity in repeated reasoning.

Through solving a variety of problems, students make sense of the meaning of multiplication and its relationship to division by identifying the number of groups and numbers of items in a group. They explain their reasoning and any strategies they use to solve problems and describe the relationship between multiplication and division. They use a variety of strategies that make sense to them to learn the basic multiplication and division facts and share these strategies with classmates. Students use various tools and models, including equal set models and arrays, to determine the product or the missing factor. Knowing and using appropriate vocabulary (*factor, missing factor, product, quotient*) will help students to associate meaning to their work and describe their thinking accurately to others. Exploring the properties and discussing what they notice helps to lay the foundation for the structure of multiplication and division not only within 100 but in future work as well.

Related Content Standards
4.NBT.B.4   4.NBT.B.5   4.NBT.B   6 5.NBT.B.5   5.NBT.B.6   5.NBT.B.7

Notes

STANDARD 7 (3.OA.C.7)

Fluently multiply and divide within 100, using strategies such as the relationship between multiplication and division (e.g., knowing that 8 × 5 = 40, one knows 40 ÷ 5 = 8) or properties of operations. By the end of Grade 3, know from memory all products of two one-digit numbers.

This culminating Standard is the outcome of multiplication and division activities from all of the previous Standards in this domain. Students begin by modeling multiplication and division situations using concrete models, pictorial representations, and number lines. They solve a variety of multiplication and division problems focusing on the meaning of numbers in the situation and identifying what they know (number of groups, number of items in a group, or total number and use that information to figure out what they do not know. They explore and use properties of multiplication. They progress to writing equations for these situations and then relating division to multiplication facts by thinking of division in terms of multiplication (that is, to determine the quotient of 45 ÷ 9, they think "What number times 9 gives 45?"). All of these Standards lead to fluently multiplying and dividing within 100.

Students should have experience with multiplication and division equations written in all forms.

$$3 \times 5 \qquad 3 \times \square = 15 \qquad 15 \div 3 \qquad 3\overline{)15}$$

Strategies that students may use to become fluent with these facts include:

- Doubling (multiplication by 2)
- Multiplying by one (identity element)
- Multiplying by five (counting by 5)
- Multiplying by ten
- Doubling doubles (multiplication by 4)
- Square numbers (2 × 2, 3 × 3, 4 × 4, etc.)
- Composing and decomposing factors to use known facts (distributive property)
- Using the commutative property
- Multiplying by nine as related to multiplication by ten
- Building fact families
- Finding missing factors

What the TEACHER does:

- Ensure that students have many opportunities in many contexts (problem solving, using concrete materials and pictorial representations, using properties) to work with multiplication and division facts.
- Provide students with activities to make explicit connections between multiplication and division followed by classroom conversations and asking purposeful questions.
- Provide experiences that elicit student strategies to learning basic facts.
- Use drill and practice after students have demonstrated conceptual understanding and have strategies for a group of facts.

What the STUDENTS do:

- Solve problems and model examples that represent multiplication and division facts.
- Relate models to written equations.
- Develop understanding of the relationship between multiplication and division by identifying information and using that information to ask themselves questions that support understanding.
- Use strategies based on properties and patterns of multiplication to learn multiplication facts.
- Use multiplication facts in terms of a missing factor to learn division facts.

Addressing Student Misconceptions and Common Errors

The development of conceptual understanding must precede drill and practice exercises. Students who struggle with facts need more experience with concrete and pictorial representations, including describing what their models represent to make connections to basic facts. They need time and experience with developing strategies that are based on patterns and properties to help support learning their facts. It is important to give students time to learn and understand these concepts before procedural skill practice takes place.

Operations and Algebraic Thinking
3.OA.D*

Cluster D

Solve problems involving the four operations, and identify and explain patterns in arithmetic.

STANDARD 8

3.OA.D.8: Solve two-step word problems using the four operations. Represent these problems using equations with a letter standing for the unknown quantity. Assess the reasonableness of answers using mental computation and estimation strategies including rounding.[3]

[3] This Standard is limited to problems posed with whole numbers and having whole-number answers; students should know how to perform operations in the conventional order when there are no parentheses to specify a particular order (Order of Operations).

STANDARD 9

3.OA.D.9: Identify arithmetic patterns (including patterns in the addition table or multiplication table), and explain them using properties of operations. *For example, observe that 4 times a number is always even, and explain why 4 times a number can be decomposed into two equal addends.*

*Major cluster

Operations and Algebraic Thinking   3.OA.D

Cluster D: Solve problems involving the four operations, and identify and explain patterns in arithmetic.
Grade 3 Overview

Third graders have many experiences solving multiplication and division problems to build conceptual understanding of those operations. These problems should be extended to situations in which students will use an operation or combinations of operations to solve two-step problems using various models and representations. Estimation strategies not only help to extend conceptual understanding, but also help students think about the numbers in a problem and whether a solution is reasonable. This cluster also includes giving students opportunities to examine patterns in multiplication and division and how those patterns relate to the properties (and vice versa).

Standards for Mathematical Practice
SFMP 1. Make sense of problems and persevere in solving them.
SFMP 2. Use quantitative reasoning.
SFMP 3. Construct viable arguments and critique the reasoning of others.
SFMP 4. Model with mathematics.
SFMP 5. Use appropriate tools strategically.
SFMP 6. Attend to precision.
SFMP 7. Look for and make use of structure.
SFMP 8. Look for and express regularity in repeated reasoning.

Students at this level use quantitative reasoning to solve single- and multi-step problems that include all four operations using models, pictures, words, and numbers. Students think about solutions in terms of reasonableness, asking themselves "Does this make sense?" Estimation strategies help to extend conceptual understanding, and to think about the numbers in a problem to determine if a solution is reasonable. Students explain their thinking using materials, pictures, words, and numbers. They listen to the reasoning of others and look for similarities and differences in various strategies used to solve a problem. Using a variety of representations and models helps students to solve problems and to deepen their understanding of the meaning of the operations. They begin to develop problem solving strategies, including make a model, draw a picture, make an organized list, and find a pattern. Students select appropriate tools, including concrete materials, graph paper, and pictures to help solve problems. They also ask themselves if a task can be completed by mental computation, estimation, or paper and pencil. For more complex situations, they might use a calculator. Using appropriate mathematical vocabulary and accurate units of measure are areas of focus as students begin to solve more sophisticated problems. They look for and extend mathematical patterns in a variety of situations, including tables and problems, and connect those patterns to the properties. These patterns help students to understand the structure of the four operations and should also be connected to the work in the Number and Operations in Base Ten (NBT) domain.

Related Content Standards

2.OA.A.1	2.MD.B.5	2.MD.C.8	3.MD.A.1	3.MD.A.2	3.MD.B.3	3.MC.C.7	3.G.A.1	4.0A.A.2
4.OA.A3	4.OA.C.5	4.MD.A.2	4.MD.B.4	4.MD.C.7				

22 The Common Core Mathematics Companion: The Standards Decoded, Grades 3–5

STANDARD 8 (3.OA.D.8)

Solve two-step word problems using the four operations. Represent these problems using equations with a letter standing for the unknown quantity. Assess the reasonableness of answers using mental computation and estimation strategies including rounding.[3]

[3] This Standard is limited to problems posed with whole numbers and having whole-number answers; students should know how to perform operations in the conventional order when there are no parentheses to specify a particular order (Order of Operations).

This Standard includes several connected mathematical ideas. Students solve two-step problems that include more than one operation by representing the information using concrete models, pictures including bar models, and number lines. Writing equations begins by making connections between the representations and the symbolic notation (equations). Although order of operations is not formally taught in Grade 3, thinking about the order in which operations should be a part of determining if answers are reasonable.

For example, consider the following problem:

Marcos bought a candy bar for 75¢ and 3 apples for 65¢ each. How much did Marcos spend?

Students need to realize that they need to find the total cost of the apples by multiplying before they add the cost of the candy bar. This begins informal thinking about order of operations (multiplication precedes addition and subtraction). Any other process would not result in a sensible solution. Explicit opportunities for discussions about possible models, strategies, and results should be an important part of this Standard.

Determining whether answers are reasonable by using number sense, understanding the context, the meaning of operations using mental computation strategies, and estimation strategies cannot be overemphasized as students work with all of the ideas imbedded in this Standard. Do not rush students through this process. It may be that one or two good problems will take a full mathematics class; assigning one or two follow-up problems for homework will encourage students to be thoughtful about their work and solution.

Using a letter standing for the unknown quantity should explicitly connect to previous work with identifying missing information that was represented by a box, underscore, or other symbols.

What the TEACHER does:

- Scaffold problems that use all four operations, including two-step problems that call for the use of different operations.
- Support students in interpreting problems, including identifying given, needed, and wanted information.
- Expect students to explain their solution strategies and to justify why their solution makes sense.

What the STUDENTS do:

- Solve problems using models, pictures, words, and numbers.
- Use a variety of problem solving strategies, including restating the problem in their own words, making models, and drawing pictures to represent their thinking.
- Explain how they solved the problem using accurate mathematical vocabulary and why their answer makes sense.

Addressing Student Misconceptions and Common Errors

Students who struggle with knowing what to do to solve problems will find it helpful to restate the problem in their own words. They should identify and underline the important information in the problem and determine what other information they might need in order to solve the problem. When they explain what the problem is asking, students will find that it will help them determine whether their answer is reasonable. Students who become easily frustrated with word problems may need carefully constructed questions to help direct them in determining what to do to solve the problem, but they should never be told what to do to reach a solution.

Notes

Identify arithmetic patterns (including patterns in the addition table or multiplication table),and explain them using properties of operations. For example, observe that 4 times a number is always even, and explain why 4 times a number can be decomposed into two equal addends.

The ability to recognize mathematical patterns is one of the most important characteristics of successful mathematics students. Mathematical ideas and concepts build on patterns, and the sooner students begin to recognize and identify patterns, the more likely mathematics will make sense to them. Identifying and explaining patterns leads students to develop the ability to make generalizations, which is the foundation of algebraic reasoning and more formal mathematical thinking.

Students should have many opportunities to explore, recognize, and talk about patterns in all of their mathematical work, but especially in addition and subtraction and the related operations of multiplication and division. Expecting students to justify their thinking is an important part of the discussion. "How do you know?" and "Does this always work?" are important questions for students to consider when describing and explaining patterns they have found.

What the TEACHER does:

- Provide students with copies of the addition or multiplication table of facts.
- Ask students to find any patterns they notice. They might color in the patterns and describe the numerical and visual pattern. Student-generated patterns are more meaningful than patterns they are shown.

What the STUDENTS do:

- Look for patterns on the addition or multiplication tables and color them. For example, if students shade all of the even numbers on the multiplication table, they will see that all of the numbers in the second, fourth, sixth, eighth, and tenth columns are shaded.
- Describe the patterns they have found.

Addressing Student Misconceptions and Common Errors

Students who have difficulty finding and describing patterns should start with simple examples and build to more complex patterns. They are more likely to notice visual patterns before numerical patterns. If possible, project the multiplication or additional tables and shaded patterns for all to see. This will help struggling students to visualize the patterns and then look at characteristics of the numbers.

Notes

Operations and Algebraic Thinking
Cluster A: Represent and solve problems involving multiplication and division.

Standard: 3.OA.A.2. *Interpret whole-number quotients of whole numbers, e.g., interpret 56 ÷ 8 as the number of objects in each share when 56 objects are partitioned equally into 8 shares, or as a number of shares when 56 objects are partitioned into equal shares of 8 objects each.* For example, describe a context in which a number of shares or a number of groups can be expressed as 56 ÷ 8.

Standards for Mathematical Practice:

SFMP 1. Make sense of problems and persevere in solving them.

Students solve division problems using both meanings of division.

SFMP 3. Construct viable arguments and critique the reasoning of others.

They explain their reasoning using pictures, words, and numbers.

SFMP 4. Model with mathematics.

Square tiles and grip paper are used to model the problems.

SFMP 7. Look for and make use of structure.

Students develop a deep understanding of the partitive and measurement meaning of division.

Goal:

Students will experience and model situations involving partitive and measurement meanings of division. They make connections to previous experiences with the meaning of multiplication.

Planning:

Materials: Square tiles or similar counters, grid paper

Sample Activity:

Students work in groups of 3 to solve each of the following problems using the tiles. They draw their representations on the grid paper and discuss how the problems are similar and how they are different.

- Anita has 42 M&M'S to put in 6 cups. If she wants to put the same number of M&M'S in each cup, how many will she put in each?
- Anita has 42 M&M'S and she wants to put 7 in a cup. How many cups will she need?

Provide similar problems for students to solve.

Notes

Questions/Prompts:

For each problem ask students what they know. Connect to previous experience with multiplication by asking questions such as:

- What number tells you the total number of M&M'S?
- What number tells you how many in a group?
- What number tells you the number of groups?

After students successfully model one set of problems, as they are working on additional problems ask them to them identify what the numbers in the problem represent (total, number of groups, or number of items in a group) and what they are looking for (number of groups or number of items in a group).

Ask students to write the equation using missing factor notation ($6 \times \underline{\hspace{1cm}} = 42$) and then relate that to writing a division equation ($42 \div 6 = \underline{\hspace{1cm}}$).

Differentiating Instruction:

Struggling Students: Provide students with many opportunities to model the problems. Have physical representations for the sets (for example, paper cups) and allow them to act out the problem. Your question will need to be very explicit so they can identify whether they know the number of groups or the number of items in a group.

Use problems with simpler numbers for struggling students.

Extension: Once students have solved several sets of problems, those who easily identify the information in the problem and make connections between previous work with multiplication and this work with division can begin to solve problems that involve remainders.

Notes

Operations and Algebraic Thinking
Cluster A: Represent and solve problems involving multiplication and division.

Standard:

Standards for Mathematical Practice:

Goal:

Planning:

Materials:

Sample Activity:

Questions/Prompts:

Differentiating Instruction:

Struggling Students:

Extension:

Operations and Algebraic Thinking

Cluster B: Understand properties of multiplication and the relationship between multiplication and division.

Standard:

Standards for Mathematical Practice:

Goal:

Planning:

Materials:

Sample Activity:

Questions/Prompts:

Differentiating Instruction:

Struggling Students:

Extension:

Operations and Algebraic Thinking
Cluster C: Multiply and divide within 100.

Standard:

Standards for Mathematical Practice:

Goal:

Planning:

Materials:

Sample Activity:

Questions/Prompts:

Differentiating Instruction:

Struggling Students:

Extension:

Operations and Algebraic Thinking

Cluster D: Solve problems involving the four operations, and identify and explain patterns in arithmetic.

Standard:

Standards for Mathematical Practice:

Goal:

Planning:

Materials:

Sample Activity:

Questions/Prompts:

Differentiating Instruction:

Struggling Students:

Extension:

Operations and Algebraic Thinking 4.OA.A*

Use the four operations with whole numbers to solve problems.

STANDARD 1 **4.OA.A.1:** Interpret a multiplication equation as a comparison, e.g., interpret $35 = 5 \times 7$ as a statement that 35 is 5 times as many as 7 and 7 times as many as 5. Represent verbal statements of multiplicative comparisons as multiplication equations.

STANDARD 2 **4.OA.A.2:** Multiply or divide to solve word problems involving multiplicative comparison, e.g., by using drawings and equations with a symbol for the unknown number to represent the problem, distinguishing multiplicative comparison from additive comparison.[1]

[1] See Table 2 in the Resources, page 256.

STANDARD 3 **4.OA.A.3:** Solve multistep word problems posed with whole numbers and having whole-number answers using the four operations, including problems in which remainders must be interpreted. Represent these problems using equations with a letter standing for the unknown quantity. Assess the reasonableness of answers using mental computation and estimation strategies including rounding.

*Major cluster

Operations and Algebraic Thinking   4.OA.A

Cluster A: Use the four operations with whole numbers to solve problems.
Grade 4 Overview

Fourth graders have worked with equal group and array/area problem situations for multiplication and division in Grade 3. Multiplication and division comparison situations are introduced in Grade 4. Students continue to work with one- and two-step problems that use all four operations, including problems in which remainders must be interpreted in terms of the question being asked in the problem.

Standards for Mathematical Practice
SFMP 1. Make sense of problems and persevere in solving them.
SFMP 2. Use quantitative reasoning.
SFMP 3. Construct viable arguments and critique the reasoning of others.
SFMP 4. Model with mathematics.
SFMP 5. Use appropriate tools strategically.
SFMP 6. Attend to precision.
SFMP 7. Look for and make use of structure.
SFMP 8. Look for and express regularity in repeated reasoning.

Students at this level use quantitative reasoning to solve single and multi-step problems that include all four operations using models, pictures, words, and numbers. In addition to equal group and area situations, they begin to solve multiplication and division comparison problems. They think about solutions in terms of reasonableness, asking themselves "Does this make sense?" Estimation strategies not only help to extend conceptual understanding but also students' thinking about the numbers in a problem to determine whether a solution is reasonable. Students explain their thinking using concrete materials, pictures, words, and numbers. They listen to the reasoning of others and look for similarities and differences in various strategies used to solve a problem. Using appropriate mathematical vocabulary and accurate units of measure are areas of focus as students begin to solve more sophisticated problems.

Students use various representations and models to help solve problems. They continue to develop problem solving strategies, including make a model, draw a picture, make an organized list, find a pattern, solve a simpler problem, and guess and check. Students select appropriate tools, including concrete materials, graph paper, and pictures to help solve problems. They also ask themselves whether a task can most efficiently completed by mental computation, estimation, or paper and pencil. For more complex situations, they might use a calculator.

Students look for and extend mathematical patterns in a variety of situations and connect those patterns to the properties. These patterns help students understand the structure of the four operations and should also be connected to the work in the Number and Operations in Base Ten (NBT) domain.

Related Content Standards

2.OA.A.1   2.MD.B.5   2.MD.C.8   3.MD.A.1   3.MD.A.2   3.MD.B.3   3.OA.D.8   3.MC.C.7   3.G.A.1

4.MD.A.2   4.MD.B.4   4.MD.C.7   5.MD.C.5   5.G.A.2

Notes

STANDARD 1 (4.OA.A.1)

Interpret a multiplication equation as a comparison, e.g., interpret 35 = 5 × 7 as a statement that 35 is 5 times as many as 7 and 7 times as many as 5. Represent verbal statements of multiplicative comparisons as multiplication equations.

In the earlier grades students worked with additive comparisons. Megan has 25¢ and Liz has 5¢. How much more does Megan have than Liz? (2.OA.1). (What amount would be *added* to Liz's money to get Megan's amount?)

Fourth graders learn to compare these quantities multiplicatively. Megan has 5 times as much money as Liz. (What factor would *multiply* Liz's money to get Megan's amount?) A multiplicative comparison is a situation in which one quantity is described as a multiple of the other.

Another way to identify multiplicative comparisons is recognizing that in these situations there are two different sets being compared. The first set contains a certain number of items. The second set contains multiple copies of the first set. The language of multiplicative situations can be difficult for students. Students should become familiar with these and similar ways to describe multiplicative comparison situations.

Darlene has seven marbles. Danny has 3 times as many.

Danny has 3 times as many marbles as Darlene.

The number of marbles Danny has divided by 3 is the number of marbles Darlene has.

Danny has 3 times fewer marbles than Darlene.

This Standard should be taught in concert with 4.OA.A.2 so that students are consistently working among problem situations, models, and equations as they work with comparisons.

What the TEACHER does:

- Provide many opportunities for students to identify and model multiplicative comparison situations (Table 2, page 256).
- Reinforce appropriate vocabulary to describe comparison situations and appropriate examples for writing equations from these situations.

What the STUDENTS do:

- Read and interpret multiplicative comparison situations identifying which quantity is being multiplied and which factor is telling how many times.
- Write and identify equations and statements for multiplicative comparisons.

    5 × 3 **Cathy has $5. Mary has three times as much. How much money does Mary have?**

- Recognize different language that describes multiplicative comparisons. (See Table 2, page 256.)

Addressing Student Misconceptions and Common Errors

Students may struggle with applying their knowledge of multiplication and division facts to multiplicative situations since all of their previous experience was with equal groups and array models. They need many experiences connecting facts to the language of multiplicative comparisons. Using concrete models will support students in making this connection.

Notes

Multiply or divide to solve word problems involving multiplicative comparison, e.g., by using drawings and equations with a symbol for the unknown number to represent the problem, distinguishing multiplicative comparison from additive comparison.[1]

[1] See Table 2 in the Resources, page 256.

In previous grades students worked with tape diagrams and other models to show additive comparison situations (see Table 1, page 254). Similar models with different representations will help with understanding multiplicative comparison situations. Early problems should involve one step and then build to multiple-step problems that involve up to three steps.

Additive Comparison (5 + m = 15)

It takes Sammy 5 minutes to wash the dishes. It takes his brother Bobby 15 minutes to wash the dishes. How much longer does it take Bobby to wash the dishes?

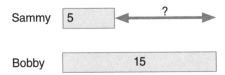

In this situation, we are finding the difference between Sammy's time and Bobby's time.

Multiplicative Comparisons

Product unknown: (3 × 5 = t)

It takes Sammy 5 minutes to wash the dishes. It takes his little brother Bobby 3 times as long. How long does it take Bobby to wash the dishes?

Think: 5 minutes 3 times would be?

Sammy | 5

Bobby | 5 | 5 | 5

← ? →

In this situation, Bobby's time is a multiple of Sammy's time.

Factor unknown (size of each group unknown) 3 × m = 15

It takes Bobby 15 minutes to wash the dishes. That is three times as long as it takes his brother Sammy. How long does it take Sammy to wash the dishes?

Think: Three groups make 15, how big is each group?

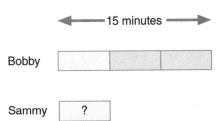

← 15 minutes →

Bobby

Sammy | ?

Factor unknown (number of groups unknown) $g \times 5 = 15$

It takes Sammy 5 minutes to wash the dishes and his little brother Bobby 15 minutes to wash the dishes. How many times as long does it take Sammy to wash the dishes?

Think: How many 5s to make 15?

Sammy | 5

Bobby | ? | ? | ?

←—— 15 minutes ——→

Table 2, page 256 in the Resources, provides various examples and models for comparison situations.

What the TEACHER does:

- Provide a variety of multiplicative comparisons (see Table 2, page 256) for students to model, describe, and solve.
- Facilitate explicit discussions in which students describe the information in the problem and use that information to represent the situation using models.
- Help students to make explicit connections between models (such as bar models), and written equations using both multiplication and division.
- Provide mixed additive and multiplicative comparison situations to help students distinguish between the two types of comparisons.
  - Additive comparisons focus on the difference between two quantities.
    - How many more?
    - How many less?
  - Multiplicative comparisons focus on comparing two quantities when one is a specified number of times greater or less than the given quantity.

What the STUDENTS do:

- Solve problems involving multiplicative comparisons using concrete materials, pictures, words, and numbers.
- Identify the information in the problem and how it relates to models.
- Write equations to represent the mathematics of the situation.

Addressing Student Misconceptions and Common Errors

Students may confuse additive and multiplicative situations. They need a variety of problems to model and discuss. Identifying what they know from the information in the problem and focusing on the question will help them to make sense of the problem. They should also consistently ask themselves if their answer makes sense.

Notes

Solve multistep word problems posed with whole numbers and having whole-number answers using the four operations, including problems in which remainders must be interpreted. Represent these problems using equations with a letter standing for the unknown quantity. Assess the reasonableness of answers using mental computation and estimation strategies including rounding.

Students continue to work with problem situations as they build fluency with all four operations. Some students may still need to use concrete and pictorial models and connect these models to numerical equations representing the unknown with a letter before solving. Others may be able to determine the equation by recognizing the information in the problem and the question that is being asked.

Students should consistently use formal and informal estimation strategies to determine whether an answer is reasonable and fits the constraints of the given situation. They should have many opportunities to explain their strategies to predict a reasonable solution or to justify why they think their answer is reasonable. Remember, good discussions take time, so it is important to have rich conversations around a small number of good problems rather than superficial discussions about a large number of problems.

This will be students' first experience with interpreting remainders. Using models, identifying the information in the problem, focusing on the question, and discussing the reasonableness of results will help students determine what to do with a whole number remainder. (They will use remainders as fractions and decimals in later work.) It is important that students have ongoing experiences with a variety of problems in which they need to determine what to do with the remainder. Encouraging students to explain their reasoning in solving such problems will also help them to think about what to do with the remainder.

Problem	Model	Equation	What to do with the remainder
Eric bought a package of 18 batteries. Each toy robot uses 4 batteries. How many toy robots can be filled with batteries?	1 robot 1 robot 1 robot 1 robot 2 left	$18 \div 4 = 4$ remainder 2 That means that 4 robots can be filled with batteries and I will have 2 batteries left over.	The solution is the quotient. Drop the remainder.
Alyssa has a new bookcase with 4 shelves. Each shelf holds 9 books. If Alyssa had 38 books how many books will not fit in the bookcase?	 $9 \times 4 = 36$ books 2 books left over	$38 \div 4 = 9$ remainder 2 Two books will not fit on the shelves.	The remainder is the solution.

Problem	Model	Equation	What to do with the remainder
Twenty-eight students are going on the class picnic. Five students can ride in each car. How many cars will be needed for the trip?		$28 \div 5 = 5$ remainder 3 That means 5 cars can hold 25 students and another car will be needed for the extra 3 students. Six cars will be needed for the trip.	Add 1 to the quotient for the solution.

What the TEACHER does:

- Provide ongoing experiences with problems, including two- and three-step problems with all four operations.
- Facilitate small group and classroom discussions in which students show and explain their strategies and solution processes using materials or pictures, words, and numbers.
- Build on previous division problem experiences by including division problem situations that include remainders.
- Lead class discussions on what to do with the remainder by focusing on the problem question, the meaning of numbers in the problems and using models.

What the STUDENTS do:

- Solve multi-step problems with all four operations using models or pictures and numbers.
- Explain their problem solving processes and compare various ways of solving problems.
- In division situations with remainders, focus on the question asked to determine what to do with the remainder.
- Ask themselves if their solution makes sense.

Addressing Student Misconceptions and Common Errors

Students who struggle in determining what operation to use to solve a problem need additional experience understanding the operations in a variety of situations (see Tables 1 and 2, pages 254 and 256). They should have explicit practice with various problem solving strategies, including:

- Restating the problem in their own words.
- Identifying given, needed, and wanted information.
- Making a model or drawing a picture.
- Making a list.
- Acting it out.
- Finding a pattern.
- Writing an equation.
- Revisiting the question and asking themselves if the solution makes sense.

Students who do not have conceptual understanding or have focused work on division procedures tend to write answers to problems using the "r" notation. For example, 16 students are going canoeing. If each canoe holds 3 canoes, how many canoes will they need? The answer 5 r 1 makes no sense in this situation. Students need to focus on the question and reasonableness of solutions using strategies including models, pictures, and acting it out.

Operations and Algebraic Thinking
4.OA.B*

Gain familiarity with factors and multiples.

STANDARD 4   **4.OA.B.4:** Find all factor pairs for a whole number in the range 1–100. Recognize that a whole number is a multiple of each of its factors. Determine whether a given whole number in the range 1–100 is a multiple of a given one-digit number. Determine whether a given whole number in the range 1–100 is prime or composite.

*Supporting cluster

Operations and Algebraic Thinking   4.OA.B

Cluster B: Gain familiarity with factors and multiples.
Grade 4 Overview

Students extend their understanding of multiplication and division to thinking about these operations in terms of composing and decomposing numbers into factors. For example, 12 can be decomposed into factors of 1, 2, 3, 4, 6, and 12 by knowing the multiplication facts that result in a product of 12. Making arrays will help students to build understanding of factors, reinforcing fluency with basic facts and extending to factor pairs beyond the basic facts. This Standard extends this understanding through recognizing prime numbers (numbers with exactly two factors) and composite numbers (number with more than two factors).

Standards for Mathematical Practice
SFMP 2. Use quantitative reasoning.
SFMP 3. Construct viable arguments and critique the reasoning of others.
SFMP 4. Model with mathematics.
SFMP 5. Use appropriate tools strategically.
SFMP 6. Attend to precision.
SFMP 7. Look for and make use of structure.
SFMP 8. Look for and express regularity in repeated reasoning.

Students extend their work with multiplication and division facts to focusing on finding factors and multiples of numbers less than 100. Although their facility with facts will help, using models and reasoning with the distributive property will help them find the factors that are not basic facts. For example, the factor pairs for 36 are 1×36, 2×18, 3×12, 4×9, and 6×6. Of these factor pairs, only 4×9 and 6×6 are considered basic facts.

Once students understand factors and multiples, they build on this understanding by defining and identifying prime and composite numbers. These concepts are important to future work with fractions. Students construct arguments based on the patterns they have found, including, for example, why 45 is a composite number and 47 is prime. They do this using models, words, and numbers.

Students extend their knowledge of basic facts by constructing arrays for numbers beyond the basic facts. For example, they can use a model of an 11×3 array to show that 3 and 11 are factors of 33 using graph paper, square tiles, and other appropriate tools. As they complete these activities, the vocabulary of multiplication is extended to include *factor, multiple, prime number,* and *composite number.* Students should be able to clearly define these words and use them in a variety of contexts.

Students recognize patterns as they explore numbers. Some numbers have exactly two factors and others have more than two factors. They will apply these structures and they begin to work with fractions. They use these patterns to make and justify generalizations such as "all even numbers other than 2 are composite because they will have more than two factors." or "All numbers other than 5 that end in 0 or 5 are composite because they will have 5 as a factor."

Related Content Standards

3.OA.B.6   3.NBT.A.3   4.NF.B.4.a   4.NF.B.4.b

Find all factor pairs for a whole number in the range 1–100. Recognize that a whole number is a multiple of each of its factors. Determine whether a given whole number in the range 1–100 is a multiple of a given one-digit number. Determine whether a given whole number in the range 1–100 is prime or composite.

This Standard builds on and extends students' knowledge of multiplication and division facts. Factor pairs include two numbers that when multiplied result in a particular product. The factor pairs of 28 include 1 × 28, 2 × 14, and 4 × 7, so the factors of 28 are 1, 2, 4, 7, and 28. Students can use square tiles to make arrays to find all of the factor pairs of a given number. They then explore patterns to build a conceptual understanding of prime numbers (numbers with exactly two factors) and composite numbers (numbers with more than two factors).

Multiples are the result of multiplying two whole numbers. Multiples can be related to factors, as shown below. Skip counting by a given number also results in the multiples of that number.

Using arrays to find the factors of 24.

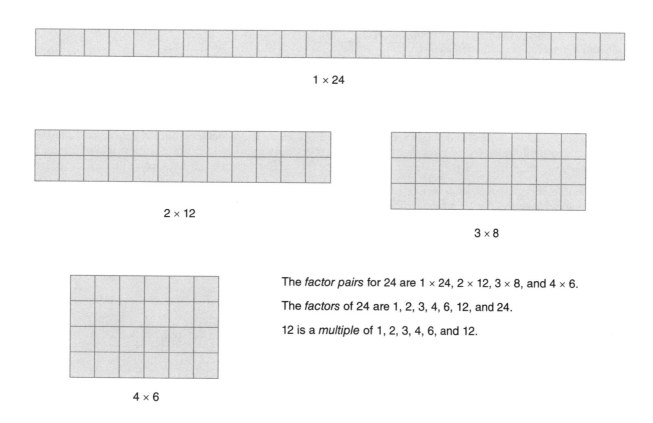

The *factor pairs* for 24 are 1 × 24, 2 × 12, 3 × 8, and 4 × 6.

The *factors* of 24 are 1, 2, 3, 4, 6, 12, and 24.

12 is a *multiple* of 1, 2, 3, 4, 6, and 12.

This Standard connects to 4.OA.C.5 in that it provides a variety of contexts for discussing number patterns that arise when students find factors and multiples. It is important to providing opportunities for students to use concrete materials, hundreds charts, and fact tables to discover patterns, followed by oral and written explanations describing those patterns, helps students develop a deeper understanding of factors, multiples, primes, and composites and to begin to make generalizations about the patterns they have found.

Such patterns include:

- Numbers that end in 0 have 10 as a factor. These numbers are multiples of 10.
- Numbers that end in 0 or 5 have 5 as a factor. These numbers are multiples of 5.
- Even numbers have 2 as a factor. These numbers are multiples of 2.
- Numbers that can be halved twice have 4 as a factor. These numbers are multiples of 4.

What the TEACHER does:

- Engage students in activities in which they use models such as arrays to find all of the factor pairs of a given number. Begin with a smaller range of numbers (1 to 20) and extend the range as students show understanding.
- Use games such as the factor game (http://illuminations.nctm.org/Activity.aspx?id=4134) to provide opportunities for students to find factors.
- As students make lists of factors, provide opportunities for them to discuss patterns.
- Use a variety of activities for students to explore finding multiples by skip counting and relate multiples to the products of a number.
- Have students connect their work with factors to identifying prime numbers (numbers with exactly two factors) and composite numbers (numbers with more than two factors). The multiples of a prime number are all composite numbers.
- Develop mathematical vocabulary including *factor, factor pair, and multiple, odd, even, prime,* and *composite.* Add these terms to the class mathematics word wall.

What the STUDENTS do:

- Students draw upon and extend their work with multiplication and division facts to determine the factors of a given number through a variety of activities.
- Discuss patterns they discover as they factor a number. (For example, all even numbers have 2 as a factor. Numbers that end in 0 or 5 have 5 as a factor.)
- List multiples of a given number using skip counting and other strategies.
- Identify and describe prime numbers as numbers that have exactly two factors.
- Identify and describe composite numbers as numbers that have more than two factors.

Addressing Student Misconceptions and Common Errors

Students often confuse the terms *factor* and *multiple*. Emphasizing the term *factor* as one of the numbers multiplied to get a product throughout all of the work with multiplication, and expecting students to use that term, should help avoid confusion. Telling students they multiply to get a *multiple* or defining *multiples* of a number as products of the number is also helpful. The more experience students have with these terms, the more accurate they will become when using them.

When listing multiples of a number, students may forget to include the number itself. Reminding students that multiples are the products of a number leads to a discussion of why a number is a factor and a multiple of itself, which is a result of the identity element of multiplication ($a \times 1 = a$).

Students may become confused about whether 1 is a prime or composite number, when actually it is neither prime nor composite because it has only one factor, itself. Developing precise definitions should help to eliminate this misconception.

Notes

Operations and Algebraic Thinking
4.OA.C*

Generate and analyze patterns.

STANDARD 5

4.OA.C.5: Generate a number or shape pattern that follows a given rule. Identify apparent features of the pattern that were not explicit in the rule itself. *For example, given the rule "Add 3" and the starting number 1, generate terms in the resulting sequence and observe that the terms appear to alternate between odd and even numbers. Explain informally why the numbers will continue to alternate in this way.*

*Additional cluster

Operations and Algebraic Thinking 4.OA.C

Cluster C: Generate and analyze patterns.
Grade 4 Overview

Finding, extending, generating, and describing patterns support developing conceptual understanding for all whole-number operations. Finding patterns is also an important strategy for solving problems. Students should have opportunities to extend and describe both physical patterns and numerical patterns.

Standards for Mathematical Practice
SFMP 1. Make sense of problems and persevere in solving them.
SFMP 2. Use quantitative reasoning.
SFMP 3. Construct viable arguments and critique the reasoning of others.
SFMP 4. Model with mathematics.
SFMP 5. Use appropriate tools strategically.
SFMP 7. Look for and make use of structure.
SFMP 8. Look for and express regularity in repeated reasoning.

Students use problems as a context for finding and extending patterns. They reason about similarities and generate rules to describe numerical and geometric patterns. Students use models and tools to describe patterns they find in problems, in numbers, and in geometric figures and to extend these patterns to other situations. They develop lists of numbers given a rule and then describe any patterns in the list using appropriate vocabulary.

In finding patterns, students are developing a deeper understanding of the structure of all four operations and begin to make generalizations by constructing rules for their patterns.

Related Content Standards

3.OA.D.9   5.OA.B.3   5.NBT.A.2

Notes

Generate a number or shape pattern that follows a given rule. Identify apparent features of the pattern that were not explicit in the rule itself. For example, given the rule "Add 3" and the starting number 1, generate terms in the resulting sequence and observe that the terms appear to alternate between odd and even numbers. Explain informally why the numbers will continue to alternate in this way.

Patterns that involve numbers or symbols can be repeating patterns or growing patterns. A repeating pattern is a cyclical repetition of an identifiable core. A linear growing pattern is a pattern that increases or decreases by a constant difference. Patterns can be shown by numeric or by geometric representations.

Number Pattern

Start with the number 4, add 5. 4, 9, 14, 19, 24, 29, . . . The numbers alternate with 4 and 9 in the ones place, which is an example of a repeating pattern. The number sequence increases by 5 which is a growing pattern.

Geometric Pattern

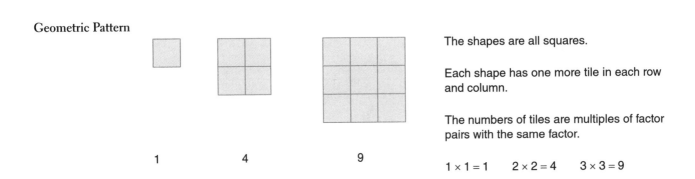

The shapes are all squares.

Each shape has one more tile in each row and column.

The numbers of tiles are multiples of factor pairs with the same factor.

$1 \times 1 = 1 \qquad 2 \times 2 = 4 \qquad 3 \times 3 = 9$

Students need a variety of opportunities in their regular mathematics work to create, extend, and describe patterns. Numerical patterns reinforce mastery of basic facts and understanding operations.

Given a geometric pattern or a numerical rule, students should extend the pattern and describe features of the pattern. They should have opportunities to describe what is happening with the pattern, but they do not need to generalize a particular rule. Describing physical patterns and connecting them to quantity supports recognition of more sophisticated patterns. Building patterns from problem situations and making an organized list are two invaluable problem solving strategies.

Finding a pattern is also an important strategy students can use to solve problems.

Example:

Anna has 5 pennies in her piggy bank. Each day she adds 6 more pennies. How many pennies will Anna have after 5 days?

Day	Pennies Added (equation)	Total Number of Pennies
0	0 + 5	5
1	1 × 6 + 5	11
2	2 × 6 + 5	17
3	3 × 6 + 5	23
4	4 × 6 + 5	29
5	5 × 6 + 5	35

Student discuss what they notice and how they can continue the pattern for more days.

What the TEACHER does:

- Provide a variety of problems and models to give students opportunities to recognize, extend, and describe patterns.
- Help students to use a variety of strategies to organize their work so that patterns are more apparent. For example, making a list, extending and describing shapes, making a model will help students to recognize and describe patterns they see.
- Facilitate student discussions about patterns they find so that students become comfortable describing and writing their ideas using words and numbers.

What the STUDENTS do:

- Look for patterns in all of their mathematical work.
- Extend and describe patterns they find.
- When appropriate, make generalizations about patterns.

Addressing Student Misconceptions and Common Errors

Some students will have difficulty recognizing and extending patterns. Others may struggle to describe the pattern. It is important for students to have many experiences with patterns and to recognize those patterns. The more patterns are explored and related to mathematical concepts, the better students will become in recognizing and describing patterns.

Some students may "recognize" a pattern when there is no pattern. Asking students to describe and continue the pattern will help them to differentiate real patterns from non-patterns.

Notes

Operations and Algebraic Thinking
Cluster B: Gain familiarity with factors and multiples.

Standard: 4.OA.B.4. *Find all factor pairs for a whole number in the range 1–100. Recognize that a whole number is a multiple of each of its factors. Determine whether a given whole number in the range 1–100 is a multiple of a given one-digit number. Determine whether a given whole number in the range 1–100 is prime or composite.*

Standards for Mathematical Practice:
SFMP 1: Make sense of problems and persevere in solving them.
Students solve this problem to identify factors of given numbers.

SFMP 4: Model with mathematics.
Using a variety of rectangular arrays will help students find factors.

SFMP 6: Attend to precision.
Students work to find all of the possible solutions and use the terms *dimensions* and *factors* in relationship to their models.

SFMP 7: Look for and make use of structure.
Students use physical models to see the structure of multiplication and in a later lesson connect their findings to identifying prime and composite numbers.

Goal:
Students use rectangular arrays to solve a problem and connect their findings to identifying the factors of a given number.

Planning:

Materials: Square tiles, grip paper, problem page, recording sheet

Sample Activity:
- Introduce students to making rectangular arrays from a given number of square tiles.
- Introduce the term *dimensions.*
- Present students with the problem and allow them time to build all the arrays they can using the tiles, draw the arrays on grid paper, and then list the dimensions of the rectangles on the recording sheet.
- Connect the dimensions they have listed to the factors of the number. Then list the factors from least to greatest.
- Discussion follows on the number of factors and the number of boxes and how they are connected.

Notes

Questions/Prompts:

Some students may see the connection between the dimensions of the boxes and the factors and not want to use the materials. Encourage them to use the materials so they can see other patterns in their work and find the "non-basic fact" factors. (For example, 36 has factors of 3 and 12 and 2 and 18.)

Following student work time, be sure to take time to discuss patterns students have found. Questions similar to the following will facilitate the conversation:

- What did you notice about the even numbers?
- Was the same thing true for all of the odd numbers?
- Look at 4, 9, and 16. What do you notice about the number of boxes you found?
- What is different about the number 1?
- What other patterns did you notice?

Differentiating Instruction:

Struggling Students: Struggling students may not have time to work all the way to 40. However, you may find that they enjoy the activity and may want to continue on their own time. Make adjustments accordingly.

It is important that struggling students—especially those who have not mastered their facts—use the concrete materials to complete the task. They also may need support in finding all of the possible rectangles. Asking questions such as *"Can you make a box that is a 4 by something?"* will encourage them to keep trying.

Extension: Check to be sure students who complete the activity early have found *all* of the possible boxes. They can work beyond 40 and may enjoy the challenge of working with larger numbers.

Notes

Yummy Doggy Treats are square in shape. They are sold in rectangular boxes with one layer of treats in a box.

A box of six treats could be any of the following shapes.

6 by 1

____ by ____

____ by ____

1 by 6

The numbers under each box show the *dimensions* of the box. The first box on the left is 1 treat wide and 6 treats high or 1 by 6. The second box is 6 treats wide and 1 treat high. Write the dimensions of the other two boxes.

Our class has been hired to find all of the possible boxes that could be made for any number of Yummy treats from 1 to 40. Work in your groups to complete the table of treats. Look for patterns as you complete the table.

Notes

Table of Treats

Number of Treats	Dimensions of Boxes	Number of Boxes	Factors
6	1 × 6, 6 × 1, 2 × 3, 3 × 2	4	1, 2, 3, 6

Operations and Algebraic Thinking

Cluster A: Use the four operations with whole numbers to solve problems.

Standard:

Standards for Mathematical Practice:

Goal:

Planning:

Materials:

Sample Activity:

Questions/Prompts:

Differentiating Instruction:

Struggling Students:

Extension:

Operations and Algebraic Thinking
Cluster B: Gain familiarity with factors and multiples.

Standard:

Standards for Mathematical Practice:

Goal:

Planning:

Materials:

Sample Activity:

Questions/Prompts:

Differentiating Instruction:

Struggling Students:

Extension:

Operations and Algebraic Thinking
Cluster C: Generate and analyze patterns.

Standard:

Standards for Mathematical Practice:

Goal:

Planning:

Materials:

Sample Activity:

Questions/Prompts:

Differentiating Instruction:

Struggling Students:

Extension:

Operations and Algebraic Thinking
5.OA.A*

Write and interpret numerical expressions.

STANDARD 1   **5.OA.A.1:** Use parentheses, brackets, or braces in numerical expressions, and evaluate expressions with these symbols.

STANDARD 2   **5.OA.A.2:** Write simple expressions that record calculations with numbers, and interpret numerical expressions without evaluating them. *For example, express the calculation "add 8 and 7, then multiply by 2" as $2 \times (8 + 7)$. Recognize that $3 \times (18932 + 921)$ is three times as large as $18932 + 921$, without having to calculate the indicated sum or product.*

*Additional cluster

Operations and Algebraic Thinking   5.OA.A

Cluster A: Write and interpret numerical expressions.
Grade 5 Overview

In Grade 5, students continue to explore and work with numerical expressions in preparation for the Expressions and Equations domain coming in middle school. Students worked informally with order of operations in grades 3 and 4 as they solved multi-step problems through modeling and writing equations. According to the standards progression document (http://ime.math.arizona .edu/progressions/), this work should be exploratory, and expressions need not include nesting symbols.

Standards for Mathematical Practice
SFMP 3. Construct viable arguments and critique the reasoning of others.
SFMP 5. Use appropriate tools strategically.
SFMP 6. Attend to precision.
SFMP 7. Look for and make use of structure.
SFMP 8. Look for and express regularity in repeated reasoning.

As students apply rules for order of operations they should explain their reasoning to others. They use scientific calculators (those that follow order of operations) to explore order of operations. Students use appropriate vocabulary to describe their work with grouping symbols and order of operations. As students explore order of operations and apply the rules in a variety of situations, they look for patterns and the structure of what is happening. They understand and apply calculating all multiplications and divisions before additions and subtractions within an expression. They make generalizations about the order of operations and grouping symbols and apply these rules to writing and solving expressions that include more than one operation and or grouping symbols.

Related Content Standards

6.EE.A.1   6.EE.A.2

Notes

STANDARD 1 (5.OA.A.1)

Use parentheses, brackets, or braces in numerical expressions, and evaluate expressions with these symbols.

Despite the traditional dependence on mnemonic phrases ("Please Excuse My Dear Aunt Sally") and mathematical convention, exploring the precedence of operations and the use of parentheses in expressions by solving a variety of multi-step problems allows students to reason about the order in which operations need to be performed. Explaining the order in which to calculate and knowing when to use parentheses can become confusing to students. Whenever possible, provide situations that model order of operations and make connections to the properties of addition and multiplication (associative and distributive).

Students need to understand that when looking at expressions, any operations in parentheses are completed first. Exponents, braces, and brackets will come later as described in the progressions document (http://ime.math.arizona.edu/progressions/).

What the TEACHER does:

- Introduce problem situations that show that multiplication and division are completed before addition and subtraction. Write and solve and equation for this problem.

  Mary bought a purse for $25 and 5 pairs of socks that cost $4 each. How much did she spend?

  $25 + (5 \times 4) = 45$

- Ask students if their answer makes sense.
- Provide students with experiences to solve equations that include parentheses with all four operations and explain their thinking.

  $5 \times (3 + 4) = 5 \times 7 = 35$ $18 - (4 + 3) = 18 - 7 = 11$
  $3 + (12 \div 4) = 3 + 3 = 6$ $(2 \times 5) + (3 \times 2) = 10 + 6 = 16$

- Provide students with equations and ask them to insert parentheses to make them true.

incorrect	$8 \div 4 \div 2 = 4$	$5 + 3 \times 7 = 56$
correct	$8 \div (4 \div 2) = 4$	$(5 + 3) \times 7 = 56$

incorrect	$4 + 8 - 4 \times 3 = 0$	$3 \times 3 + 6 \div 9 = 3$
correct	$(4 + 8) - (4 \times 3) = 0$	$3 \times (3 + 6) \div 9 = 3$

- Explain that multiplication and division are calculated in order from left to right before any addition or subtraction calculations. Have students use scientific calculators to solve equations with two to four operations. Students explain how the calculator solved the problem. This introduces students to the idea of order of operations, with multiplication or division being calculated from left to right and then additions and subtractions being performed.

For example, when solving $4 + 6 \times 4$ the calculator will give an answer of 28, although most students will expect the answer to be 40. Students should reason that because multiplication is done before addition, 6×4 is calculated and then the 4 is added. $24 + 4 = 28$

- Students should work in small groups to solve equations with up to 4 operations by applying order of operations. They explain their solutions by describing how they solved the equations.

  $12 \div 4 + 3 \times 6$ Multiplications and divisions have equal weight, so $12 \div 4$ is calculated and then 3×6. The final answer is found by adding $3 + 18 = 21$.

  $16 - 8 \div 2 \times 4$ Divide 8 by 2 and multiply the result by 4. Subtract the result from 16.

  $16 - 16 = 0$

  $18 - 14 \div 2 + 5 \times 2$ Divide 14 by 2 and then multiply 5×2. Think $18 - 7 + 10 = 21$.

What the STUDENTS do:

- Solve problems and equations that include parentheses.
- Solve problems and equations that employ order of operations.
- Explain their thinking as they use order of operations to solve a variety of examples.

Addressing Student Misconceptions and Common Errors

Some students will have the misconception that all multiplications are calculated before divisions and additions are calculated before subtractions. Scaffold examples for students to practice solving multiplications and/or divisions in order from left to right and then additions and/or subtractions in order from left to right. Although parentheses are not necessary when the equation is written accurately, some students will find it helpful to add grouping symbols in order to solve equations and word problems.

Write simple expressions that record calculations with numbers, and interpret numerical expressions without evaluating them. For example, express the calculation "add 8 and 7, then multiply by 2" as 2 × (8 + 7). Recognize that 3 × (18932 + 921) is three times as large as 18932 + 921, without having to calculate the indicated sum or product.

This Standard extends the work of the previous Standard by having students write and interpret numerical expressions. Moving from expressions to words and from words to expressions will reinforce understanding of order of operations.

What the TEACHER does:

- After students have had experiences solving many examples following order of operations, offer opportunities to play target number games in which they have to write equations using order of operations to make a target number and explain their reasoning (http://www.mathwire.com/games/numbsensegames.html, http://illuminations.nctm.org/Lesson.aspx?id=2962).
- Encourage games such as "I have who has" with an expression written in numbers and written in words to give students additional opportunities to understand how to read and interpret expressions without evaluating them (finding the solution).

What the STUDENTS do:

- Given a mathematical expression in words, write the numerical expression.

  Three times six added to seven would be written $7 + 3 \times 6$

- Given a numerical expression, translate it into words.

  $12 - (14 \div 7)$ could be read as *the quotient of 14 and 7 subtracted from 12.*

Addressing Student Misconceptions and Common Errors

Struggling students should begin with simple expressions. Because there may be several ways to write or read an expression, they should justify how they arrived at their answers.

Notes

GRADE 5

Operations and Algebraic Thinking
5.OA.B*

Analyze patterns and relationships.

STANDARD 3   **5.OA.B.3:** Generate two numerical patterns using two given rules. Identify apparent relationships between corresponding terms. Form ordered pairs consisting of corresponding terms from the two patterns, and graph the ordered pairs on a coordinate plane. *For example, given the rule "Add 3" and the starting number 0, and given the rule "Add 6" and the starting number 0, generate terms in the resulting sequences, and observe that the terms in one sequence are twice the corresponding terms in the other sequence. Explain informally why this is so.*

*Additional cluster

Operations and Algebraic Thinking   5.OA.B

Cluster B: Analyze patterns and relationships.
Grade 5 Overview

Students extend the work of the previous cluster to graphing ordered pairs on a one quadrant coordinate plane and discussing the visual patterns on the graph.

Standards for Mathematical Practice
SFMP 1. Make sense of problems and persevere in solving them.
SFMP 2. Use quantitative reasoning.
SFMP 3. Construct viable arguments and critique the reasoning of others.
SFMP 4. Model with mathematics.
SFMP 5. Use appropriate tools strategically.
SFMP 6. Attend to precision.
SFMP 7. Look for and make use of structure.
SFMP 8. Look for and express regularity in repeated reasoning.

Students use problems as a context for finding and extending patterns. They reason to find similarities and determine rules to identify numerical and geometric patterns and describe patterns they find in problems and in numbers and in geometric figures. They compare descriptions and look for counterexamples. Students use models and tools to help extend and describe shape patterns. Given a rule, students develop lists of numbers and describe any patterns in the list using appropriate vocabulary. In finding patterns, students are developing a deeper understanding of the structure of all four operations and begin to make generalizations by constructing rules for their patterns.

Related Content Standards

3.OA.D.9   4.OA.C.5

Notes

Generate two numerical patterns using two given rules. Identify apparent relationships between corresponding terms. Form ordered pairs consisting of corresponding terms from the two patterns, and graph the ordered pairs on a coordinate plane. For example, given the rule "Add 3" and the starting number 0, and given the rule "Add 6" and the starting number 0, generate terms in the resulting sequences, and observe that the terms in one sequence are twice the corresponding terms in the other sequence. Explain informally why this is so.

This Standard relates to previous work in Grade 4 with patterns and includes several skills beyond solving the problem and identifying a pattern. Students need experience identifying, recording, and graphing ordered pairs on a coordinate plane (positive numbers only). In solving problems, they begin by making a list to find a solution and then graph the ordered pairs in that list. It is appropriate to begin with graphing a single rule, then discuss and describe the graph and how it relates to the problem situation. Proceed with situations in which two rules are generated. After graphing the ordered pairs for each rule, students analyze and discuss the relationship between the two results.

Example 1:

Berto is going on a bike trip. If he travels 1.5 miles every 15 minutes, how far will he ride in 2 hours?

Example 2:

Louise and Tom are working on a science project. They both plant seeds and measure the height of the plant every day. Louise's plant grows 1 inch a day and Tom's plant grows 2 inches each day. Draw a graph of their seeds' growth for the first week. Describe what you notice about each person's plant.

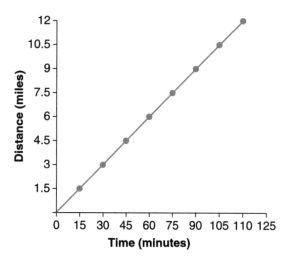

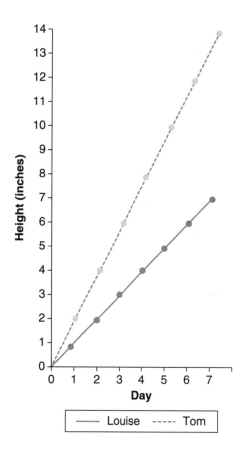

What the TEACHER does:

- Provide students with problems to solve in which students make a T-table and generate numerical patterns (see examples above), including problems with two rules or two patterns.
- Provide students with "mathematical rules" that give them additional opportunities to make a table and generate a sequence of numbers based on the rule.

  - Rule: Double the number and add 1.
  - Rule: Find $\frac{1}{2}$ of the number.

- Facilitate student discussions describing patterns in their tables.
- Support students as they list ordered pairs from the tables and plot the points on a coordinate grid.
- Facilitate student discussions in which they informally describe the visual patterns of their graphs (for example, "The graph is a line that starts at 0" or "The line goes up and to the right.")

What the STUDENTS do:

- Make a table to solve problems.
- Describe patterns.
- Plot pairs on a coordinate grid.
- Describe the graphs.

Addressing Student Misconceptions and Common Errors

Students often reverse coordinates when plotting them on a coordinate plane. They use the first number to count up the y-axis and then count over the second number in the ordered pair on the x-axis. Have students identify and label the x-axis and the y-axis on their coordinate planes. Remind them that since x is before y alphabetically, they move across the x-axis first and then up the y-axis. Students should also describe the difference of the location of (3,5) and (5,3) on the coordinate plane. Give students many opportunities to describe how to plot a point using a variety of ordered pairs.

Notes

Operations and Algebraic Thinking
Cluster A: Write and interpret numerical expressions.

Standard: 5.OA.A.1. *Use parentheses, brackets, or braces in numerical expressions, and evaluate expressions with these symbols.*

Standards for Mathematical Practice:
SFMP 6. Attend to precision.
Students apply previous work with order of operations and pay close attention to the use of parentheses and the order of operations.

Goal:
Students will practice using order of operations to play a game in which they need to write expressions to make a given number.

Planning:

Materials: Dice or spinner with numbers 1 through 9, teacher-made cards with numbers from 15 to 30.

Sample Activity:
Students play in groups of four. Each person spins the spinner or rolls a die. They record the four numbers for that round. The teacher draws a card and gives the target number. Groups work together to make expressions using their four numbers following order of operations, including using parentheses, that will make the target number. They may use two, three, or all four of the numbers.

Students share their expressions and explain how they make the target using order of operations.

Sample: Playing numbers 2, 3, 3, 5 Target 16

$3 + 3 + (2 \times 5)$ or $3 + 3 + 2 \times 5$

Questions/Prompts:

As students share their expressions, you may find that as they explain what they did, it does not match how they wrote the equation. Ask questions to clarify student thinking, such as, "What did you do first? How did you write that in your equation?" You may also want to have them clarify why.

$3 + 3 + 2 \times 5$ is not equal to 40.

Differentiating Instruction:

Struggling Students: Work with a smaller range of numbers or use three numbers to make the target number.

Although parentheses may not be needed, students may find it easier to include parentheses in their expressions.

Extension: Students who easily find expressions should be encouraged to find more expressions. They can also write their expressions in different ways. For example, $3 + 3 + (2 \times 5)$ could also be written as

$2 \times 5 + 3 + 3$.

These students also work on being precise in their explanations of how their expressions are accurate.

Operations and Algebraic Thinking
Cluster A: Write and interpret numerical expressions.

Standard:

Standards for Mathematical Practice:

Goal:

Planning:

Materials:

Sample Activity:

Questions/Prompts:

Differentiating Instruction:

Struggling Students:

Extension:

Operations and Algebraic Thinking
Cluster B: Analyze patterns and relationships.

Standard:

Standards for Mathematical Practice:

Goal:

Planning:

Materials:

Sample Activity:

Questions/Prompts:

Differentiating Instruction:

Struggling Students:

Extension:

Reflection Questions: Operations and Algebraic Thinking

1. How does the use of problem situations help students to develop a conceptual understanding of multiplication and division?

2. Discuss each problem situation in Table 2: Multiplication and Division Situations, Grades 3–5, in the Resources. As a group, develop a set of grade-level-appropriate problems you can use for each situation. What are some developmentally appropriate models for your grade level? Refer to Standards in this domain to determine the range of numbers with which students will be working at your grade level, and include fractions and mixed numbers.

3. Discuss strategies for introducing the problem types and how this progresses across grade levels so that you can build upon each other's work.

4. How do the properties of multiplication help students to develop a deeper understanding of multiplication and division as well as become fluent with procedural skills?

5. What are some activities you can use to help students "discover" the properties so they understand and use them? (Remember that students do not need to know a property's formal name at this level.)

6. How does the expectation for fluency with facts develop across grade levels in this domain? Talk about strategies that students can use to become fluent with facts using understanding rather than rote memorization.

Part 2

Number and Operations in Base Ten

Number and Operations in Base Ten

Domain Overview

GRADE 3

In Grade 3 students use place value to extend previous work in addition and subtraction to 1,000. They use number line models to develop an understanding of rounding numbers. They build on multiplication facts and understanding to multiply one-digit numbers times multiples of 10.

GRADE 4

Fourth graders extend their work with place value to add and subtract multi-digit numbers using an efficient algorithm. They use strategies based on properties and place value to multiply and divide multi-digit numbers.

GRADE 5

Fifth graders extend their work with place value to include decimal numbers to the thousandths place.
They use efficient algorithms to multiply multi-digit whole numbers. They begin to divide whole numbers with two-digit divisors. They extend their understanding of whole number operations to adding, subtraction, multiplying, and dividing decimals to hundredths.

This domain is not taught in isolation from the Operations and Algebraic Thinking domain. Students work across domains to develop a deep understanding of addition and subtraction by focusing on the instructional shift of rigor, that is, developing conceptual understanding, building skill and fluency, and applying all four operations in problem contexts.

SUGGESTED MATERIALS FOR THIS DOMAIN

3	4	5	
✓	✓	✓	Objects for counting, such as beans, linking cubes, two-color counter chips, coins
✓	✓	✓	Straws or coffee stirrers and small rubber bands
✓	✓	✓	Number lines
✓	✓	✓	Digit cards
✓	✓	✓	Base-ten blocks (Reproducible 4)

KEY VOCABULARY

3	4	5	
✓	✓	✓	**algorithm** a step-by-step procedure used to calculate an answer
✓	✓	✓	**area model** a concrete model for multiplication or division made up of a rectangle. The length and width represent the factors, and the area represents the product.

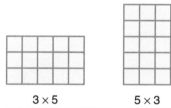

3×5 5×3

3	4	5	
✓	✓	✓	**benchmark** a number or numbers that help to estimate a value. Sample benchmarks include 10, 100, 0, $\frac{1}{2}$, 1.
✓	✓	✓	**compare** to identify similarities or differences among numbers in order to determine which of two numbers is larger, smaller, or if they are equal in value
	✓	✓	**compatible numbers** numbers that are close in value to the actual numbers in an expression, which make it easy to do mental arithmetic
			Example: To divide 37 ÷ 7 start by thinking of 36 ÷ 6 or 35 ÷ 7
✓	✓	✓	**decimal number** a number based on 10 and powers of ten
✓	✓	✓	**dividend** in division, the number being divided, product
✓	✓	✓	**divisor** in division, the number that divides another number factor
✓	✓	✓	**estimate** to make an approximation or calculate using closer but easier numbers
✓	✓	✓	**expanded form** a way of writing numbers that shows place value, expanded notation
			300 + 20 + 7 + 0.8 = 327.8
			(3 × 100) + (2 × 10) + (7 × 1) + (8 × 0.1) = 327.8

(Continued)

(Continued)

3	4	5		
		✓	**exponent**	the small number placed to the upper right of a number indicating how many times the base number is multiplied by itself

2^4 2 is the base number, 4 is the exponent

$2^4 = 2 \times 2 \times 2 \times 2 = 32$

3	4	5		
		✓	**exponential notation**	a shortened way to represent a number using an exponent
✓	✓	✓	**factor**	one of the numbers multiplied to find a product
	✓	✓	**factor pair**	a pair of numbers that when multiplied give a product; for example, 1, 15, and 3, 5 are factor pairs for 15
✓	✓	✓	**fluency**	having efficient, flexible, and accurate ways to calculate
		✓	**hundredth**	one part when a whole is divided into 100 equal parts
✓	✓	✓	**midpoint**	a point that divides a line segment into halves
	✓	✓	**multiple**	the result of multiplying a whole number by other whole numbers multiples of 5 are 0, 5, 10, 15, 20, 25, 30 . . .
	✓	✓	**partial product**	a part of the product in multiplication calculation, usually based on place value and the distributive property
	✓	✓	**partial quotient**	a part of the quotient in division calculation, usually based on place value and the distributive property
✓	✓	✓	**pattern**	a set of numbers or objects that can be described by a specific rule
✓	✓	✓	**place value**	the value of a digit depending on its place in a number
		✓	**power**	exponent, the number of times a base number is multiplied by itself
✓	✓	✓	**product**	the result when two numbers are multiplied
✓	✓	✓	**quotient**	the result when two numbers are divided; the missing factor
✓	✓	✓	**remainder**	the amount left over after dividing a number
✓	✓	✓	**round**	to change a number to a less exact number that is more convenient for computation
✓	✓	✓	**strategy**	a plan to find an answer or solve a problem that makes sense
	✓	✓	**tenth**	one part when one whole is divided into ten equal parts
		✓	**thousandth**	one part when one whole is divided into one thousand equal parts

Number and Operations in Base Ten
3.NBT.A*

Use place value understanding and properties of operations to perform multi-digit arithmetic.[1]

[1] A range of algorithms may be used.

STANDARD 1   **3.NBT.A.1:** Use place value understanding to round whole numbers to the nearest 10 or 100.

STANDARD 2   **3.NBT.A.2:** Fluently add and subtract within 1000 using strategies and algorithms based on place value, properties of operations, and/or the relationship between addition and subtraction.

STANDARD 3   **3.NBT.A.3:** Multiply one-digit whole numbers by multiples of 10 in the range 10–90 (e.g., 9×80, 5×60) using strategies based on place value and properties of operations.

*Additional cluster

Number and Operations in Base Ten   3.NBT.A

Cluster A: Use place value understanding and properties of operations to perform multi-digit arithmetic.[1]

[1] A range of algorithms may be used.

Grade 3 Overview

Students enter third grade with knowledge of place value through hundreds and with experience adding and subtracting through 100 using a variety of strategies, concrete materials, and various representations. In Grade 3 they extend their knowledge of place value to include rounding numbers. They add and subtract fluently through 1000 using place value, properties, and the relationship between addition and subtraction. They extend their understanding of multiplication to include multiplying one-digit numbers times multiples of 10.

Standards for Mathematical Practice
SFMP 1. Make sense of problems and persevere in solving them.
SFMP 2. Use quantitative reasoning.
SFMP 3. Construct viable arguments and critique the reasoning of others.
SFMP 4. Model with mathematics.
SFMP 5. Use appropriate tools strategically.
SFMP 6. Attend to precision.
SFMP 7. Look for and make use of structure.
SFMP 8. Look for and express regularity in repeated reasoning.

Problem solving continues to provide a context for ongoing work with place value in rounding experiences as well as in adding and subtracting through 1000. Students use quantitative reasoning throughout this cluster as they use representations, including number lines, bundling straws into groups of tens and groups of one hundred, to model and explain their thinking. They continue to develop appropriate vocabulary and use that vocabulary in their explanations. As students extend their previous work with addition and subtraction, they use the structure of place value (composing and decomposing tens and hundreds) to develop efficient strategies to add and subtract. They explore and discuss the structure of multiplication by using models to see what happens when multiplying by multiples of 10. After many opportunities to multiply by 10 and multiples of 10, students generalize that when multiplying by 10, for example 3×10, they have three 10s, which is written as 30. It is important that students recognize this pattern and why it works rather than being given a shortcut to avoid other misconceptions. They extend this understanding to all multiples of 10, making generalizations to find efficient ways to multiply.

Related Content Standards

3.OA.C.8   4.OA.A.3   4.NBT.A.3   5.NBT.A.4

Use place value understanding to round whole numbers to the nearest 10 or 100.

Students need to consider the value of the digits in the ones and tens places to determine how to round a number to the nearest ten and the value of the digits in the tens and hundreds places to round a number to the nearest hundred. Placing the number on a number line between the closest tens or the closest hundreds will help students to see whether the number is closest to the given ten or the next ten (or hundred). Using the midpoint as a benchmark on the number line will help students to determine the closer ten or hundred.

Round 34 to the nearest 10.

Explanation: The number 34 is between 30 and 40. It is closer to 30. Therefore it would be rounded to 30.

Round 47 to the nearest ten.

Explanation: The number 47 is between 40 and 50. It is closer to 50. Therefore it would be rounded to 50.

Round 327 to the nearest hundred.

Explanation: The number 327 is between 300 and 400. It is closer to 300. Therefore the nearest hundred is 300.

Round 456 to the nearest hundred.

Explanation: The number 456 is between 400 and 500. It is closer to 500. Therefore the nearest hundred is 500.

What the TEACHER does:

- Ask students to identify the tens a two-digit number falls between.
- Provide opportunities for students to place that number on a number line between the two closest tens.
- Have students discuss which ten the number is nearest to and justify their thinking.
- Provide many experiences with two-digit numbers and ask students to describe any patterns they see.
- Discuss what happens when there is a 5 in the ones place. (The number automatically rounds up even though it is in the middle.)
- Repeat this process with three-digit numbers rounding to the hundreds place.

What the STUDENTS do:

- Given a two-digit number, identify the tens that the number falls between.

  o 54 falls between 50 and 60.
  o 78 falls between 70 and 80.

- Plot the number on a number line between the tens.
- Determine which ten the number is closer to and justify their reasoning.
- Given a three-digit number, identify the hundreds that the number falls between.

  o 745 falls between 700 and 800.
  o 269 falls between 200 and 300.

(continued)

What the STUDENTS do (continued):

- Identify the closest hundreds and plot the number on a number line between the closest hundreds.
- Determine which hundred the number is closer to and justify their reasoning.

- After many experiences, students discuss any patterns they find to determine when to round to the lesser ten (or hundred) or round to the next ten (or hundred).

Addressing Student Misconceptions and Common Errors

The rounding "rules" can cause students a variety of misconceptions. Rounding up to the nearest ten means the digit in the tens place will increase by one. Rounding down can lead students to believe the digit in the tens place would decrease by one when in reality it remains the same. Following rules that do not make sense can be more complicated than the number line representation. Students should have many experiences using number line models and justifying their solutions.

Notes

Fluently add and subtract within 1000 using strategies and algorithms based on place value, properties of operations, and/or the relationship between addition and subtraction.

In second grade students built conceptual understanding and procedural skills adding and subtracting within 100. They used concrete models and the number line to explore addition and subtraction within 1000. This Standard extends previous experiences to becoming fluent, which include being accurate and efficient (in a reasonable amount of time). In Grade 3 students continue adding and subtracting within 1000, extending their understanding of place value by composing and decomposing tens and hundreds. They develop and apply strategies based on place value, properties of operations, and the relationship between addition and subtraction. Practice and refining strategies that make sense lead to fluency with addition and subtraction and lay the foundation for developing efficient algorithms in Grade 4. Whenever possible, use problems to provide a context for addition and subtraction to reinforce the meaning of the operations and to enable students to determine whether their solutions make sense.

Strategies for addition and subtraction through 1000 will vary depending on the problem. Some students may need review and ongoing experiences with concrete materials such as bundling straws or open number lines. Other students may have mental strategies that help them to calculate. It is most important that students understand what they are doing rather than following a series of rote steps that do not make sense.

Models and strategies include, but are not limited to the following:

Example 1:

Kevin and Randy have been putting pennies in their piggy banks to see how much they can save in one month. At the end of the month, they open their banks and count the pennies. Kevin has 289 pennies and Randy has 345 pennies. How many pennies did they both collect?

Strategy: Model with a place value chart.

hundreds	tens	ones
Kevin		
Randy		

5 hundreds	12 tens	14 ones =
5 hundreds	13 tens	4 ones =
6 hundreds	3 tens	4 ones =

Strategy: Open number line.

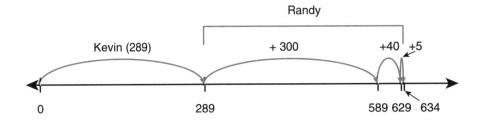

How many more pennies did Randy collect than Kevin?

Strategy: Open number line (counting on).

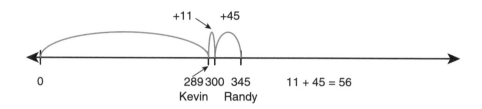

Strategy: Bar model.

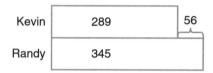

Example 2:

Michelle is reading a book that has 300 pages. She has read 199 pages so far. How many pages does she need to read to finish her book?

Although students may use an algorithmic approach using written calculations, this problem provides an example of how mental strategies can be much more efficient.

Strategy: Counting on and using mental mathematics.

If Michelle reads 1 more page she will have read 200 pages. Then she needs to read 100 more pages to finish the book, so she needs to read a total of 101 pages.

What the TEACHER does:

- Assess student conceptual understanding of adding to determine appropriate materials and activities for differentiation to meet individual student needs when adding and subtracting within 1000.

  o Provide concrete materials for students who are developing understanding of composing and decomposing tens and hundreds. (straws and place value chart, number lines, 100 chart)
  o Scaffold examples of addition and subtraction situations to build understanding of regrouping strategies.

    o Regroup ones to tens (addition) and tens to ones (subtraction).

      425 + 317   552 − 427

    o Regroup tens to hundreds (addition) and hundreds to tens (subtraction).

      374 + 465   628 − 337

    o Double regroup ones to tens and tens to hundreds (addition).

      479 + 567

    o Double regroup tens to ones and hundreds to tens (subtraction).

      423 − 248

- Give students a variety of problem situations in which they add and subtract within 1000 using various strategies and representations.
- Provide subtraction that includes the digit 0 in the hundreds, tens, and/or ones place and discuss efficient strategies to calculate.

  o 980 − 457
  o 908 − 457
  o 900 − 457

- Ask explicit questions that promote connections between conceptual understanding (Why does that work?) to procedural skills (How can you write that?).
- Ask students to show their work and explain their thinking.

What the STUDENTS do:

- Use a variety of models, representations, and strategies to solve addition and subtraction examples and problems within 1000.
- Ask themselves if their answers make sense.
- Explain their strategies and make sense of the strategies of others.
- Write equations vertically and horizontally.
- Make connections between conceptual understanding and procedures for adding and subtracting.

Students who learn to add and subtract procedurally without a deep understanding of place value and regrouping will struggle to determine whether their answers are reasonable. They also make common errors when subtracting with zero in the sum or take the smaller number from the larger as shown in the following examples. Students who make these errors need more experience with concrete models, using place value charts with bundling/unbundling straws. They should make explicit connections from models to written work. They should also explain their reasoning in composing and decomposing numbers when regrouping using pictures, numbers, and words.

Common Errors in Subtraction

```
  7|36        6|00
- 2|59      - 4|65
---------   ---------
  5|23        2|65
```

Notes

STANDARD 3 (3.NBT.A.3)

Multiply one-digit whole numbers by multiples of 10 in the range 10–90 (e.g., 9 × 80, 5 × 60) using strategies based on place value and properties of operations.

Students extend their understanding of multiplying two single-digit numbers to multiplying a single-digit number by a multiple of 10. They begin using concrete models and groups of 10, for example, showing 3 × 10 as 3 bundles of 10 or 30. Using the commutative property, they conclude that 10 × 3 is also 30. Students discuss patterns linking previous understanding that 30 means 30 ones or 3 tens. Additional representations including number lines and skip counting support their thinking.

They continue with other multiples of 10 within the range of 10 to 90 using models, reasoning, and patterns to generalize a method or algorithm for finding the product of a one-digit number times a multiple of 10.

It is important for students to have many experiences to model, explain, and generalize rather than to be shown tricks about adding zeros. Such tricks and short cuts hinder understanding of place value's role in multiplication, a concept that will become very important as students work with more complex multiplication examples.

What the TEACHER does:

- Begin with examples of multiplying a one-digit factor by 10. Provide opportunities for students to model the examples, explain their reasoning including connecting the meaning of 30 to 30 ones or 3 tens.
- Ask questions that help students to generalize that when they multiply a one-digit number by 10, the product will be that number of tens.
- Extend examples to multiplication by 20, 30, up to 90 using models, skip counting, number lines.
- Ask questions that help students to generalize what happens when they multiply a one-digit number by a multiple of 10.
- Require students to explain their thinking, generalize, and justify their generalizations using a variety of strategies.

What the STUDENTS do:

- Use their understanding of the meaning of multiplication to model examples of multiplying a one-digit number by 10.
- Demonstrate an understanding that a one-digit number multiplied by ten gives a multiple of 10 (for example, 6 × 10 = 60), which is the same as that number of ones (60) or that number of tens (6 tens).
- Model multiplication of a one-digit number by a multiple of 10 (from 10 to 90) using concrete materials, number lines, skip counting, and the distributive property.
- Discuss patterns and make generalizations.

Addressing Student Misconceptions and Common Errors

Teaching shortcuts (adding a zero to the product of the two non-zero whole numbers) rather than understanding the relationship between the product and its place value does not establish the underlying importance of place value in multiplication. Understanding that multiplying 4 × 30 means I have 4 groups of 3 tens and that is 12 tens or 120 (rather than multiply 4 × 3 and "add a zero at the end") is fundamental to ongoing work with multiplication and working with partial products. Students who recognize and can explain a pattern rather than following a rule begin to understand the structure of multiplication rather than a meaningless shortcut.

Notes

Number and Operations in Base Ten

Cluster A: Use place value understanding and properties of operations to perform multi-digit arithmetic.[1]

[1] A range of algorithms may be used.

Standard: 3.NBT.A.2. *Fluently add and subtract within 1000 using strategies and algorithms based on place value, properties of operations, and/or the relationship between addition and subtraction.*

Standards for Mathematical Practice:

SFMP 2. Reason abstractly and quantitatively.
Students build on previous experiences with concrete materials to apply efficient algorithms to adding three-digit numbers.

SFMP 6. Attend to precision.
Students consider place value and add accurately.

SFMP 7. Look for and make use of structure.
Students apply their understanding of place value to work to make the greatest (or least) sum.

Goal:
To provide practice with adding and subtracting whole numbers.

Planning:

Materials: Deck of cards (with 10 and face cards removed), paper and pencil

Sample Activity:
Ask students to draw the following on a piece of paper:

$$\underline{\qquad} \quad \underline{\qquad} \quad \underline{\qquad}$$
$$+ \underline{\qquad} \quad \underline{\qquad} \quad \underline{\qquad}$$
$$\overline{\rule{6cm}{0.4pt}}$$

Randomly choose a card and say the number on the card. Students write that digit on one of the lines on their papers. Once a digit has been recorded, it cannot be moved. Repeat until 6 numbers have been drawn. The object is to get the greatest (or least) sum. Play several times.

Questions/Prompts:

Following each round, ask students to describe how they decided where to put the digits. Talk about how they can be sure the greatest possible sum was found (or maybe not).

Change the object of the game to finding the lowest sum. Discuss how that changed students' strategies.

Another variation of the game is to subtract and look for the greatest (or least) possible difference.

Differentiating Instruction:

Struggling Students: This game should be played after students have had enough experience with concrete representations and explicitly connecting those experiences to written equations. Students who have not yet mastered the algorithm can play and should explain their strategies for adding.

Play adding a three-digit number and a two-digit number.

Be sure to recognize answers that may not be the greatest sum and give students opportunities to explain their work.

Extension: Extend the game to more than two addends or to using four-digit numbers.

Number and Operations in Base Ten
Cluster A: Use place value understanding and properties of operations to perform multi-digit arithmetic.[1]

[1] A range of algorithms may be used.

Standard:

Standards for Mathematical Practice:

Goal:

Planning:

Materials:

Sample Activity:

Questions/Prompts:

Differentiating Instruction:

Struggling Students:

Extension:

Number and Operations in Base Ten[1]
4.NBT.A*

[1] Grade 4 expectations in this domain are limited to whole numbers less than or equal to 1,000,000.

Generalize place value understanding for multi-digit whole numbers.

STANDARD 1   **4.NBT.A.1:** Recognize that in a multi-digit whole number, a digit in one place represents ten times what it represents in the place to its right. *For example, recognize that 700 ÷ 70 = 10 by applying concepts of place value and division.*

STANDARD 2   **4.NBT.A.2:** Read and write multi-digit whole numbers using base-ten numerals, number names, and expanded form. Compare two multi-digit numbers based on meanings of the digits in each place, using >, =, and < symbols to record the results of comparisons.

STANDARD 3   **4.NBT.A.3:** Use place value understanding to round multi-digit whole numbers to any place.

*Major cluster

Number and Operations in Base Ten[1]   4.NBT.A

Cluster A: Generalize place value understanding for multi-digit whole numbers.

[1] Grade 4 expectations in this domain are limited to whole numbers less than or equal to 1,000,000.

Grade 4 Overview

Fourth graders extend their understanding of place value to 1,000,000. They develop an understanding of the relationship among places in a number, and they use that understanding to read and write numbers from 1 to 1,000,000. Writing numbers in expanded notation reinforces the relationship among places as well as how to decompose a number in various ways. Students compare numbers by focusing on the value of a digit in a given place. They extend earlier work with rounding numbers to rounding numbers to any given place and using rounding to estimate in real-life situations.

Standards for Mathematical Practice
SFMP 1. Make sense of problems and persevere in solving them.
SFMP 2. Use quantitative reasoning.
SFMP 3. Construct viable arguments and critique the reasoning of others.
SFMP 4. Model with mathematics.
SFMP 5. Use appropriate tools strategically.
SFMP 6. Attend to precision.
SFMP 7. Look for and make use of structure.
SFMP 8. Look for and express regularity in repeated reasoning.

Using models and quantitative reasoning will help students understand the relationship between places as the value of a digit moves to the left or to the right. A digit in the tens place is ten times as great as the same digit in the ones place. Understanding that as a place moves to the left it becomes ten times greater and as a place moves to the right it is one tenth the value is a fundamental structure of our place value system. Providing a variety of contexts for students to consider will help them to develop understanding. Using models for lesser numbers will help student to recognize patterns and make generalizations for working with larger numbers and for comparing numbers.

Students read and write numbers from 1 to 1,000,000 using precision and recognizing the structure of our number system. Recognizing and understanding the role of commas in written numbers and the regularity of the sequence of numbers between commons (hundreds, tens, ones) will help students "chunk" large numbers into smaller parts and become fluent in reading and writing numbers.

Proficient students use quantitative reasoning to round numbers to a given place. They realize that rounding numbers can be useful in solving problems and making sure their answers are reasonable. They can justify their thinking about rounding. They use the structure of the place value system to round numbers.

Related Content Standards
3.OA.C.8   4.OA.A.3   5.NBT.A.1   5.NBT.A.3   5.NBT.A.4

Recognize that in a multi-digit whole number, a digit in one place represents ten times what it represents in the place to its right. For example, recognize that 700 ÷ 70 = 10 by applying concepts of place value and division.

Note: Grade 4 expectations in this domain are limited to whole numbers less than or equal to 1,000,000.

Students need a variety of experiences and focused questions to understand the relationship among place values. This Standard relates the relationship of the value of a digit, based on its place in a number, to multiplication and division by multiples of 10. Build on previous experiences with models and the place value chart and make connections to multiplication and division by multiples of ten.

Consider the digit 3. Each time it moves one place to the left its value becomes ten times greater.

- In the ones place (3) it is 3 ones.
- When moved one place to the left, the tens place (30), it is ten times greater than 3.
- When moved one place to the left, the hundreds place (300), it is ten times greater than 30.
- When moved one more place to the left, the thousands place (3,000), it is ten times greater than 300.

We can also prove that using the relationship between multiplication and division. Each time we move one place to the right, it becomes one-tenth of the previous value.

$3,000 \div 10 = 300$

$300 \div 10 = 30$

$30 \div 10 = 3$

What the TEACHER does:

- Provide students with a variety of experiences to compare the value of digits as they appear in different places in numerals and to explain the relationship.

  o How does the value of the 2 in 528 compare with the value of the 2 in 582?

  o How does the value of the 7 in 275 compare with the value of the 7 in 725?

  o If you were to win the lottery and could win $70 or $700, which would you prefer? Explain your thinking including the value of the 7 in each amount.

- Give students numbers in a pattern such as 5, 50, 500, 5,000. Have them extend the pattern and describe what happens to the value of the number as the pattern continues.

- Give students time to explore and describe similar patterns based on the place value of a given digit.

What the STUDENTS do:

- Extend and explore patterns that involved moving digits to different places in a given numeral.
- Explain what is happening to the value of a digit as it appears within various places in a numeral.
- Identify the relationship among places by multiplying by 10 (moving one place to the left) and dividing by 10 (moving one place to the right).

Addressing Student Misconceptions and Common Errors

Students may become confused with extending patterns and focus on the zeros rather than the value of the digit based on its place. Concrete models comparing ones, tens, and hundreds and using appropriate language (ten times greater, one-tenth, or divided by ten) will help students recognize, extend, and describe patterns based on understanding rather than what the number looks like.

Notes

GRADE 4

Read and write multi-digit whole numbers using base-ten numerals, number names, and expanded form. Compare two multi-digit numbers based on meanings of the digits in each place, using >, =, and < symbols to record the results of comparisons.

Note: Grade 4 expectations in this domain are limited to whole numbers less than or equal to 1,000,000.

Students read and write numbers from 1 to 1,000,000. They think of numbers as "families" that are made up of hundreds, tens, and ones. Each family is separated by a comma. The family on the far right is the ones family, the next family to the left is thousands, and the family to the left of thousands is millions. If students read the numbers in groups of 3 using the comma to separate the families, they can think of the number in smaller parts to make reading and writing manageable.

1, 382, 425 is read as one million, three hundred eighty-two thousand, four hundred twenty-five.

A similar pattern can help to write numerals from words.

One million, two hundred sixty-five thousand, four hundred fifty-five is written as 1, 265, 455.

Students use place value understanding to write numbers in expanded notation.

376 = 3 hundreds + 7 tens + 6 ones (or variations such as 37 tens + 6 ones)

$$300 + 70 + 6 \qquad\qquad 370 + 6$$

12, 387 = 1 ten thousand + 2 thousands + 3 hundreds + 8 tens + 7 ones (or variations such as 12 thousands + 38 tens + 7)

$$10,000 + 2,000 + 300 + 80 + 7 \qquad\qquad 12,000 + 380 + 7$$

Based on their understanding of place value, students compare numbers and use <, >, = symbols to show their comparisons. Students need to practice explicit strategies, including lining up numbers by place value and describing the place value of given digits to justify their thinking when comparing numbers. The number line provides a model to help students compare two numbers based on their location (lesser numbers are to the left of greater numbers).

What the TEACHER does:

- Use many contexts in which students read and write numbers based on place value and the use of commas.
- Use a variety of activities to have students model numbers using digit cards and reading those numbers.
- Provide opportunities for students to read and write numbers up to 1,000,000.
- Demonstrate writing numbers in expanded notation using place value and words.

  o Provide place value cards that enable students to show a number in expanded notation.

- Once students have the opportunity to talk about comparisons, discuss strategies for comparing numbers, including expanded notation, writing numbers in a vertical list, and eventually comparing numbers by looking at the numbers and comparing places.
- Use a variety of activities for students to make the greatest and least numbers possible from given digits and activities in which students compare numbers from given digits.
- Use interesting situations and data as a context for reading, writing, and comparing numbers.

813,461

$$800,000 \; + \; 10,000 \; + \; 3,000 \; + \; 400 \; + \; 60 \; + \; 1$$

8 [hundred thousands] + 1 [ten thousand] + 3 [thousands] + 4 [hundreds] + 6 [tens] + 1 [one]

- Give students numbers to compare using <, >, =.

  o Compare numbers with the same place value. (Compare 295 and 259)
  o Compare numbers with different place values. (Compare 4,254 and 14,372)

What the STUDENTS do:

- Accurately read and write numbers from 1 to 1,000,000 based on place value understanding.
- Write numbers using various forms of expanded notation.
- Compare numbers using place value and use <, >, = symbols to show the comparison.

Addressing Student Misconceptions and Common Errors

Students need practice reading and writing numbers. Students who struggle should focus on the groups of digits before, between, and after commas. The comma preceding the units group represents the thousands group, the comma preceding the thousands group represents the millions group. Once students know this, they can focus on reading the numbers as usual and then name the group by naming the comma. Some students will need more practice to relate understanding to developing skill reading and writing numbers.

When comparing numbers, students may focus on the number furthest to the left to determine the greater number rather than considering place value. For example, a student may say 952 is greater than 2,354 because 9 is greater than 2. Approximating the location of numbers on the number line will help students to focus on the overall place value to help them determine which number is greater. Later, identifying place value by writing numbers using graph paper and aligning the digits starting with the ones place will help students to see that 2,000 is greater than 900. It is important that students realize they are lining up numbers in column by place value and not by a random rule.

Notes

Use place value understanding to round multi-digit whole numbers to any place.

Note: Grade 4 expectations in this domain are limited to whole numbers less than or equal to 1,000,000.

We use rounding as one of many strategies in everyday situations when we do not need an exact answer. The situation often determines the way to round or the best place to round to. Students need to have an understanding of rounding as one of several strategies to make estimates and to determine whether answers are reasonable. Once they have developed a conceptual understanding of rounding and use this to generalize a procedural understanding, they need to use number sense to determine the best method of rounding given a situation. Is it best to round to the nearest hundred? The nearest ten? Can I just round up (for example, when determining if I have enough money)? How should I round to determine if my answer to a division example is reasonable? These are all questions students need to consider as they apply rounding to real problem situations.

Students in Grade 3 learned to round numbers to their greatest place (example, round 376 to the nearest hundred) by placing them on number lines and determining which hundred the number is closer to. In Grade 4 students extend that understanding to rounding to any given place using number lines, 100 charts, and making generalizations to develop meaningful procedures to round numbers.

Example:

Round 258 to the nearest ten.

Use a number line:

Focus on the tens place. Notice that 258 falls between 250 and 260 on the number line. It is closer to 260 so it would be rounded to 260.

Using a 100 chart:

Focus on the tens place. Notice that 58 is between 50 and 60 on the 100 chart. It is 8 away from 50 and 2 away from 60. Therefore 250 is closer to 260 and would be rounded to 260.

What the TEACHER does:

- Provide opportunities and contexts for students to round numbers to a given place value using models including number lines and the 100 chart.
- Ask explicit questions that help students to generalize meaningful strategies and rules for rounding numbers to a given place.
- Provide problem situations that call for estimation and rounding, including examples in which students need to determine the best place for rounding.

Example:

Marsha went to the store for her mom and bought the following items:

    Dish soap $2.48

    Paper towels $1.95

    Napkins $1.75

She gave the clerk $10.00. About how much change did she receive?

What the STUDENTS do:

- Identify and explain situations that call for rounding numbers.
- Place the number on a number line.
- Depending on the place to be rounded, identify the two numbers between which the given number falls.

  o For example, to round 382 to the nearest ten, identify that it falls between 380 and 390.
  o Plot those two numbers on the number line.
  o Determine which rounded number is closer to the original number.

    o 382 is 2 away from 380 and 8 away from 390.
    o Therefore 382 rounded to the nearest ten is 380.

- Use other models that make sense for rounding strategies.
- Explain their reasoning.
- Make generalizations that will help them to round without using models.
- Use rounding in a variety of situations, including estimation, solving problems, and determining if their answers make sense.

Addressing Student Misconceptions and Common Errors

Rounding to a place within a number can be difficult for students. For example, rounding 1,266 to the nearest ten means that students must recognize that it falls between 1,260 and 1,270. Understanding place value and thinking flexibly about the meaning of places in a number along with practice will help students to be successful rounding to any place. It is important that students make generalizations and use steps that make sense to them. Giving students meaningless rules about rounding up or rounding down often causes much confusion.

Number and Operations in Base Ten[1]
4.NBT.B*

[1] Grade 4 expectations in this domain are limited to whole numbers less than or equal to 1,000,000.

Use place value understanding and properties of operations to perform multi-digit arithmetic.

STANDARD 4 **4.NBT.B.4:** Fluently add and subtract multi-digit whole numbers using the standard algorithm.

STANDARD 5 **4.NBT.B.5:** Multiply a whole number of up to four digits by a one-digit whole number, and multiply two two-digit numbers, using strategies based on place value and the properties of operations. Illustrate and explain the calculation by using equations, rectangular arrays, and/or area models.

STANDARD 6 **4.NBT.B.6:** Find whole-number quotients and remainders with up to four-digit dividends and one-digit divisors, using strategies based on place value, the properties of operations, and/or the relationship between multiplication and division. Illustrate and explain the calculation by using equations, rectangular arrays, and/or area models.

*Major cluster

Number and Operations in Base Ten[1]   4.NBT.B

Cluster B: Use place value understanding and properties of operations to perform multi-digit arithmetic.

[1] Grade 4 expectations in this domain are limited to whole numbers less than or equal to 1,000,000.

Grade 4 Overview

Students apply the understanding of operations they have built in previous grades, place value understanding, and properties of addition and multiplication to add and subtract multi-digit numbers, multiply a one-digit number by a number up to four digits, as well as multiplying a two-digit number by a two-digit number. They apply and extend the strategies they have been using to develop fluent (accurate and efficient) procedures.

Standards for Mathematical Practice
SFMP 1. Make sense of problems and persevere in solving them.
SFMP 2. Use quantitative reasoning.
SFMP 3. Construct viable arguments and critique the reasoning of others.
SFMP 4. Model with mathematics.
SFMP 5. Use appropriate tools strategically.
SFMP 6. Attend to precision.
SFMP 7. Look for and make use of structure.
SFMP 8. Look for and express regularity in repeated reasoning.

Problem solving siutations continue to provide contexts as students apply and extend work with whole number operations from previous grades. The problem situations in Table 1, page 254, and Table 2, page 256, should be used to provide students more experience with all types of problems situations. Students explain the strategies they use to solve problems and compare their strategies with others. They use concrete materials to model when needed, and they continue to develop the vocabulary of mathematics and apply it to their explanations. Problem contexts help students associate meaning to the numbers and the operations. Requiring students to label answers with the unit helps them focus on the meaning of the problem and determine whether the answer makes sense. As students extend previous experiences, particularly with multiplication (multiplying with one multi-digit factor) and division (multi-digit dividends), they apply their knowledge of the structure of place value in these operations.

Related Content Standards

3.OA.B.5   3.OA.B.6   3.OA.C.7   5 NBT.A.5   5 NBT.A.6

Fluently add and subtract multi-digit whole numbers using the standard algorithm.

Note: Grade 4 expectations in this domain are limited to whole numbers less than or equal to 1,000,000.

Students apply conceptual understanding developed previously using concrete and pictorial models and properties of operations to build procedural understanding and skills in addition and subtraction. Although they continue to use efficient strategies, the goal of this Standard is to use an accurate and efficient (fluent) procedure that makes sense to them. They explain their thinking (which is usually longer than the actual procedure) to show they understand the algorithm they are using.

Most students will automatically develop the standard algorithm by connecting the work they did with concrete and pictorial models to writing numeric computations. The United States is one of the only countries in the world that has focused instruction around one traditional algorithm. Students may find other efficient ways to represent their work that are also appropriate, just as they may find some cases in which using mental strategies is much more efficient than writing out the work. Becoming flexible thinkers and building understanding through making sense of mathematical ideas should always be the main goals for students.

Consider $30.00 – $29.98.

$$\begin{array}{r} {\scriptstyle 2\ 9\ 9} \\ \$\ \cancel{3}\ \cancel{0}.\cancel{0}{}^{1}0 \\ -\ 2\ 9.9\ 8 \\ \hline \$\ 0\ 0.0\ 2 \end{array}$$ Traditional algorithm

think

$29.98 + \underline{\hspace{1cm}} = \$30.00$

$29.98 + \underline{\$.02} = \$30.00$

The difference is $0.02

This is most easily solved by thinking about the value of the numbers and knowing that if I add $.02 to $29.98 I get $30.00.

What the TEACHER does:

- Provide students with problem situations and practice examples involving multi-digit addition and subtraction.
- Scaffold examples so that students begin with simpler exercises (numbers to hundreds and thousands) and building to multi-digit numbers (up to 1,000,000).
- As students explore algorithms, make explicit connections to previous experiences with concrete materials, pictorial representations, and number lines.
- Provide students opportunities to use efficient mental strategies to compute when appropriate (counting up; adding tens, then adding ones; open number lines).
- Consistently expect students to justify their reasoning, understand the reasoning of classmates, and see the connections among different ways to solve a problem.

What the STUDENTS do:

- Make connections between previous work with addition and subtraction from using models and other representations to developing an efficient algorithm to add and subtract multi-digit numbers.
- Explain their thinking as they employ procedural steps to add or subtract, including composing and decomposing

place values (regrouping) to demonstrate understanding of the procedural steps.

$$\begin{array}{r} {\scriptstyle 1}2,{\scriptstyle 1}5\ {\scriptstyle 1}6\ 7 \\ +3,\ 6\ 9\ 5 \\ \hline 6\ 2\ 6\ 2 \end{array}$$

- o I began by adding 7 + 5 in the ones place which is 12. I wrote the 2 in the ones place and added 1 to the tens place since 12 is 1 ten and 2 ones.
- o I added 6 + 9 +1 in the tens place and got a total of 16 which is 16 tens. I wrote the 6 in the tens place and made 1 hundred out of the 10 tens in 16 since 16 tens is 1 hundred and 6 tens.
- o I added 5 + 6 + 1 in the hundreds place which is 12 (hundreds). I wrote down the 2 in the hundreds place and added 1 to the thousands place since 12 hundreds is 1 thousand and 2 hundreds.
- o I added 2 + 3 + 1 in the thousands place which is 6. I wrote 6 in the thousands place.
- o My sum is 6,262.

(continued)

What the STUDENTS do (continued):

$$\begin{array}{r} {\scriptstyle 21315} \\ \cancel{3},\cancel{4}\cancel{5}\,5 \\ -\ 8\ 9\ 5 \\ \hline 2,5\ 6\ 0 \end{array}$$

Traditional algorithm approach:

- ○ I began by subtracting 5 from 5 in the ones place. The difference is 0.
- ○ Because I cannot take 9 from 5 in the tens place, I took apart 1 hundred and made it 10 tens. I now have 15 tens and can subtract 9 tens. The difference is 6 tens.
- ○ I now have 3 hundreds since I took one hundred apart to make tens. I cannot subtract 8 from 3, so I need to take apart 1 thousand to make 10 hundreds. I now have 13 hundreds and can subtract 8 hundreds. The difference is 5 hundreds.
- ○ I have 2 thousands left.
- ○ The final answer is 2,560.

- Use efficient mental strategies to compute when appropriate.

Another algorithm using a different strategy:

$$3{,}455 - 895$$

$$\begin{array}{r} 3{,}455 + 5 = 3{,}460 \\ -\ 895 + 5 = 900 \\ \hline 2{,}560 \end{array}$$

- ○ I decided to add 5 to 895 making it 900.
- ○ Because I added 5 to what I am subtracting, I should add 5 to what I started with to keep the problem balanced. So I also added 5 to 3,455 to make it 3,460.
- ○ 3,460 minus 900 is 2,560.

Addressing Student Misconceptions and Common Errors

Students who struggle with the algorithm need more experience with concrete materials (place value charts, bundling and unbundling straws into tens and hundreds). Be sure to scaffold examples so that students are comfortable with place value to hundreds, including one regrouping and two regroupings, and can explain their work before they work with four- and five-digit numbers or multiple addends.

Watch for students who subtract the smaller digit from the larger regardless of their positions in the problem. These students need additional work with concrete models and decomposing tens or hundreds. Make connections between the work with models and the written equations explicit.

Notes

Multiply a whole number of up to four digits by a one-digit whole number, and multiply two two-digit numbers, using strategies based on place value and the properties of operations. Illustrate and explain the calculation by using equations, rectangular arrays, and/or area models.

Note: Grade 4 expectations in this domain are limited to whole numbers less than or equal to 1,000,000.

In Grade 3 students worked with multiplying a single-digit factor times a multiple of ten. A major focus of Grade 4 is to extend previous experiences to multiplying a single-digit factor times multi-digit factors. Students should understand arrays and area models as well as the properties of multiplication in order to use models and mental strategies to multiply a single-digit factor by a multi-digit factor. Although connections should be made between models and written equations (written vertically), it is not necessary for students to use or write a standard algorithm at this time. Rather, they should be developing and explaining efficient strategies that make sense to them. Problem situations should be used whenever possible as a context for multiplication work.

Use an area model to multiply a single-digit factor times a two-digit factor:

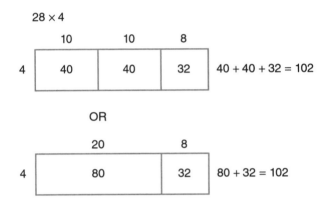

Use an area model to multiply a single-digit factor times a three-digit factor:

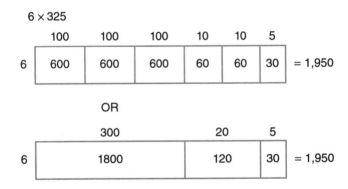

Once students show an understanding of multiplication by a single-digit factor, extend to multiplying by a two-digit factor that is a multiple of 10 and then any two-digit factor. Discuss patterns and why they work rather than showing students short cuts with no conceptual understanding as a basis.

Use an area model to multiply 2 two-digit factors:

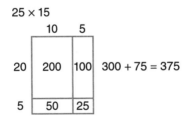

Examples of using the distributive property.

$$25 \times 16 \qquad\qquad 25 \times 16$$

$25 \times 10 = 250$	$20 \times 16 = 320$
$25 \times \ 4 = 100$	$\underline{\ 5 \times 16 = \ \ 80}$
$\underline{25 \times \ 2 = \ \ 50}$	$25 \times 16 \quad 400$
$25 \times 16 = 400$	

Use partial products to multiply:

```
        25
      × 16
      -----
        30    (6 × 5)
       120    (6 × 20)
        50    (10 × 5)
       200    (10 × 20)
      -----
       400
```

Note that students are not expected to understand and use the standard algorithm in Grade 4.

What the TEACHER does:

- Carefully plan and scaffold multiplication situations involving a one-digit factor times a multi-digit factor.
- Provide activities that require students to model and use sensible strategies to show their understanding of multiplication.
- Use formative assessment activities to determine whether students have a conceptual understanding of multiplication by a one-digit factor using pictures, words, and numbers.
- Extend previous work to multiplying a two-digit factor by a two-digit multiple of 10 using models and strategies based on place value and the properties of multiplication.
- Facilitate discussions based on patterns and why they work.
- Provide situations and examples in which students can model and connect previous strategies to multiplication of a two-digit factor by a two-digit factor.

What the STUDENTS do:

- Use a variety of models (arrays and area models) and strategies to represent multi-digit factors times a one-digit factor.
- Explain their reasoning using pictures, numbers, and words.
- Make connections to written equations.
- Extend this work to multiplication of 2 two-digit factors using pictures, words, and numbers.

Addressing Student Misconceptions and Common Errors

Students may ignore place value when multiplying multi-digit numbers, as shown in the following example. Use concrete materials to review place value understanding (multiplying by a multiple of ten will give a product that is expressed as tens; $6 \times 70 = 6 \times 7$ tens $= 42$ tens $= 420$). At this time the use of partial products and the distributive property will help to reinforce each part of a multiplication equation.

```
    50          46          46          33
  × 46        × 32        × 32        × 52
  ----        ----        ----        ----
   300          12        1212         156
   200           8
  ----          18
   500          12
                50
```

Extending simple area models to area models for multi-digit multiplication examples will also reinforce the role of partial products.

Find whole-number quotients and remainders with up to four-digit dividends and one-digit divisors, using strategies based on place value, the properties of operations, and/or the relationship between multiplication and division. Illustrate and explain the calculation by using equations, rectangular arrays, and/or area models.

Note: Grade 4 expectations in this domain are limited to whole numbers less than or equal to 1,000,000.

Previous work with division in Grade 3 focused on the meaning of division (determining the number of groups or the number of items in a group) using examples of dividing a number up to 100 by a one-digit number (primarily basic facts) and relating division to multiplication. By the end of Grade 4 students should be able to model, write, and explain division by a one-digit divisor.

Students should continue to become fluent with extending basic facts to efficient recall of situations with remainders.

Example:

I have 38 pennies. If each gum stick costs 5¢, how many can I buy?

(*Think:* How many groups of 5 can I make out of 38?) I can make 7 groups of 5. I can buy 7 gum sticks and I will have 3¢ left over. 38 ÷ 5 = 7 remainder 3.

They extend their work beyond situations with basic facts, asking themselves questions that relate to the meaning of division using place value and estimation.

Example:

Tony's mother made 84 cookies. She wants to put them in bags with 3 cookies in each bag. How many bags will she fill?

Students may begin by modeling, but this can become cumbersome and very inefficient. Rather, have students consider the situation and use conceptual understanding of division, so they can proceed by narrowing in on the quotient using multiples of 10.

- Can she fill 10 bags? Yes. How many cookies will it take? 30
- Can she fill 20 bags? Yes. How many cookies will it take? 60
- Can she fill 30 bags? No. How many cookies will it take? I would need 90 cookies.
- So 20 bags uses 60 cookies, how many cookies are left? 24
- How many bags can she fill with 24 cookies? 8
- So how many bags can she fill altogether? 28

Tony's mother will fill 28 bags with cookies.

As students transition from concrete models to putting their ideas in writing, they can use partial products to show their thinking.

Some students may find their work with area models to be helpful in thinking about division. Using this model, they need to remember that they are looking for the missing factor and therefore need to break the dividend (product) into smaller parts.

Students who have a sense of compatible numbers (for example, 42 ÷ 5 is close to 40÷5 or 45÷5) have better estimation skills and can apply these skills because they have more experience with solving division problems.

What the TEACHER does:

- Select division problems to scaffold student learning.

  - Begin building on division facts by providing examples that enable students to identify compatible numbers.
  - Provide examples including two- and three-digit numbers divided by single-digit divisors.
  - Model questioning that relates the meaning of division to the example.
  - Support student thinking as they work to translate their models into written notation (for example, using partial quotients).

- Facilitate class discussion in which students explain their reasoning as they develop conceptual understanding of division and connect that understanding to procedures and skills.
- Use formative assessment activities to assess student understanding of division.

What the STUDENTS do:

- Use models that make sense to represent division situations.
- Connect previous work with division facts to finding compatible numbers.
- Explain their reasoning in small groups and with the whole class as they solve division problems.

Watch for students who get the place value of digits confused when dividing. Use the relationship between multiplication and division and students' previous experiences with estimation to help students realize the place value of the quotient.

Consistently model questions such as the following to help students hone in on the quotient.

Example:

Martin has 183 Hot Wheels cars in his collection. He has boxes that each hold 8 Hot Wheels cars. How many boxes will he need to store the cars?

- Can he fill 10 boxes? Yes. How many cars will 10 boxes hold? 80 cars
- Can he fill 20 boxes? Yes. How many cars will 20 boxes hold? 160 cars
- Can he fill 30 boxes? No. How many cards would 30 boxes hold? 240 cars
- So if 20 boxes will hold 160 cars, how many cars still need to be put in a box? 23 cars
- How many boxes will hold 23 cars? 2 boxes
- So how many boxes will be full? 20+2 = 22 boxes
- Are there any cars that are not in a box? 1 car
- If he wants to put all of the cars in a box, how many boxes will he need? 23 boxes

Use partial quotients to allow students to chunk the numbers into smaller pieces, make the problem more manageable, and avoid mistakes when there is a zero in the quotient.

Give students opportunities to find and use compatible numbers in determining the quotient.

Example:

For example: $4\overline{)263}$

Think $4\overline{)240}$ first because 4 and 24 are compatible numbers.

Notes

Number and Operations in Base Ten
Cluster B: Use place value understanding and properties of operations to perform multi-digit arithmetic.

Note: Grade 4 expectations in this domain are limited to whole numbers less than or equal to 1,000,000.

Standard: 4.NBT.B.6. *Find whole-number quotients and remainders with up to four-digit dividends and one-digit divisors, using strategies based on place value, the properties of operations, and/or the relationship between multiplication and division. Illustrate and explain the calculation by using equations, rectangular arrays, and/or area models.*

Standards for Mathematical Practice:
SFMP 2. Reason abstractly and quantitatively.

Students use their knowledge of division and place value to estimate quotients using strategies that make sense to them.

SFMP 3. Construct viable arguments and critique the reasoning of others.

Students explain their thinking to partners and to the class.

SFMP 7. Look for and make use of structure.

Practice with estimating by rounding, using compatible numbers, and other strategies prepares students to find exact quotients of division examples.

Goal:
To give students opportunities to find an estimated quotient of a three-digit (or four-digit) number divided by a one-digit number using compatible numbers, rounding, or other strategies to prepare for finding actual quotients.

Planning:

Materials: Digit cards (1–9) for each set of partners, paper and pencil

Sample Activity:
Students write the following set-up on their papers.

$$\_)\overline{\_\ \_\ \_}$$

Work with a partner. Each pair copies the division template shown above on their paper. They turn over four cards and fill in the blanks with the digits they have turned over (in order). They work together to determine the place value of the quotient (hundreds or tens) and the digit that belongs in that place. For example, if the cards are 5 3 4 6 their problem would look like this:

$$5)\overline{346}$$

They would determine the quotient has a 6 in the tens place.

Notes

Questions/Prompts:

Ask students to justify their thinking as they determine the place value of the quotient.

- How do you know the quotient will be in the tens (or hundreds place)?
- What numbers did you use to estimate the first digit of the quotient?
- What strategy did you use to solve this problem?
- Explain your thinking to your partner/ group/the class.

Differentiating Instruction:

Struggling Students: Questions connecting this work to physical models will help students to estimate

- Can you make 100 groups of 5? How many would you need?
- Can you make 10 groups of 5? How many would you need?
- Can you make 20 groups of 5? How many would you need?

Continue with similar questions. Work toward having students ask themselves these questions.

Extension: Students who complete this task fluently can begin to work on finding the actual quotient.

Notes

Number and Operations in Base Ten

Cluster A: Generalize place value understanding for multi-digit whole numbers.

Note: Grade 4 expectations in this domain are limited to whole numbers less than or equal to 1,000,000.

Standard:

Standards for Mathematical Practice:

Goal:

Planning:

Materials:

Sample Activity:

Questions/Prompts:

Differentiating Instruction:

Struggling Students:

Extension:

Number and Operations in Base Ten
Cluster B: Use place value understanding and properties of operations to perform multi-digit arithmetic.

Note: Grade 4 expectations in this domain are limited to whole numbers less than or equal to 1,000,000.

Standard:

Standards for Mathematical Practice:

Goal:

Planning:

Materials:

Sample Activity:

Questions/Prompts:

Differentiating Instruction:

Struggling Students:

Extension:

Number and Operations in Base Ten
5.NBT.A*

Understand the place value system.

STANDARD 1   **5.NBT.A.1:** Recognize that in a multi-digit number, a digit in one place represents 10 times as much as it represents in the place to its right and $\frac{1}{10}$ of what it represents in the place to its left.

STANDARD 2   **5.NBT.A.2:** Explain patterns in the number of zeros of the product when multiplying a number by powers of 10, and explain patterns in the placement of the decimal point when a decimal is multiplied or divided by a power of 10. Use whole-number exponents to denote powers of 10.

STANDARD 3   **5.NBT.A.3:** Read, write, and compare decimals to thousandths.

   a. Read and write decimals to thousandths using base-ten numerals, number names, and expanded form, e.g., $347.392 = 3 \times 100 + 4 \times 10 + 7 \times 1 + 3 \times \frac{1}{10} + 9 \times \frac{1}{100} + 2 \times \frac{1}{1000}$.

   b. Compare two decimals to thousandths based on meanings of the digits in each place, using >, =, and < symbols to record the results of comparisons.

STANDARD 4   **5.NBT.A.4:** Use place value understanding to round decimals to any place.

*Major cluster

Number and Operations in Base Ten   5.NBT.A

Cluster A: Understand the place value system.
Grade 5 Overview

Fifth graders expand on previous work with place value to understand the relationship between adjacent places both to the left and to the right of a given place value. Connecting previous work with 10s, 100s, and 1,000s to powers of ten gives students a sense of the magnitude of numbers and reinforces the relationship among place values.

Students begin to extend knowledge of place value to decimal numbers, including writing numbers to thousandths in expanded form and comparing decimals to the thousandths place.

Standards for Mathematical Practice
SFMP 2. Use quantitative reasoning.
SFMP 3. Construct viable arguments and critique the reasoning of others.
SFMP 4. Model with mathematics.
SFMP 5. Use appropriate tools strategically.
SFMP 6. Attend to precision.
SFMP 7. Look for and make use of structure.

This cluster contains various aspects of using place value with both whole numbers and decimal numbers. Different mathematical practices help students develop understanding and apply the mathematics in each Standard. Using models and quantitative reasoning will help students to understand the relationship between adjacent places in both whole numbers and decimals and reinforce conceptual understanding of individual places as well as the magnitude of a number across place values on both sides of the decimal point. The use of exponents in expressing powers of ten is new to this grade level, and precision in writing and explaining powers of ten is critical. Students also connect this new written notation with exponents to the structure of our place value system.

Related Content Standard

4.NBT.A.1

Recognize that in a multi-digit number, a digit in one place represents 10 times as much as it represents in the place to its right and $\frac{1}{10}$ of what it represents in the place to its left.

This Standard extends work from Grade 4 in which students explored and generalized that when a digit moves one place to the left (for example, from tens to hundreds) it becomes ten times greater. In Grade 5 they look at what happens as the digit moves to the right (10 is $\frac{1}{10}$ of 100).

What the TEACHER does:

- Provide students with multiple activities and games to determine the value of digits in different places—working from left to right and from right to left.
- Develop conceptual understanding through models and tasks that requires students to compare and describe digits in different places.

  o How is the value of 2 in 625 different from the value of 2 in 652?

    o Use bundled straw and place value chart to model
    o Explain the value of the 2 in each number.

  o Describe the value of the 4 in each place of 444 using expanded notation.

    o $400 + 40 + 4 = 444$
    o 4 hundreds + 4 tens + 4 ones = 444

- As students are ready, extend their understanding to include decimals to the thousandths place.

  o Use models such as base-ten blocks in which the flat represents one whole, the long represents one tenth, and the cube represents one hundredth as important representations to help build students' number sense about the size of decimals.

  o Reinforce words and spelling of decimal place value names.

- Use a variety of tasks, activities, and games that reinforce the meaning of whole number and decimal places and the relationships among them (for example, 300 is one hundred times more than 3).

What the STUDENTS do:

- Compare the value of digits based on their placement in a given number and explain their thinking.

  o The value of 3 in 435 is 30 or 3 tens.

  o The value of 3 in 365 is 300 or 3 hundreds.

  o 300 is ten times greater than 30 and 30 is $\frac{1}{10}$ of 300.

- Use models, including a place value chart and base-ten blocks, to support discussions.
- Use numeral cards, playing cards, dice, and money to generate numbers, including decimals, to compare the values of various places.

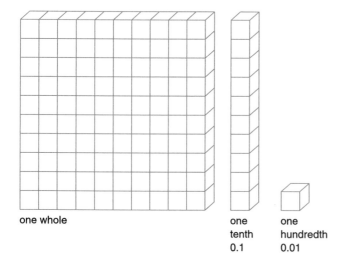

one whole

one tenth 0.1

one hundredth 0.01

GRADE 5

Students can get confused with the language describing the relationship between place values for whole numbers and decimal numbers. For example, when moving from ones to tens (one place to the left), the value is ten *times* greater, not ten greater or ten more. When moving from tenths to hundredths (one place to the right), the value is $\frac{1}{10}$ the value and not ten less than. Working with concrete models and pictorial representations and practicing with appropriate language will help students avoid confusion.

Notes

Explain patterns in the number of zeros of the product when multiplying a number by powers of 10, and explain patterns in the placement of the decimal point when a decimal is multiplied or divided by a power of 10. Use whole-number exponents to denote powers of 10.

This Standard contains several important ideas. As students explore products of expressions with multiple factors of 10 (that is, $10 \times 10 \times 10$), they easily see patterns with the number of zeroes in the product but also need to recognize that each time I multiply by ten, the place value of product shifts one place to the left, which is the basis of our base-ten system.

$$10 \times 10 = 100 \qquad 10 \times 10 \times 10 = 1,000 \qquad 10 \times 100 = 1,000$$

Students also learn the notation of exponents to express powers of ten with the exponent telling the number of times 10 is used as a factor.

$$10 = 10^1 \qquad 10 \times 10 = 10^2 \qquad 10 \times 10 \times 10 = 10^3$$

Students extend this work to exploring what happens when they multiply a number times a power of ten written in multiple ways.

$$5 \times 1 = 5 \qquad 5 \times 10 = 50 \qquad 5 \times 10 \times 10 = 500 \qquad 5 \times 10 \times 10 \times 10 = 5,000$$
$$5 \times 100 = 500 \qquad 5 \times 1000 = 5,000$$
$$5 \times 10^1 = 50 \qquad 5 \times 10^2 = 500 \qquad 5 \times 10^3 = 5,000$$

It is important that students focus not only on the number of zeros in the product but even more so on why the pattern of zeroes works: each time you multiply by ten, the place value of the product moves one place to the left (is ten times greater).

Once students understand and can explain the pattern, continue with decimal examples. Base-ten blocks and coins provide concrete models and contexts for students.

$10 \times \$.01 = \$.10$ (ten pennies make a dime, $.10) $\qquad 10 \times \$.05 = \$.50$

$10 \times \$.10 = \$1.00$ (ten dimes make 1 dollar, $1.00) $\quad 10 \times \$.50 = \$5.00$

What the TEACHER does:

- Provide a variety of experiences for students to explore multiplying a number by a power of ten using concrete models, pictures, and words. Begin with whole-number examples, and once students demonstrate understanding move to decimal numbers to the thousandths place.

  o $5 \times 10 = 50$
  o $5 \times 100 = 500$
  o $5 \times 1000 = 5,000$

- Facilitate student discussions using questions that help students find and understand patterns when multiplying by a power of ten. For example, "What do you notice about the product of 6×10?" "Why do you think that works?" "Will that always be true when you multiply a number by 10?" "Can you find an example of when that is not true?"

- Continue with similar questions for multiplying by 100 and 1,000.
- Introduce writing powers of 10 using notation with exponents. Have students describe patterns and relationships between the exponent and the number of times 10 is used as a factor.

  o $10 = 10^1$
  o $100 = 10 \times 10 = 10^2$
  o $1,000 = 10 \times 10 \times 10 = 10^3$
  o $10,000 = 10 \times 10 \times 10 \times 10 = 10^4$

What the STUDENTS do:

- Explore multiplication of whole numbers and decimal numbers by powers of 10 (10; 100; 1,000; 10,000) using concrete materials, pictures, numbers, and words.
- Describe patterns they find and justify why those patterns work.
- Write powers of ten using exponential notation.

Addressing Student Misconceptions and Common Errors

It is of major importance that students understand the relationship between the number of zeros in the power of ten, or the exponent, and the number of zeros in the product beyond just noticing that they are the same. For example, when multiplying 62×100, students should be able to justify that the product represents 62 groups of 100, which is written as 6,200. This understanding is critical as students move to multiplying by decimals. The use of concrete materials and pictorial representations will help students to make these important connections.

As students begin to work with exponents they must understand that the exponent tells them the number of times the base (in this case 10) is used as a factor. Some students may think of addition ($10^2 = 10 + 10$ instead of 10×10). Students need a variety of experiences including concrete and pictorial representations connected to skill practice to build understanding and skill working with exponential notation.

GRADE 5

Read, write, and compare decimals to thousandths.

Reading and writing decimals should be part of the total experience of working with decimal place value, which is explored in this Standard. Students connect previous experience comparing whole numbers to comparing decimals.

> a. *Read and write decimals to thousandths using base-ten numerals, number names, and expanded form, e.g.,*
> $347.392 = 3 \times 100 + 4 \times 10 + 7 \times 1 + 3 \times \frac{1}{10} + 9 \times \frac{1}{100} + 2 \times \frac{1}{1000}.$

As students begin to work with decimals by extending their place value understanding of whole numbers and the relationship among decimal places, reading and writing decimals are essential skills. Extending previous work with expanded notation to include decimals to thousandths will help to support the meaning of decimal place value.

It is important that students read decimals appropriately. Reading 13.45 as *thirteen point forty-five* has no meaning and does not support understanding of decimal place value or the meaning of .45 as forty-five hundredths, which can also be written as a fraction. Students should read decimals completely, for example, 13.45 is read *thirteen and forty-five hundredths*. It is critical that teachers read decimals in the same way to model for students.

What the TEACHER does:

- Provide a variety of experiences and activities in which students model and write base-ten numerals on a place value chart. Connect those experiences to writing decimal numbers in expanded notation.

24.69

What the STUDENTS do:

- Recognize and name place values for base-ten numerals to the thousandths place using place value charts and expanded form.
- Demonstrate understanding of decimal place values:

  o tenth   0.1 $\frac{1}{10}$ of 1 whole

  o hundredth   0.01 $\frac{1}{100}$ of 1 whole

  o thousandth 0.01 $\frac{1}{1000}$ of 1 whole

- Read and write decimals (to thousandths) using numerals, words, and expanded form.

- Model reading decimal numbers and writing decimal names in words.
- Add decimal place names (*tenths, hundredths, thousandths*) to the mathematics word wall.

Addressing Student Misconceptions and Common Errors

It is imperative that students read decimal numbers correctly to reinforce the meaning of the decimal and its place value. For example, 1.12 should be read as "one and twelve hundredths" and not "one point twelve." Teachers should model this and the expectation should be clear. This not only reinforces the value of the decimal number but also explicitly connects decimal numbers to fraction numbers.

b. *Compare two decimals to thousandths based on meanings of the digits in each place, using >, =, and < symbols to record the results of comparisons.*

Students use various representations and understandings of decimal place value and fractions to compare decimals. When the decimals have the same number of places, comparisons can be made based on the value of the digits starting in the tenths place.

a. 0.246 < 0.567 because 2 tenths is less than 5 tenths.

b. 0.246 < 0.567 because 246 thousandths is less than 567 thousandths.

This may become confusing to students when the number of places differs between the decimal numbers being compared. Using grid models or base-ten blocks will help students to focus on the value of the tenths and then move to hundredths if necessary.

a. 0.5 > 0.24 because 5 tenths is greater than 2 tenths.

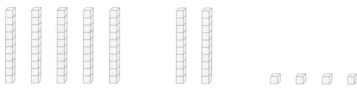

0.5   is greater than 0.24

What the TEACHER does:

- Provide experiences that reinforce the value of decimal places and how they connect to the previous place value work with whole numbers.
- Include both concrete experiences and written activities in which students write a decimal number to an equivalent decimal with additional places. Modeling these equations with concrete materials will help students understand that they are equivalent because they represent the same amount.

  ○ 0.5 = 0.50 = 0.500
  ○ 0.34 = 0.340

- Scaffold student experiences beginning with concrete models to build an understanding of the size of various decimals.

  ○ Compare numbers with like places (that is, tenths to tenths; hundredths to hundredths; and thousandths to thousandths).
  ○ Compare numbers with 1 decimal place to numbers with 2 decimal places using models, pictures, and words.

    ◦ 0.5 > 0.45
    ◦ 0.32, 0.6

- Facilitate classroom discussions in which students justify their reasoning when comparing decimal numbers.

What the STUDENTS do:

- Demonstrate understanding of the equivalence of decimal numbers and fractions by connecting models to reading and writing equivalent numbers. $0.5 = \frac{5}{10}$
- Demonstrate understanding of equivalent decimal numbers by generating lists of equivalent decimals with different place values. 0.3 = 0.30 = 0.300
- Use a place value chart to compare decimals by comparing the digits in each decimal place.
- Explain their reasoning when comparing decimals numbers using objects, pictures, numbers, and words.

Addressing Student Misconceptions and Common Errors

When comparing two decimals with different place values, students may have the misconception that 0.345 > 0.57 because 345 is greater than 57 without considering the value of each place after the decimal point. Modeling these numbers using drawings or base-ten blocks will help students to see that 0.57 is greater because there are more tenths. They should have many opportunities to use models and drawings and explain their thinking. Once students demonstrate understanding using concrete materials, they should begin to explore why 0.57 is equivalent to 0.570 using models, place value understanding, and previous experience with equivalent fractions. If both decimal numbers have the same number of places, thousandths for example, students can then compare the number of thousandths in each decimal number to determine which is greater and which is less.

Use place value understanding to round decimals to any place.

Building on previous experiences rounding whole numbers, students generalize those experiences and understandings to include decimal numbers. Teachers should provide activities in which students round to a given place, for example, round 2.36 to the nearest tenth, noting that, in real life, people need to determine to what place a number should be rounded in a particular context. Presenting problem situations and letting students discuss what place make most sense for rounding in that situation connects the mathematics to everyday life applications.

Example:

The price of a gallon of gasoline is $3.459. Nancy thinks this is a strange way to write money. What would the cost of gasoline be rounding to the nearest cent (hundredth)?

Students begin by determining the hundredths that this number falls between. Illustrating it on a number line would look like the following:

To the nearest cent, the cost of a gallon of gasoline is $3.46.

What the TEACHER does:

- Provide real-world examples in which students must round decimals to the appropriate place.
- Extend previous experiences with rounding whole numbers using the number line to rounding with decimal numbers on the number line.
- Model using benchmark numbers to help students determine the location of a number on the number line.

  Round 12.73 to the nearest tenth.

  o 12.73 falls between 12.7 and 12.8.
  o 12.75 is halfway between 12.7 and 12.8.
  o 12.73 is closer to 12.7.

What the STUDENTS do:

- Use place value understanding and number line models to round decimal numbers to a given place.
- Examine various situations to determine where to round in a given situation.
- Give clear explanations to justify their thinking.

Addressing Student Misconceptions and Common Errors

Students who are taught to round decimals by using a rule rather than place value understanding have difficulty determining places when rounding up or down. This is true with both whole numbers and decimals. For example, when rounding to the nearest tenth, a student might round 15.28 to 15.38. When using a number line model, students need to determine the numbers that the given number falls between. In the previous case it would be between 15.2 and 15.3. Using benchmark numbers such as 15.25, which falls exactly in the middle, will help students determine the closest tenth. By plotting the given point on the number line, students can determine to which tenth it is closer. Scaffold examples for students who are struggling with this concept.

Notes

Number and Operations in Base Ten
5.NBT.B*

Perform operations with multi-digit whole numbers and with decimals to hundredths.

STANDARD 5   **5.NBT.B.5:** Fluently multiply multi-digit whole numbers using the standard algorithm.

STANDARD 6   **5.NBT.B.6:** Find whole-number quotients of whole numbers with up to four-digit dividends and two-digit divisors, using strategies based on place value, the properties of operations, and/or the relationship between multiplication and division. Illustrate and explain the calculation by using equations, rectangular arrays, and/or area models.

STANDARD 7   **5.NBT.B.7:** Add, subtract, multiply, and divide decimals to hundredths, using concrete models or drawings and strategies based on place value, properties of operations, and/or the relationship between addition and subtraction; relate the strategy to a written method and explain the reasoning used.

*Major cluster

Number and Operations in Base Ten   5.NBT.B

Cluster B: Perform operations with multi-digit whole numbers and with decimals to hundredths.
Grade 5 Overview

In Grade 5, students continue to add and subtract whole numbers with fluency. They apply previous experiences using models, strategies, place value, and problem contexts in multiplication to an efficient algorithm. Students continue to work with various division examples and explore to find efficient procedures for division. (Note that use of a division algorithm is not expected until Grade 6.) Students extend their understanding of decimals to solve problems and calculation examples to add, subtract, multiply, and divide decimals. They apply their understanding of the meaning of these operations from whole number experiences to using decimals.

Standards for Mathematical Practice
SFMP 1. Make sense of problems and persevere in solving them.
SFMP 2. Use quantitative reasoning.
SFMP 3. Construct viable arguments and critique the reasoning of others.
SFMP 4. Model with mathematics.
SFMP 5. Use appropriate tools strategically.
SFMP 6. Attend to precision.
SFMP 7. Look for and make use of structure.
SFMP 8. Look for and express regularity in repeated reasoning.

Although this cluster does not explicitly address expecting students to solve problems, providing contexts for computation will support students in extending the meaning of multiplication and division from whole numbers to operations with decimals. Students think quantitatively as they apply earlier strategies to a standard algorithm in multiplication. Models and tools, including area models, the number line, and partial products, will help to connect conceptual understanding to procedural skills. Students explain their thinking using precise vocabulary. As they move from previous multiplication strategies to using an efficient algorithm, students are making use of the structure of mathematics, including the use of place value and properties.

Related Content Standards
3.NBT.A.2   3.NBT.A.3   4.NBT.B.4   4.NBT.B.5

Fluently multiply multi-digit whole numbers using the standard algorithm.

This Standard is a culmination of the foundational work in grades 3 and 4. Third graders began with modeling and exploring the meaning of whole number multiplication. In Grade 4 students focused work on multiplying a multi-digit factor times a one-digit factor and multiplying a two-digit factor times a two-digit factor. In Grade 5, they extend this work to multiplying a multi-digit factor times a two-digit factor using an efficient algorithm. Models such as the area model can be used help students visualize the components of the product and connect the partial products in the model to an efficient algorithm that makes sense.

What the TEACHER does:

- Provide a variety of activities and experiences in which students multiply multi-digit whole numbers explicitly connecting previous models to efficient algorithms, such as using partial products or by regrouping.

```
    273
  ×  52
```

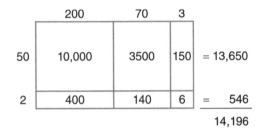

```
      273
    ×  52
       6  (2 × 3)
     140  (2 × 70)
     400  (2 × 200)
     150  (50 × 3)
   3500  (50 × 70)
 10,000  (50 × 200)
  14,196
```

```
      273
    ×  52
     546  (2 × 273)
  13650  (50 × 273)
  14,196
```

- Present students with various problem solving situations for multiplication.
- Facilitate student discussions in which they explain their reasoning in multiplication computation.

What the STUDENTS do:

- Connect previous work with the meaning of multiplication to activities and problem solving situations, asking themselves if their answer is reasonable by estimating and calculating an exact product.
- Connect previous models such as area models to a standard algorithm, including finding partial products or using regrouping in multiplication.
- Explain their reasoning when using a standard algorithm, which should include use of the properties of multiplication and place value.

Addressing Student Misconceptions and Common Errors

Students who become confused with regrouping in multi-digit multiplication need additional experiences with the partial product algorithm. Once they are proficient multiplying using partial products, they can begin to consider how using regrouping can save several steps. Scaffold examples for these students and give them time to understand how both the partial product and the regrouping algorithms are alike.

Notes

Find whole-number quotients of whole numbers with up to four-digit dividends and two-digit divisors, using strategies based on place value, the properties of operations, and/or the relationship between multiplication and division. Illustrate and explain the calculation by using equations, rectangular arrays, and/or area models.

Fourth graders explored and developed strategies for dividing multi-digit numbers by a one-digit number. In Grade 5 students extend this work to dividing by two-digit numbers. Using relationship between multiplication and division, estimation, rounding divisors, place value understanding, and connecting strategies to the meaning of division all contribute to an understanding of the process that is meaningful rather than having students follow a series of rote steps.

It would be very helpful to read over the Standards related to division from grades 3 and 4 in order to understand students' previous experiences developing understanding of the meaning of division through the use of partitive and measurement models for division. Because this is students' first experience with two-digit divisors, building on earlier work will help students develop understanding of what is happening when they divide and apply this to more difficult division examples.

As you prepare for this Standard, begin with dividing by multiples of 10 so students can get accustomed to dividing with compatible numbers. Estimation and rounding are using critical skills as students move to any two-digit divisor.

It is not expected that students will master a particular strategy or division procedure. It is important for students to use the strategy that makes the most sense to them. Students are expected to know a standard (efficient) algorithm for division in Grade 6. The use of compatible numbers and partial products will make sense for most students and is an acceptable goal for Grade 5.

Division Models

Area model with compatible numbers:

$$28,682 \div 80$$

	300	50	8	358 r 42
80	24,000	4,000	640	42

Rounding:

$$78\overline{)6,472} \rightarrow \text{think} \rightarrow 80\overline{)6,472}$$

Partial quotient:

```
52)6,432
   5,200   100
   ------
   1,232
   1,040   20     123 r 36
   -----
     192   3
     156
   -----
      36
```

GRADE 5

What the TEACHER does:

- Make connections from previous work with one-digit to divisors by dividing by multiples of 10, having students use concrete materials such as straws and rubber bands using place value to decompose the dividend.
- Use the division and missing factor problem solving situations (Table 2, page 256) as a context for division.
- Ask students questions that will help them to use estimation as they work to find partial quotients.
- Use formative assessment tasks to determine when students are successful with division by multiples of 10.
- Provide a variety of division examples. Use questions to support students as they use strategies, such as area models and partial products, for dividing by any two-digit number.

What the STUDENTS do:

- Connect previous experience with division to dividing by multiples of 10 using place value and estimation.
- Develop strategies for division by multiples of 10.
- Explain their reasoning using pictures, words, and numbers.
- Use rounding and estimation to divide by any two-digit number.
- Solve problems that include various division situations.

Addressing Student Misconceptions and Common Errors

Division is a complex operation, and students who depend on following rote steps cannot determine whether their answer is reasonable. Emphasis on place value and connections to multiplication will help students to develop a deeper understanding of division. All division experience should be developed in the context of asking question such as "How many groups of 20 can you make from 700?" and then allowing students to estimate and identify the number of objects (for example, If I make 30 groups of 20 that would be 600, and if I make 40 groups that would be 800, and that is too high). Such reasoning will help students to hone in on a good estimate and use partial products to determine the exact quotient.

Students may still need additional experiences with the meaning of the remainder built on previous work in Grade 4. Problems in which the remainder is the answer, in which the remainder is dropped, or in which the quotient should be one more because of a remainder should all be included in division problems students are asked to solve.

Notes

Add, subtract, multiply, and divide decimals to hundredths, using concrete models or drawings and strategies based on place value, properties of operations, and/or the relationship between addition and subtraction; relate the strategy to a written method and explain the reasoning used.

Students extend previous experiences with adding and subtracting whole numbers and their understanding of decimal place value to add and subtract decimals. They begin with modeling using base-ten blocks or grid paper models and relate those models to written equations. They explain their thinking in composing and decomposing numbers. It is important that conceptual understanding is built on place value rather than to simply line up the decimal points and compute. Problem situations extending from those used with whole numbers will provide a context for thinking about reasonableness of results.

The meaning of multiplication and division with decimals is *not* a new topic for students. These operations mean the same thing whether students are multiplying whole numbers, decimals, or fractions. Too often multiplication and division of decimals are taught as a series of rules developed around moving the decimal point with little connection to the meaning of the operations.

What the TEACHER does:

- Provide explicit connections between addition and subtraction of whole numbers and addition and subtraction of decimals, emphasizing the importance of place value.
- Make a variety of concrete materials such as base-ten blocks and grid paper models available to students as they add and subtract decimal numbers.
- Scaffold addition and subtraction examples, beginning with adding and subtracting tenths from tenths, hundredths from hundredths, tenths from hundredths, and hundredths from tenths.
- Provide a variety of problem situations that include decimal numbers for students to solve.
- Provide opportunities for students to make explicit connections from concrete and pictorial models to solving written equations.
- Include problems and examples to make explicit connections between the meaning of multiplication and division of whole numbers to multiplication and division of decimals. Have students estimate products and quotients based on the meaning of the operation.
- Ask students to describe place value patterns from multiplication examples:

  o Tenths time tenths equals hundredths.
  o Tenths times hundredths equals thousandths.
  o Hundredths times hundredths equals ten thousandths.

- Discuss why when multiplying a decimal by a decimal (or a decimal by a whole number), the product is smaller than at least one of the factors.
- Scaffold division examples using problem situations beginning with dividing a decimal by a whole number and progressing to dividing by tenths and hundredths.
- Provide division examples connecting whole number examples to decimals examples to have students recognize and describe place value patterns.
- Expect students to use estimation, the meaning of division, and a variety of contexts to explain why their answer is reasonable.

What the STUDENTS do:

- Connect previous experiences with the meaning of addition and subtraction of whole numbers to addition and subtraction of decimal numbers using concrete models and place value structure.
- Solve a variety of addition and subtraction problems involving decimal numbers.
- Explain their reasoning using concrete models, pictures, words, and numbers.
- Connect previous experiences with the meaning of multiplication and division of whole numbers to multiplication and division of decimals using estimation, models, and place value structure.
- Describe place value patterns in multiplication examples.

  o When I multiply tenths by tenths, the product is in the hundredths.
  o When I multiply tenths by hundredths, the product is in the thousandths.
  o When I multiply hundredths by hundredths, the product is in the ten thousandths.

- Describe place value patterns in division examples.
- Solve a variety of multiplication and division problems involving decimal numbers.
- Explain their reasoning using models, pictures, words, and numbers.

Addressing Student Misconceptions and Common Errors

Student misconceptions when working with decimal numbers are usually based on place value. Simply telling students to line up the decimal points when adding and subtracting decimals does not build the important understanding that similar place values are to be added or subtracted and can lead to errors such as the following:

$$\begin{array}{r} 2.5 \\ -1.75 \\ \hline 0.85 \end{array}$$

Building on whole-number experiences using concrete materials and place value charts will help students to relate previous work with composing and decomposing whole numbers to composing and decomposing decimals.

Since the "rules" for multiplication and division of decimals are much easier to teach than developing place value understanding, we are often tempted to provide students with these rules at some point. Don't do it! Students need time to see the structure of multiplication and division of decimals and how it relates to whole-number multiplication and division. Without this foundation, students may move decimal points when it is convenient rather than when it is necessary. Place value understanding also allows students to determine whether answers are reasonable. It is far more meaningful to students when they can generalize rules after many experiences and good questions from the teacher.

Notes

Number and Operations in Base Ten
Cluster B: Perform operations with multi-digit whole numbers and with decimals to hundredths.

Standard: 5.NBT.B.7. *Add, subtract, multiply, and divide decimals to hundredths, using concrete models or drawings and strategies based on place value, properties of operations, and/or the relationship between addition and subtraction; relate the strategy to a written method and explain the reasoning used.*

Standards for Mathematical Practice:

SFMP 2. Reason abstractly and quantitatively.
Students make connections between previous work with whole-number multiplication and division to estimate reasonableness of answers with decimals (before any formal instruction takes place).

SFMP 3. Construct viable arguments and critique the reasoning of others.
Students justify their thinking and make connections between their solutions and the solutions of classmates.

SFMP 7. Look for and make use of structure.
Students connect the structure of whole-number multiplication and division to using those operations with decimals.

Goal:
This lesson precedes any formal work with multiplication and division of decimals. The main purpose is for students to see that the meaning of multiplication and division is the same whether working with whole numbers or decimals.

Planning:

Materials: Problems for students to consider (see below), technology to project examples for the class to see.

Sample Activity:
Use what you know about multiplication and division to help you place the decimal point in the answer.

- $7.8 \times 4.9 = 3822$
- $53.4 \times 0.55 = 29937$
- $49.5 \div 6.25 = 792$
- $4.82 \div .95 = 4579$

Provide additional examples for students to solve on their own or in small groups. Once students place the decimal point, they should explain their reasoning.

Notes
_____
_____
_____

Questions/Prompts:

As students determine where the decimal point belongs, ask them to explain their reasoning. Ask questions such as

- How do you know the decimal point belongs between the 8 and the 2? Explain your reasoning.

At this point students should not have had experience with the algorithm, so rounding and relating the product or quotient of these examples to whole numbers is critical to helping students to understand that the meaning of the operation does not change when they are working with decimals.

Differentiating Instruction:

Struggling Students: Have students connect the decimal numbers in these examples to whole numbers:

7.8×4.9 is close to 8×5.

Use the product of 8×5 to determine where the decimal point belongs.

Talk about how the numbers are similar and how they are different.

Extension: Students who solve these examples and can clearly explain their thinking can use a calculator to make up similar problems to give their classmates.

Notes

Number and Operations in Base Ten
Cluster A: Understand the place value system.

Standard:

Standards for Mathematical Practice:

Goal:

Planning:

Materials:

Sample Activity:

Questions/Prompts:

Differentiating Instruction:

Struggling Students:

Extension:

Number and Operations in Base Ten
Cluster B: Perform operations with multi-digit whole numbers and with decimals to hundredths.

Standard:

Standards for Mathematical Practice:

Goal:

Planning:

Materials:

Sample Activity:

Questions/Prompts:

Differentiating Instruction:

Struggling Students:

Extension:

Reflection Questions: Number and Operations in Base Ten

1. Discuss how this domain relates to the Operations and Algebraic Thinking domain.

2. Look at the Related Content Standards listed in each cluster overview. Make a chart with a sequence of Standards across your grade level. Share your ideas with colleagues who teach the other grades in 3–5. From this work, discuss how ideas grow from one grade to the next and within a specific grade.

3. Select one of the following examples. Talk about the strategies students would use to solve this example. Discuss the concrete models students can use to develop conceptual understanding.

   a. Grade 3: $3 \times 6 = ?$ $15 \div 5 = ?$

   b. Grade 4: $423 \times 7 = ?$ $462 \div 6 = ?$

   c. Grade 5: $381 \times 26 = ?$ $565 \div 15 = ?$

Part 3

Number and Operations—Fractions

Number and Operations—Fractions

Domain Overview

GRADE 3

Students use visual models, including area models, fraction strips, and the number line, to develop conceptual understanding of the meaning of a fraction as a number in relationship to a defined whole. They work with unit fractions to understand the meaning of the numerator and denominator. They build equivalent fractions and use a variety of strategies to compare fractions. In Grade 3, denominators are limited to 2, 3, 4, 6, and 8.

GRADE 4

Fourth graders extend understanding from third grade experiences, composing fractions from unit fractions and decomposing fractions into unit fractions, and apply this understanding to add and subtract fractions with like denominators. They begin with visual models and progress to making generalizations for addition and subtraction fractions with like denominators. They compare fractions that refer to the same whole using a variety of strategies. Using visual models and making connections to whole number multiplication supports students as they begin to explore multiplying a whole number times a fraction. In Grade 4, denominators are limited to 2, 3, 4, 5, 6, 8, 10, 12, and 100. Students build equivalent fractions with denominators of 10 and 100 and connect that work to decimal notation for tenths and hundredths.

GRADE 5

Fifth graders build on previous experiences with fractions and use a variety of visual models and strategies to add and subtract fractions and mixed numbers with unlike denominators. Problem solving provides contexts for students to use mathematical reasoning to determine whether their answers make sense. They extend their understanding of fractions as parts of a whole to interpret a fraction as a division representation of the numerator divided by the denominator. Students use this understanding in the context of dividing whole numbers with an answer in the form of a fraction or mixed number. They continue to build conceptual understanding of multiplication of fractions using visual models and connecting the meaning to the meaning of multiplication of whole numbers. The meaning of the operation is the same; however, the procedure is different. Students use visual models and problem solving contexts to develop understanding of dividing a unit fraction by a whole number and a whole number by a unit fraction. Once conceptual understanding is established, students generalize efficient procedures for multiplying and dividing fractions.

3	4	5	
	✓	✓	Decimal models (base-ten blocks) (Reproducible 4)
✓	✓	✓	Fraction area models (circular) (Reproducible 5)
✓	✓	✓	Fraction area models (rectangular) (Reproducible 6)
✓	✓	✓	Fraction strips/bars (Reproducible 7)
✓	✓	✓	Grid paper (Reproducible 3)
✓	✓	✓	Objects for counting, such as beans, linking cubes, two-color counter chips, coins
✓	✓	✓	Place value chart (Reproducible 8)

KEY VOCABULARY

3	4	5	
✓	✓	✓	**area model** a concrete model for multiplication or division made up of a rectangle. The length and width represent the factors, and the area represents the product.

3×5 5×3

3	4	5	
✓	✓	✓	**benchmark** a number or numbers that help to estimate or determine the reasonableness of an answer. Sample benchmarks for fractions include $0, \frac{1}{2}, 1$.
	✓	✓	**decimal fraction** a fraction whose denominator is a power of 10, written in decimal form (for example, 0.4, 0.67)
✓	✓	✓	**denominator** the number of equal-sized pieces in a whole, the number of members of a set with an identified attribute. The bottom number in a fraction.
	✓	✓	**equivalent fractions** fractions that name the same amount or number but look different (*Example:* $\frac{2}{3}$ and $\frac{6}{9}$ are equivalent fractions)
	✓	✓	**hundredth** one part when a whole is divided into 100 equal parts
	✓	✓	**like denominator (common denominator)** having the same denominator
	✓	✓	**like numerator (common numerator)** having the same numerator

(Continued)

(Continued)

3	4	5	
✓	✓	✓	**measurement division (equal groups model)** a division model in which the total number of items and the number of items in each group is known. The number of groups that can be made is the unknown. *Example:* I have 3 yards of ribbon. It takes $\frac{1}{6}$ of a yard to make a bow. How many bows can I make? (How many groups of $\frac{1}{6}$ yards can I make from 3 yards?)
	✓	✓	**mixed number** a number that is made up of a whole number and a fraction (for example, $2\frac{3}{4}$)
✓	✓	✓	**numerator** the number in a fraction that indicates the number of parts of the whole that are being considered. The top number in a fraction.
✓	✓	✓	**partitive division (fair share model)** a division model in which the total number and the number of groups is known and the number of items in each group is unknown. *Example:* Erik has $\frac{1}{2}$ of a gallon of lemonade. He wants to pour the same amount in 5 glasses. How much lemonade will he pour into each glass if he uses all of the lemonade?
		✓	**scale (multiplication)** compare the size of a product to the size of one factor on the basis of the size of the other factor *Example:* Compare the area of these rectangles. When you double *one* dimension, the area is doubled.

10 in

5 in

5 in

5 in

3	4	5	
	✓	✓	**tenth** one part when one whole is divided into 10 equal parts
✓	✓	✓	**unit fraction** a fraction with a numerator of one, showing one of equal-sized parts in a whole (for example, $\frac{1}{2}, \frac{1}{3}, \frac{1}{4}$)

Number and Operations—Fractions[1]
3.NF.A*

[1] Grade 3 expectations in this domain are limited to fractions with denominators 2, 3, 4, 6, and 8.

Develop understanding of fractions as numbers.

STANDARD 1 **3.NF.A.1:** Understand a fraction $\frac{1}{b}$ as the quantity formed by 1 part when a whole is partitioned into b equal parts; understand a fraction $\frac{a}{b}$ as the quantity formed by a parts of size $\frac{1}{b}$.

STANDARD 2 **3.NF.A.2:** Understand a fraction as a number on the number line; represent fractions on a number line diagram.

    a. Represent a fraction $\frac{1}{b}$ on a number line diagram by defining the interval from 0 to 1 as the whole and partitioning it into b equal parts. Recognize that each part has size $\frac{1}{b}$ and that the endpoint of the part based at 0 locates the number $\frac{1}{b}$ on the number line.

    b. Represent a fraction $\frac{a}{b}$ on a number line diagram by marking off a lengths $\frac{1}{b}$ from 0. Recognize that the resulting interval has size $\frac{a}{b}$ and that its endpoint locates the number $\frac{a}{b}$ on the number line.

STANDARD 3 **3.NF.A.3:** Explain equivalence of fractions in special cases, and compare fractions by reasoning about their size.

    a. Understand two fractions as equivalent (equal) if they are the same size, or the same point on a number line.

    b. Recognize and generate simple equivalent fractions, e.g., $\frac{1}{2} = \frac{2}{4}$, $\frac{4}{6} = \frac{2}{3}$. Explain why the fractions are equivalent, e.g., by using a visual fraction model.

    c. Express whole numbers as fractions, and recognize fractions that are equivalent to whole numbers.

       Examples: Express 3 in the form $3 = \frac{3}{1}$; recognize that $\frac{6}{1} = 6$; locate $\frac{4}{4}$ and 1 at the same point of a number line diagram.

    d. Compare two fractions with the same numerator or the same denominator by reasoning about their size. Recognize that comparisons are valid only when the two fractions refer to the same whole. Record the results of comparisons with the symbols >, =, or <, and justify the conclusions, e.g., by using a visual fraction model.

*Major cluster

Number and Operations—Fractions[1]   3.NF.A

Cluster A: Develop understanding of fractions as numbers.

[1] Grade 3 expectations in this domain are limited to fractions with denominators 2, 3, 4, 6, and 8.

Grade 3 Overview

As students begin to develop understanding of fractions as a special group of numbers, they work with area models (circles, rectangles, and squares), fraction strips and fraction bars, and the number line to explore the meaning of the denominator and the meaning of the numerator. Unit fractions, fractions with a numerator of 1, form the foundation for initial fraction work. Students extend work with unit fractions to comparing fractions and finding simple equivalent fractions. Grade 3 expectations in this domain are limited to fractions with denominators 2, 3, 4, 6, and 8, which provides an opportunity to develop deep understanding of these foundational concepts.

Standards for Mathematical Practice
SFMP 2. Use quantitative reasoning.
SFMP 3. Construct viable arguments and critique the reasoning of others.
SFMP 4. Model with mathematics.
SFMP 5. Use appropriate tools strategically.
SFMP 6. Attend to precision.
SFMP 7. Look for and make use of structure.
SFMP 8. Look for and express regularity in repeated reasoning.

As third graders begin formal work with fractions, first and foremost they understand that fractions are numbers. They reason with physical models including area models, fraction strips, and number lines to understand unit fractions, such as $\frac{1}{4}$, as one part of a defined whole cut into four equivalent parts. They begin to develop an understanding of the meaning of the numerator and the denominator. Students extend their understanding of the structure of fractions beyond unit fractions, using visual representations to explain their thinking. They use repeated reasoning to compose other fractions from unit fractions including fractions equal to or greater than 1. Connecting area models to fraction strip models and to number lines provides a meaningful progression of models. This helps students to make generalizations as they build understanding of the meaning of common fractions extended to fractions greater than one. They use this understanding to compare and find equivalent fractions.

Related Content Standards

1.G.A.3   2.G.A.3   3.G.A.2   4.NF.A.1   4.NF.A.2   4.NF.B.3   4.NF.C.5

Notes

STANDARD 1 (3.NF.A.1)

Understand a fraction $\frac{1}{b}$ as the quantity formed by 1 part when a whole is partitioned into b equal parts; understand a fraction $\frac{a}{b}$ as the quantity formed by a parts of size $\frac{1}{b}$.

Note: Grade 3 expectations in this domain are limited to fractions with denominators 2, 3, 4, 6, and 8.

A fundamental goal throughout work across fraction clusters is for students to understand that fractions are numbers. They represent a quantity or amount that happens to be less than, equal to, or greater than 1. Too often we project the notion of fractions as parts of a whole without emphasizing that they are special numbers that allow us to count pieces that are part of a whole. Fractions in third grade are about a whole being divided (partitioned) into equal parts. Suggested models for Grade 3 include area models (circles, squares, rectangles), strip or fraction bar models, and number line models. Set models (parts of a group) are not models used in Grade 3. This Standard is about understanding unit fractions (fractions with a numerator of 1) and how other fractions are composed of unit fractions.

Folding a strip into 2 equal parts (one fold), each part or section would be $\frac{1}{2}$.

$\frac{1}{2}$	$\frac{1}{2}$

Folding a strip into 4 equal parts (three folds), each part or section would be $\frac{1}{4}$.

$\frac{1}{4}$	$\frac{1}{4}$	$\frac{1}{4}$	$\frac{1}{4}$

The fraction $\frac{3}{4}$ is the quantity formed by 3 parts that are each $\frac{1}{4}$ of the whole.

$\frac{1}{4}$	$\frac{1}{4}$	$\frac{1}{4}$	$\frac{1}{4}$

$\frac{3}{4}$

Important ideas for students to consider as they begin their work with fractional parts include:

- When working with any type of area model (circles, squares, rectangles) or strip models, fractional parts must be of equal size (but not necessarily equal shape). Using grid paper or geoboards can help students to determine when two pieces are the same size even if they are not the same shape.

- The denominator represents the number of equal size parts that make a whole.
- The more equal pieces in the whole (greater denominator), the smaller the size of the piece.

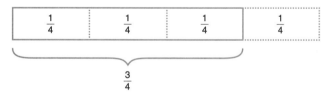

- The numerator of a fraction represents the number of equal pieces in the whole that are counted.

$\frac{1}{4}$	$\frac{1}{4}$
$\frac{1}{4}$	$\frac{1}{4}$

$\frac{3}{4}$ are shaded.

What the TEACHER does:

- Begin with strip models. These can simply be strips of construction paper about 2 inches by 11 inches. It is important that students understand that one strip represents one whole. If it is possible to use different colors it will help students to identify and compare fractions.
- Have students fold one strip into 2 equal parts and label each part $\frac{1}{2}$.
  - Ask students to make a conjecture about the meaning of the 2 in $\frac{1}{2}$ (the number of equal-size parts the whole strip).
  - Ask students to make a conjecture of the meaning of the 1 in $\frac{1}{2}$ (each piece is one part of the whole).
- Repeat the process folding and labeling strips for fourths, eighths, thirds, and sixths.
- Introduce the terms *numerator* and *denominator*. Ask students to explain what each term means based on this activity.
- Show students $\frac{3}{4}$ of a strip. Ask them what part (fraction) of one whole strip that amount represents. Students should use the terminology *numerator* and *denominator* in justifying their reasoning (that is, I know it is $\frac{3}{4}$ because it is made up of $\frac{1}{4} + \frac{1}{4} + \frac{1}{4}$).
- Prepare other activities in which students name parts of a whole and describe them as the sum of unit fractions.
- Use a variety of concrete representations for activities in which students compare the size of various unit fractions and then develop an understanding that the larger the denominator, the smaller the size of the piece. Using the same size whole is an important part of this understanding.
- When students are ready, use two different size wholes to have them talk about when $\frac{1}{4}$ might be greater than $\frac{1}{2}$. (When $\frac{1}{4}$ is part of a larger whole than $\frac{1}{2}$.)
- Give examples of fraction models that are equal size but not equal shape. Use area models or geoboards to have students represent unit fractions that are equal sized but not equal shape.

What the STUDENTS do:

- Make models of fractions (with denominators of 2, 3, 4, 6, and 8) using fraction strips. Label each part with the correct unit fraction.
- Describe the meaning of the denominator and the numerator using pictures, numbers, and words.
- Name various parts of the whole using fractions and explain that the fraction is made up of that number of unit pieces.

$$\frac{5}{8} = \frac{1}{8} + \frac{1}{8} + \frac{1}{8} + \frac{1}{8} + \frac{1}{8}$$

- Demonstrate an understanding that given the same size whole, the larger the denominator the smaller the size of the pieces because there are more pieces in the whole. Students demonstrate understanding by explaining their reasoning using concrete materials, pictures, numbers, and words.
- Identify and demonstrate fractional parts of a whole that are the same size but not the same shape using concrete materials.

Addressing Student Misconceptions and Common Errors

There are many foundational fraction ideas in this Standard, and it is important to take the time necessary to develop student understanding of each idea. This is best accomplished through extensive use of concrete representations, including fraction strips, area models, fraction bars, geoboards, and similar items. Do not work with too many representations at the same time. Begin with activities that use area models and reinforce those idea with fraction strips and then number lines. For most students one experience with a concept will not be adequate to develop deep understanding.

Students who demonstrate any of the following misconceptions need additional experiences connecting concrete representations to fraction concepts:

- Given the same size whole, the smaller the denominator, the smaller the piece.
- Fraction pieces must be the same shape and size.

- Students write a fraction numeral based on the number of pieces in a whole even if they are not the same sized pieces.

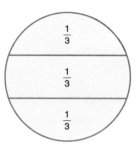

Misconception: Student considers the number of pieces in the whole but does not understand they must be the same size.

- Student label fractions as $\frac{\text{part}}{\text{part}}$ rather than as $\frac{\text{part}}{\text{whole}}$.

Misconception: Student writes the fraction as a part to part relationship rather than $\frac{1}{3}$ (part to whole).

Notes

Understand a fraction as a number on the number line; represent fractions on a number line diagram.

Note: Grade 3 expectations in this domain are limited to fractions with denominators 2, 3, 4, 6, and 8.

a. *Represent a fraction $\frac{1}{b}$ on a number line diagram by defining the interval from 0 to 1 as the whole and partitioning it into b equal parts. Recognize that each part has size $\frac{1}{b}$ and that the endpoint of the part based at 0 locates the number $\frac{1}{b}$ on the number line.*

Students have had previous experience with whole numbers on the number line. They extend this understanding by focusing on subdividing the distance from 0 to 1. Representing $\frac{1}{4}$ on the number line requires students to understand the distance from 0 to 1 represents one whole. When they partition this distance, the whole, into 4 equal parts, each part has the size of $\frac{1}{4}$. They also reason and justify the location of unit fractions by folding strips or on the number line. Previous work with fraction strips or fraction bars can be extended to developing parts on the number line.

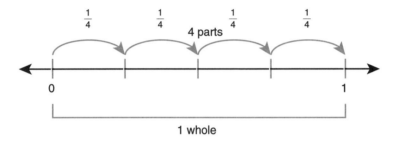

b. *Represent a fraction $\frac{a}{b}$ on a number line diagram by marking off a length $\frac{1}{b}$ from 0. Recognize that the resulting interval has size $\frac{a}{b}$ and that its endpoint locates the number $\frac{a}{b}$ on the number line.*

As students develop conceptual understanding of unit fractions they extend this to work counting unit fractions to represent and name other fractions on the number line.

For example, represent the fraction $\frac{3}{4}$ on a number line by marking off lengths of $\frac{1}{4}$ starting at 0. They can explain that 3 pieces of $\frac{1}{4}$ ($\frac{1}{4} + \frac{1}{4} + \frac{1}{4}$) or that the distance from 0 to that point represents $\frac{3}{4}$ on the number line.

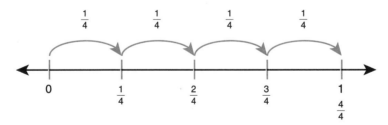

This Standard also includes work with improper fractions, not as a special group of fractions but as a continuation of counting unit fractions. By extending the number line, students develop the understanding that fractions equal to 1 have the same numerator and denominator and fractions greater than 1 have a numerator that will be greater than the denominator. They develop this understanding by counting on the number line using unit factions and recognizing patterns with fractional numbers.

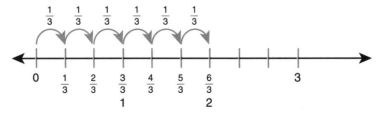

What the TEACHER does:

- Provide students with fraction strips (Reproducible 7) and number lines and ask students to transfer the parts from the fraction strip to the number line.
- Model labeling unit fraction intervals on the number line.
- Ask students to use the unit fraction intervals to "count" and label the fraction name for each division from zero to one.

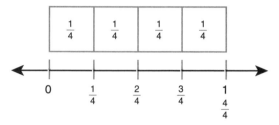

- Facilitate discussions in which students explain their reasoning as they label the number line.
- Repeat this process for fractions with denominators of 2, 3, 4, 6, and 8.
- Extend the number line to numbers greater than 1 using the same rationale for naming points on the number line.
- Provide students with many opportunities to describe patterns they see as they label number lines.

What the STUDENTS do:

- Use fraction strips to find fractional parts on the number line.
- Label intervals and points on the number lines. Intervals are unit fractions. Points on the number line represent the distance from 0 to that specific point and are made up of the number of unit fraction intervals.
- Demonstrate how they labeled the number line and explain their thinking.
- Extend number lines and activities to include fractions greater than 1.

Addressing Student Misconceptions and Common Errors

Although it is not critical for students to differentiate between the intervals between points and actual points on the number line, you want to be careful not to cause any misconceptions. The fraction that names a point on the number line describes the distance of that point from 0 and not the point itself.

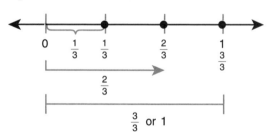

Notes

Explain equivalence of fractions in special cases, and compare fractions by reasoning about their size.

Note: Grade 3 expectations in this domain are limited to fractions with denominators 2, 3, 4, 6, and 8.

a. *Understand two fractions as equivalent (equal) if they are the same size, or the same point on a number line.*

The number line is one of several models such as area models and fraction bar models that can help students to develop conceptual understanding of equivalent fractions. Concrete experiences drawing area models and folding fraction strips should gradually transition to equivalent fractions on the number line.

b. *Recognize and generate simple equivalent fraction, e.g., $\frac{1}{2} = \frac{2}{4}$, $\frac{4}{6} = \frac{2}{3}$. Explain why the fractions are equivalent, e.g., by using a visual fraction model.*

Patterns with visual models help students to reason and justify why two fractions are equivalent. The use of procedures or algorithms is not a third grade expectation.

c. *Express whole numbers as fractions, and recognize fractions that are equivalent to whole numbers.* Examples: Express 3 in the form $3 = \frac{3}{1}$; recognize that $\frac{6}{1} = 6$; locate $\frac{4}{4}$ and 1 at the same point of a number line diagram.

The foundational understanding of this Standard is established by providing experiences for students to recognize that any whole number can be expressed as a fraction with a denominator of 1. Previous experiences developing the understanding that the denominator tells the number of pieces into which one whole has been partitioned now extends to situations in which the whole is not divided and remains in 1 piece, resulting in a denominator of 1.

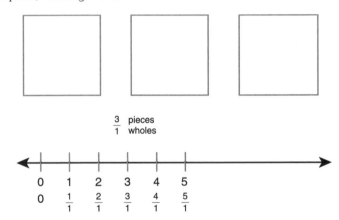

Students extend this understanding to dividing a number of area models that are wholes into parts and determining the resulting fraction.

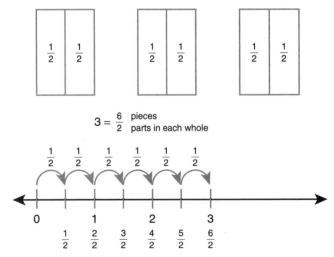

Classroom discussions and visual representations lead students to make the connection between fraction representations and division. For example, the fraction $\frac{6}{2}$ represents 6 pieces that are each $\frac{1}{2}$ of one whole. Two pieces are needed to make one whole. Modeling by putting the wholes back together with each whole representing one group shows that I can make 3 wholes or groups, each of which is $\frac{2}{2}$. Therefore $\frac{6}{2}$ is the same as $6 \div 2$. Note that students are just beginning to make this connection, and multiple activities will help students to develop this understanding rather than teaching it by simply giving them a rule.

> d. *Compare two fractions with the same numerator or the same denominator by reasoning about their size. Recognize that comparisons are valid only when the two fractions refer to the same whole. Record the results of comparisons with the symbols >, =, or <, and justify the conclusions, e.g., by using a visual fraction model.*

Students work with models and the number line to compare fractions with the same numerator. Models should refer to the same whole and include examples of how different size wholes impact the size of the fraction. Students explain their reasoning using pictures, words, and numbers, focusing on the meaning of the denominator as describing the number of pieces in one whole or size of the pieces and the numerator as the number of pieces or count. If the pieces are the same size (denominator), then the number of pieces (numerator) will determine which fraction is greater.

$\frac{3}{6}$ < $\frac{3}{4}$ because sixths are smaller than fourths

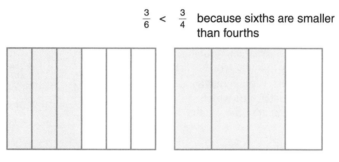

Students extend their reasoning to compare fractions with different denominators and the same numerator using models and the number line, and explain their reasoning using pictures, words, and numbers. They generalize that when the number of pieces (numerator) is the same, the number of pieces in a whole (denominator) will determine which fraction is greater. The larger the denominator, the smaller the size of the piece.

$\frac{5}{8}$ > $\frac{3}{8}$

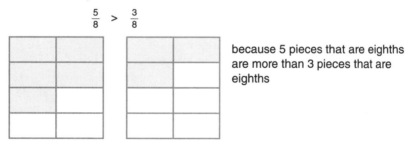

because 5 pieces that are eighths are more than 3 pieces that are eighths

What the TEACHER does:

- Provide a variety of activities with visual models, including area models, fraction strips, and the number line, to give students experience developing conceptual understanding that

  o Many fractions can describe the same quantity or point on a number line.
  o Fractions that represent the same amount are called *equivalent fractions*.

- Use purposeful questions to help students recognize patterns in equivalent fractions.

  o What do you notice about the numerators in equivalent fractions?

  o What do you notice about the denominators in equivalent fractions?
  o What patterns do you see in the numerators and denominators in two equivalent fractions?

- Connect concrete experiences to building sets of equivalent fractions using numerals. This should not be based on a procedure or algorithm, rather by looking for patterns and having students describe what is happening to the visual representation and numbers as they find equivalent fractions.
- Provide activities and experiences in which students use visual representations to express whole numbers as fractions.

(continued)

What the TEACHER does (continued):

- ○ Cutting one whole into fourths shows that $\frac{4}{4}$ equals one whole.
- ○ Generating fractions from more than one whole. Cutting 4 wholes into thirds will result in 12 pieces. Because each piece is $\frac{1}{3}$ of a whole, the resulting fraction is $\frac{12}{3}$. Therefore $\frac{12}{3}$ is equivalent to four wholes.
- ○ Leaving several wholes intact shows that 4 can be represented as $\frac{4}{1}$ since there are 4 pieces that are each 1 whole piece.
- Provide concrete experiences for students to compare parts of the same size whole with the same numerator and different denominators. Ask questions that will help students to generalize that when the size of the piece (denominator) is the same, the number of pieces (numerator) will determine which is the greater fraction.
- Provide concrete experiences for students to compare fractions of the same size whole with the same denominator and different numerators and generalize that when the number of pieces in the whole is the same (denominator), the number of pieces (numerator) will determine which fraction is greater. The larger the denominator, the smaller the size of the piece.

- Build sets of equivalent fractions from visual models and by recognizing patterns.
- Explain their reasoning in building sets of equivalent fractions. For example, $\frac{3}{4}$ is equivalent to $\frac{6}{8}$ because doubling the number of pieces in the whole (denominator) then will also double the count of pieces (numerator).
- Use visual representations to find fractional names for 1.
- Use visual representations to find fractional names for several wholes that are not partitioned (denominator is 1).
- Use visual representations to find fractional names for several wholes that are partitioned into pieces.
- Explain patterns they see as they are working with wholes and their equivalent fractions.
- Provide experiences that help students to make the following generalizations:

  - ○ When the numerator and denominator are the same, the value of the number is one whole.

    $$\frac{6}{6} = 1 \qquad 1 = \frac{8}{8} \qquad \frac{4}{4} = 1$$

  - ○ When the denominator is 1, the fraction represents wholes. The number of wholes is the same as the numerator.

    $$\frac{8}{1} = 8 \qquad 7 = \frac{7}{1} \qquad 3 = \frac{3}{1}$$

  - ○ When the numerator is a multiple of the denominator, the number of wholes is their quotient.

  - ○ $\frac{12}{4} = 3 \qquad \frac{10}{2} = 5 \qquad 6 = \frac{18}{3}$

What the STUDENTS do:

- Use visual representations including rectangular and circular area models, fraction bars, and the number line to find various (equivalent) fractions that name the same quantity or point.

Addressing Student Misconceptions and Common Errors

As students work with equivalent fractions, it is important that they understand that different fractions can name the same quantity and there is a multiplicative relationship between equivalent fractions. Students need multiple experiences using concrete materials as they explore each of these important concepts. They need to explain their reasoning and explicitly connect visual representations (concrete and pictorial) to numerical representations. It is important that students have time to make these connections, describe patterns, and make generalizations rather than by practicing rote rules.

The following misconceptions indicate that students need more work with concrete and then pictorial representations:

- The numerator cannot be greater than the denominator.
- The larger the denominator, the larger the piece.
- Fractions are a part of a whole; therefore, you cannot have a fraction that is greater than 1 whole.
- In building sets of equivalent fractions, students use addition or subtraction to find equivalent fractions.

Notes

Number and Operations—Fractions

Cluster A: Develop understanding of fractions as numbers.

Note: Grade 3 expectations in this domain are limited to fractions with denominators 2, 3, 4, 6, and 8.

Standard: 3.NF.A.1. *Understand a fraction $\frac{1}{b}$ as the quantity formed by 1 part when a whole is partitioned into b equal parts; understand a fraction $\frac{a}{b}$ as the quantity formed by a parts of size $\frac{1}{b}$.*

Standards for Mathematical Practice:

SFMP 4. Model with mathematics.

Students make fraction strips to use as they begin to explore the meaning of fractional parts of a whole.

SFMP 6. Attend to precision.

Initial experiences with fractions emphasize that a fraction is a number. Students develop fraction-related vocabulary, starting with *numerator* and *denominator*.

Goal:

Students use physical models as they begin to work with fractions, focusing on the meaning of fractions as a number as well as the meanings of the numerator and the denominator.

Planning:

Materials: 3 inch by 12 inch construction paper strips for each student. If possible provide each student with five strips that are different colors. Be sure to have extra strips on hand for students who make a mistake. Color marking pens.

Sample Activity:

Begin with one strip. Designate that strip as one whole and label it 1 WHOLE.

Have students take a strip of a color (for example, red) and fold it into two parts that are the same size. Talk about the pieces. Have students describe the pieces. Have students label each piece $\frac{1}{2}$. Talk about the meaning of the 1 (it is 1 part) and the meaning of the number 2 (there are 2 parts in the whole strip).

Introduce the terms *whole, fraction, unit fraction, numerator,* and *denominator*. Add them to your mathematics word wall.

Continue with another color, asking students to fold the piece into four equal parts. Have a similar discussion about the pieces. Proceed with eighths, thirds, and sixths.

Notes

Questions/Prompts:

Ask questions that directly relate new vocabulary to the work students are doing.

Be sure to give students plenty of time to talk about what they noticed. Important ideas that should come out of the discussion include:

- The whole is the same size for each fraction.
- A fraction is a part of the whole.
- The smaller the denominator the larger the piece (thirds are greater than fourths).
- The numerator indicates it is one part of the whole. These are called unit fractions.
- The denominator indicates the number of equal-size pieces in the whole.

Save these fraction strips for future work with comparing fractions.

Differentiating Instruction:

Struggling Students: Watch for students who may struggle with figuring out how to fold the fractions, particularly thirds and sixths.

Students need to label each part with a unit fraction. Give struggling students the opportunity to talk about the size of unit fractions. It may help these students to cut the pieces apart after labeling them. Ask them to reconstruct the whole.

Have extra prepared strips for students who are not successful in folding the fraction strips into equal parts. It is important to let them try—several times.

Extension: Although it is not expected at this grade level, some students may want to experiment folding fractions with other denominators.

Notes

Number and Operations—Fractions
Cluster A: Develop understanding of fractions as numbers.

Note: Grade 3 expectations in this domain are limited to fractions with denominators 2, 3, 4, 6, and 8.

Standard:

Standards for Mathematical Practice:

Goal:

Planning:

Materials:

Sample Activity:

Questions/Prompts:

Differentiating Instruction:

Struggling Students:

Extension:

Number and Operations—Fractions[1]
4.NF.A*

[1] Grade 4 expectations in this domain are limited to fractions with denominators 2, 3, 4, 5, 6, 8, 10, 12, and 100.

Cluster A

Extend understanding of fraction equivalence and ordering.

STANDARD 1

4.NF.A.1: Explain why a fraction $\frac{a}{b}$ is equivalent to a fraction $\frac{(n \times a)}{(n \times b)}$ by using visual fraction models, with attention to how the number and size of the parts differ even though the two fractions themselves are the same size. Use this principle to recognize and generate equivalent fractions.

STANDARD 2

4.NF.A.2: Compare two fractions with different numerators and different denominators, e.g., by creating common denominators or numerators, or by comparing to a benchmark fraction such as $\frac{1}{2}$. Recognize that comparisons are valid only when the two fractions refer to the same whole. Record the results of comparisons with symbols >, =, or <, and justify the conclusions, e.g., by using a visual fraction model.

*Major cluster

Number and Operations—Fractions[1]   4.NF.A

Cluster A: Extend understanding of fraction equivalence and ordering.

[1] Grade 4 expectations in this domain are limited to fractions with denominators 2, 3, 4, 5, 6, 8, 10, 12, and 100.

Grade 4 Overview

Fourth graders continue to work with equivalence beginning with models and using those models to generalize a pattern and eventually a rule for finding equivalent fractions. They justify their reasoning using pictures numbers and words. In Grade 3, students compared fractions with like numerators or like denominators. They now extend that understanding to comparing fractions with different numerators and denominators reinforcing the important comparison concept that fractions must refer to the same whole.

Standards for Mathematical Practice
SFMP 2. Use quantitative reasoning.
SFMP 3. Construct viable arguments and critique the reasoning of others.
SFMP 4. Model with mathematics.
SFMP 5. Use appropriate tools strategically.
SFMP 7. Look for and make use of structure.
SFMP 8. Look for and express regularity in repeated reasoning.

Fourth graders extend their understanding of equivalent fractions reasoning with visual models. They look for patterns both physical (when I double the number of pieces in the whole pizza, I double the number of pieces that I ate.) and think about these patterns in terms of the meaning of the numerator and the denominator. Providing experiences with appropriate visual models will help students to develop understanding rather than just following a rule that has no meaning. Through finding and discussing patterns students construct mathematical arguments to explain their thinking as they build sets of equivalent fractions. All of this work supports the fundamental structure of fractional numbers that is critical to all future work with fractions in this domain.

Related Content Standards

3.NF.A.2   3.NF.A.3

Explain why a fraction $\frac{a}{b}$ is equivalent to a fraction $\frac{(n \times a)}{(n \times b)}$ by using visual fraction models, with attention to how the number and size of the parts differ even though the two fractions themselves are the same size. Use this principle to recognize and generate equivalent fractions.

Note: Grade 4 expectations in this domain are limited to fractions with denominators 2, 3, 4, 5, 6, 8, 10, 12, and 100.

Previous work in Grade 3 included exploring to find equivalent fractions using area models, fraction strips, and the number line. Although students looked for patterns, a formal algorithm for finding equivalent fractions was not developed. Fourth graders build on prior experiences, beginning with area models, to formally describe what happens to the number of pieces in the whole and the number of pieces shaded when they compare $\frac{1}{2}$, $\frac{2}{4}$, $\frac{3}{6}$ and $\frac{4}{8}$ using models, pictures, words and numbers.

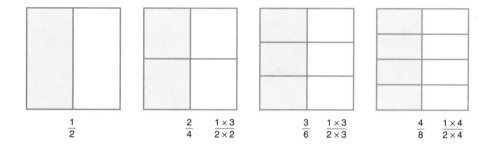

Students should be able to explain that when the number of pieces in the whole is doubled, the number of pieces in the count (the numerator) also doubles. This is true when multiplying by any factor.

Note that the Standards do not require students to simplify fractions although students may find fractions written in simpler form easier to understand. For example, if they recognize that $\frac{50}{100}$ is equivalent to $\frac{1}{2}$, they may choose to use $\frac{1}{2}$ since the two fractions are equivalent. Having students find equivalent fractions "in both directions" may help students to realize that fractions can be written in simpler form without formally simplifying fractions.

What the TEACHER does:

- Provide students with different models to use in building sets of equivalent fractions for visual representations and then write the fractions as numerals.
- Facilitate student discussions about patterns they see in sets of equivalent fractions.
- Expect students to use models and written numerals to generate a rule for finding equivalent fractions.
- Provide a variety of activities to help students build and recognize equivalent fractions.

What the STUDENTS do:

- Connect visual representations of equivalent fractions to numerical representations.
- Use pictures, words, and numbers to explain why fractions are equivalent.
- Generate a rule for finding equivalent fractions and follow that rule.
- Recognize equivalent fractions.

Addressing Student Misconceptions and Common Errors

Students who use addition or subtraction instead of multiplication to develop sets of equivalent fractions need additional experiences with visual representations including fraction bars, areas models, and the number line. Explanations of why one multiplies or divides to find an equivalent fraction should begin with visual representations and eventually connect to the rule/algorithm.

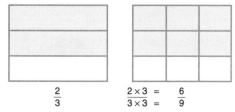

If I triple the number of pieces in the whole, that triples the number of pieces in my count.

Compare two fractions with different numerators and different denominators, e.g., by creating common denominators or numerators, or by comparing to a benchmark fraction such as $\frac{1}{2}$. Recognize that comparisons are valid only when the two fractions refer to the same whole. Record the results of comparisons with symbols >, =, or <, and justify the conclusions, e.g., by using a visual fraction model.

Note: Grade 4 expectations in this domain are limited to fractions with denominators 2, 3, 4, 5, 6, 8, 10, 12, and 100.

Students compare two fractions with different denominators by creating equivalent fractions with a common denominator or with a common numerator. Using benchmarks such as 0, $\frac{1}{2}$, or 1 will help students to determine the relative size of fractions.

Students justify their thinking using visual representations (fraction bars, area models, and number lines), numbers, and words. It is important for students to realize that size of the wholes must be the same when comparing fractions.

Use benchmark fractions,

Compare $\frac{5}{6}$ and $\frac{7}{12}$.

think

$\frac{5}{6}$ is almost 1

So $\frac{7}{12}$ is a little more than $\frac{1}{2}$ $\left(\frac{6}{12}\right)$

$$\frac{5}{6} > \frac{7}{12}$$

Use common denominators,

Compare $\frac{5}{6}$ and $\frac{3}{4}$.

think

So $\frac{5}{6} = \frac{10}{12}$ and $\frac{3}{4} = \frac{9}{12}$ and $\frac{10}{12} > \frac{9}{12}$

$$\frac{5}{6} > \frac{3}{4}$$

Use common numerators.

Compare $\frac{3}{6}$ and $\frac{5}{8}$.

think

$\frac{3}{6} = \frac{15}{25}$ $\frac{5}{8} = \frac{15}{24}$

Since 25ths are less than 24ths, $\frac{15}{25} < \frac{15}{24}$

So

$$\frac{3}{5} < \frac{5}{8}$$

Students should have opportunities to justify their thinking as well as which strategy is the most efficient to use.

What the TEACHER does:

- Provide a variety of concrete materials for students to use in comparing fractions.
  - Use 0, $\frac{1}{2}$, 1 as benchmarks to compare fractions.
  - Find common denominators to compare fractions.
  - Find common numerators to compare fractions.

    Note: Students should determine which method makes the most sense to them, realizing that they will use different methods for different situations.

- Engage students in a variety of activities and problem solving situations in which they compare fractions and justify their reasoning using pictures, words, and numbers.

What the STUDENTS do:

- Use a variety of representations to compare fractions including concrete models, benchmarks, common denominators, and common numerators.
- Determine which method makes the most sense for a given situation and justify their thinking.
  - Louisa and Linda went to the movies. Each bought a small box of popcorn. Linda ate $\frac{5}{6}$ of her popcorn and Louisa at $\frac{5}{8}$ of her popcorn. Who ate more?
  - Linda ate more. Because sixths are larger than eighths, $\frac{5}{6} > \frac{5}{8}$.
  - Mrs. Multiple made two pans of brownies. One pan had nuts and the other was plain. Each pan was the same size. The pan of brownies with nuts has $\frac{5}{12}$ left. The pan of plain brownies has $\frac{5}{8}$ left. Which pan has less left?

    I know that $\frac{5}{12}$ is less than $\frac{1}{2}$ (which is $\frac{6}{12}$). I know that $\frac{5}{8}$ is more than $\frac{1}{2}$ (which is $\frac{4}{8}$). Therefore the pan of brownies with nuts has less than the pan with the plain brownies because $\frac{5}{12} < \frac{5}{8}$.
  - Terri has collected $\frac{2}{3}$ of the money she needs to buy her mom's birthday present. Her brother Timmy has collected $\frac{5}{6}$ of the money he needs to buy his gift. Who is closer to their goal?

    I know that $\frac{2}{3}$ is equivalent to $\frac{4}{6}$. Timmy has $\frac{5}{6}$, Terry has $\frac{4}{6}$. Timmy is closer to his goal because $\frac{5}{6} > \frac{2}{3}$ ($\frac{4}{6}$).

Addressing Student Misconceptions and Common Errors

It is important for students to use reasoning and number sense to compare fractions and justify their thinking. Students who forget that the larger the number in the denominator, the smaller the piece, may base their comparisons on incorrect notions. These students need additional practice with concrete models and making connections to the written numerals. When comparing fractions, students must consider the size of the whole. One-half of a large box of popcorn is greater than $\frac{1}{2}$ of a small box of popcorn. Take time to provide a variety of experiences for students to make sense of these important concepts.

Number and Operations—Fractions[1]
4.NF.B*

[1] Grade 4 expectations in this domain are limited to fractions with denominators 2, 3, 4, 5, 6, 8, 10, 12, and 100.

Build fractions from unit fractions by applying and extending previous understandings of operations on whole numbers.

STANDARD 3   **4.NF.B.3:** Understand a fraction $\frac{a}{b}$ with $a > 1$ as a sum of fractions $\frac{1}{b}$.

    a. Understand addition and subtraction of fractions as joining and separating parts referring to the same whole.

    b. Decompose a fraction into a sum of fractions with the same denominator in more than one way, recording each decomposition by an equation. Justify decompositions, e.g., by using a visual fraction model. *Examples:*

$$\frac{3}{8} = \frac{1}{8} + \frac{1}{8} + \frac{1}{8}$$

$$\frac{3}{8} = \frac{1}{8} + \frac{2}{8}$$

$$2\frac{1}{8} = 1 + 1 + \frac{1}{8} = \frac{8}{8} + \frac{8}{8} + \frac{1}{8}$$

    c. Add and subtract mixed numbers with like denominators, e.g., by replacing each mixed number with an equivalent fraction, and/or by using properties of operations and the relationship between addition and subtraction.

    d. Solve word problems involving addition and subtraction of fractions referring to the same whole and having like denominators, e.g., by using visual fraction models and equations to represent the problem.

STANDARD 4   **4.NF.B.4:** Apply and extend previous understandings of multiplication to multiply a fraction by a whole number.

    a. Understand a fraction $\frac{a}{b}$ as a multiple of $\frac{1}{b}$. *For example, use a visual fraction model to represent $\frac{5}{4}$ as the product $5 \times \frac{1}{4}$, recording the conclusion by the equation $\frac{5}{4} = 5 \times \frac{1}{4}$.*

    b. Understand a multiple of $\frac{a}{b}$ as a multiple of $\frac{1}{b}$, and use this understanding to multiply a fraction by a whole number. *For example, use a visual fraction model to express $3 \times \frac{2}{5}$ as $6 \times \frac{1}{5}$, recognizing this product as $\frac{6}{5}$. (In general, $n \times \frac{a}{b} = \frac{(n \times a)}{b}$.)*

    c. Solve word problems involving multiplication of a fraction by a whole number, e.g., by using visual fraction models and equations to represent the problem. *For example, if each person at a party will eat $\frac{3}{8}$ of a pound of roast beef, and there will be 5 people at the party, how many pounds of roast beef will be needed? Between what two whole numbers does your answer lie?*

*Major cluster

Cluster B: Build fractions from unit fractions by applying and extending previous understandings of operations on whole numbers.

[1] Grade 4 expectations in this domain are limited to fractions with denominators 2, 3, 4, 5, 6, 8, 10, 12, and 100.

Grade 4 Overview

Fourth graders continue to develop understanding of fractions as numbers composed of unit fractions (for example,

$\frac{3}{4} = \frac{1}{4} + \frac{1}{4} + \frac{1}{4}$). They also extend their understanding that fractions greater than 1 can be expressed as mixed numbers

(for example, $\frac{12}{5} = \frac{5}{5} + \frac{5}{5} + \frac{2}{5} = 2\frac{2}{5}$). They connect their understanding of addition and subtraction of whole numbers as

adding to/joining and taking apart/separating to fraction contexts using fractions with like denominators. They begin with visual representations, including area models, fraction strips, and number lines, and connect these representations to written equations.

First experiences with multiplication of a fraction by a whole number begin with connecting the meaning of multiplication

of whole numbers to multiplication of a fraction by a whole number (for example, $5 \times \frac{1}{4}$ means 5 groups of $\frac{1}{4}$) using visual

representations. Following many experiences modeling multiplication with unit fractions by whole numbers, students continue to work with other fractions. They solve problems by modeling using area models, fraction strips, and number lines and explain their reasoning to others.

Standards for Mathematical Practice
SFMP 1. Make sense of problems and persevere in solving them.
SFMP 2. Use quantitative reasoning.
SFMP 3. Construct viable arguments and critique the reasoning of others.
SFMP 4. Model with mathematics.
SFMP 5. Use appropriate tools strategically.
SFMP 6. Attend to precision.
SFMP 7. Look for and make use of structure.
SFMP 8. Look for and express regularity in repeated reasoning.

Students extend their work with unit fractions to composing and decomposing non-unit fractions. In doing so, they reason about fractions as numbers (quantitatively) and understand that fractions, like whole numbers, represent a "count" of something. The main difference is the "something" includes part of a whole. Problem solving contexts reinforce the meaning of addition and subtraction, presenting opportunities for students to relate previous work with addition and subtraction situations with whole numbers to adding and subtracting fractions. They use models including area models, fraction strips, and number lines, and connect those visual models to written equations when they are ready. They build on previous understandings of the meaning of the numerator and denominator (precision) to see the structure of addition and subtraction and explain what is happening when they add and subtract fractions (for example, why they add or subtract numerators but keep the same denominator).

Related Content Standards
1.OA.A.1   2.OA.A.1   3.NF.A.2   3.G.A.2   5.NF.A.1   5.NF.A.2

Notes

GRADE 4

Understand a fraction $\frac{a}{b}$ with a > 1 as a sum of fractions $\frac{1}{b}$.

Note: Grade 4 expectations in this domain are limited to fractions with denominators 2, 3, 4, 5, 6, 8, 10, 12, and 100.

Unit fractions are fractions with a numerator of 1. Third graders' experiences with fractions focused on unit fractions. Their work with non-unit fractions was limited to using visual models such as fraction strips and number lines to see that fractions such as $\frac{3}{4}$ are composed of three jumps of $\frac{1}{4}$ on the number line. This is an important concept as students prepare to add and subtract fractions. Fourth grade experiences extend to composing and decomposing fractions greater than 1 (improper fractions) and mixed numbers into unit fractions Students use prior knowledge of using concrete fraction representations for whole numbers to move between mixed numbers and fractions.

What the TEACHER does:

- Provide a variety of experiences for students to compose and decompose fractions, including fractions greater than 1 and mixed numbers, into unit fractions using concrete and pictorial representations, words, and numbers.

What the STUDENTS do:

- Compose and decompose fractions, including fractions greater than 1 and mixed numbers, into unit fractions using concrete and pictorial representations including the number line.
- Explain their reasoning using pictures, words, and numbers.

Representations for $\frac{5}{6}$

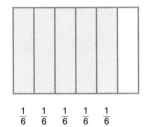
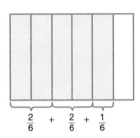

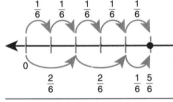

Representations for $3\frac{2}{3}$

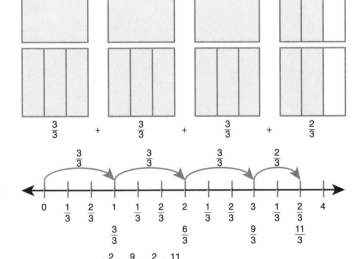

Addressing Student Misconceptions and Common Errors

Although students may be able to decompose a fraction into unit fractions (that is, $\frac{4}{5} = \frac{1}{5} + \frac{1}{5} + \frac{1}{5} + \frac{1}{5}$), when given the unit fractions to compose into a fraction, they may think they need to add denominators as well as numerators. This misconception can be avoided by giving students multiple opportunities with various concrete models, pictures, and the number line and making explicit connections to written equations.

a. *Understand addition and subtraction of fractions as joining and separating parts referring to the same whole.*

This Standard begins with an understanding that addition and subtraction of fractions has the same meaning as addition and subtraction of whole numbers, although the process of adding and subtracting is different with fractions. Remember expectations in this domain are limited to fractions with denominators 2, 3, 4, 5, 6, 8, 10, 12, and 100. Addition and subtraction work is limited to examples with like denominators.

What the TEACHER does:

- Give students activities that relate the meaning of addition and subtraction of fractions to addition and subtraction of whole numbers.
- Use problem solving situations with addition and subtraction of fractions relating to the same whole, and have the students determine which operation should be used to solve the problem. (See Table 1, page 254.)

What the STUDENTS do:

- Use a variety of materials to model and describe various problem situations that require adding and subtracting fractions.

Addressing Student Misconceptions and Common Errors

Students need not actually add or subtract fractions at this point, although many of them will be ready. Students who struggle with identifying a situation as an addition situation or a subtraction situation need more experience solving problems that require addition or subtraction. Modeling such situations using fraction pieces will help them to relate these operations to previous work with whole numbers (Table 1, page 254).

Notes

GRADE 4

b. *Decompose a fraction into a sum of fractions with the same denominator in more than one way, recording each decomposition by an equation. Justify decompositions, e.g., by using a visual fraction model.*

Examples: $\frac{3}{8} = \frac{1}{8} + \frac{1}{8} + \frac{1}{8}$; $\frac{3}{8} = \frac{1}{8} + \frac{2}{8}$

$2\frac{1}{8} = 1 + 1 + \frac{1}{8} = \frac{8}{8} + \frac{8}{8} + \frac{1}{8}$

This Standard includes work with improper fractions and mixed numbers.

What the TEACHER does:

- Provide a variety of activities in which students must decompose a fraction into fractions with the same denominator. Use a variety of denominators.

  o Begin with decomposing a fraction into unit fractions.

  $$\frac{5}{12} = \frac{1}{12} + \frac{1}{12} + \frac{1}{12} + \frac{1}{12} + \frac{1}{12}$$

  o Ask students to combine the unit fractions to show other addends that compose the fraction.

  $$\frac{5}{12} = \frac{1}{12} + \frac{1}{12} + \frac{3}{12}$$

  $$\frac{5}{12} = \frac{2}{12} + \frac{3}{12}$$

- Facilitate discussions in which students use visual models, including area models and the number line, to justify their thinking.
- As students demonstrate understanding with fractions less than one, extend to activities with fractions greater than 1 and mixed numbers.

$$\frac{5}{4} = \frac{1}{4} + \frac{1}{4} + \frac{1}{4} + \frac{1}{4} + \frac{1}{4}$$

$$\frac{5}{4} = \frac{2}{4} + \frac{3}{4}$$

$$\frac{5}{4} = \frac{4}{4} + \frac{1}{4}$$

$$2\frac{3}{8} = \frac{8}{8} + \frac{8}{8} + \frac{3}{8}$$

$$2\frac{3}{8} = \frac{16}{8} + \frac{3}{8}$$

- Encourage students to find many different ways to decompose fractions and explain their reasoning.

What the STUDENTS do:

- Decompose fractions less than 1 into fractional parts with the same denominator using models, pictures, words, and numbers.
- Explain their reasoning using visual models.
- Decompose fractions greater than 1 into fractional parts with the same denominator using models, pictures, words, and numbers.
- Explain their reasoning using visual models and equations.
- Decompose mixed numbers into fractional parts with the same denominator using models, pictures, words, and numbers.
- Explain their reasoning using visual models and equations.

Addressing Student Misconceptions and Common Errors

Although this work may seem obvious to some students, it is important to take the time to build this concept because it lays the foundation for adding and subtracting fractions. Students who see fractions as composed of smaller parts develop the understanding that when they add or subtract fractions, the numerator describes the count of pieces and the denominator describes the piece. Carefully developing this concept now will avoid misconceptions many students have when adding two fractions with unlike denominators.

c. *Add and subtract mixed numbers with like denominators, e.g., by replacing each mixed number with an equivalent fraction, and/or by using properties of operations and the relationship between addition and subtraction.*

After students have had ample experience composing and decomposing various fractions and mixed numbers, they work with adding and subtracting fractions with like denominators. This Standard includes work with fractions less than one, fractions greater than one, and mixed numbers. At this point students do not need to regroup or decompose mixed numbers. When adding and subtracting mixed numbers, students should use concrete materials and develop strategies that make sense to them.

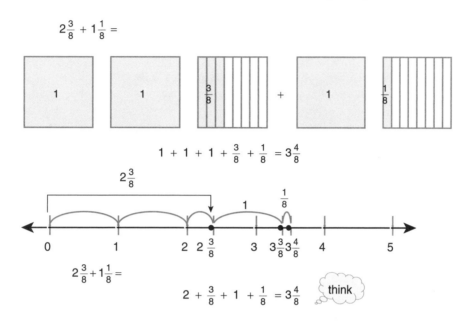

Note that this Standard and 4.NF.B.3.d should be taught simultaneously so that students have contexts in which to build understanding and determine whether their answers make sense.

d. *Solve word problems involving addition and subtraction of fractions referring to the same whole and having like denominators, e.g., by using visual fraction models and equations to represent the problem.*

(Refer to Table 1, page 254.) Students have experienced all of these situations using whole numbers in earlier grades. Use similar situations that involve fractions and mixed numbers with like denominators for students to solve as they continue to add and subtract fractions using pictures, words, and numbers. Be sure to give students many opportunities to consider the reasonableness of their answers.

What the TEACHER does:

- Provide students with fraction models, including area models, fraction bars, and number lines, to use as they solve addition and subtraction of fraction problems.
- Scaffold examples and problems.

  o Adding and subtracting fractions less than 1.
  o Adding and subtracting fractions greater than 1.
  o Adding and subtracting mixed numbers (with no regrouping).

- Expect students to solve problems using visual representations and provide opportunities to have them make explicit connections to numerical representations.
- Facilitate discussions in which students explain their thinking using materials, pictures, words, and numbers.

What the STUDENTS do:

- Use concrete materials and pictures to solve a variety of problems involving addition and subtraction of fractions and mixed numbers.
- Connect visual models to addition and subtraction equations.
- Explain their thinking using models, pictures, numbers, and words.

Watch for students who may add or subtract denominators when adding and subtracting fractions. These students need additional concrete experiences and specific questions about whether their answer is reasonable. For example, if a student adds $\frac{2}{3} + \frac{3}{3}$ and gets a sum of $\frac{5}{6}$, talk about the value of the addends and the value of the sum to realize that the answer should be greater than 1.

Number lines and visual models will also reinforce correct thinking. It is important that students understand that the numerator tells the count (how many pieces) and the denominator describes the piece. Since the pieces are the same size, the numerator (count) is added and the description of the pieces does not change. When I add 2 pieces that are thirds to 3 pieces that are thirds I will get 5 pieces that are thirds.

Notes

STANDARD 4 (4.NF.B.4)

Apply and extend previous understandings of multiplication to multiply a fraction by a whole number.

Note: Grade 4 expectations in this domain are limited to fractions with denominators 2, 3, 4, 5, 6, 8, 10, 12, and 100.

Students need a variety of experiences to understand that the meaning of multiplication with fractions is the same as the meaning of multiplication with whole numbers. They begin by thinking about a whole number of fractional pieces or the number of groups of a given fraction. Note that Standard 4.NF.B.4.d should be taught at the same time as Standards 4.NF.B.4.a and 4.NF.B.4.b, using appropriate numbers so that students have contexts in which to build understanding rather than focusing only on the numbers.

a. *Understand a fraction $\frac{a}{b}$ as a multiple of $\frac{1}{b}$.* For example, use a visual fraction model to

represent $\frac{5}{4}$ as the product $5 \times \frac{1}{4}$, recording the conclusion by the equation $\frac{5}{4} = 5 \times \frac{1}{4}$.

This Standard builds on experiences with decomposing fractions into unit fractions and connecting that understanding to multiplication.

$\frac{5}{4} = \frac{1}{4} + \frac{1}{4} + \frac{1}{4} + \frac{1}{4} + \frac{1}{4}$ or 5 groups of $\frac{1}{4}$, which can be represented as $5 \times \frac{1}{4}$.

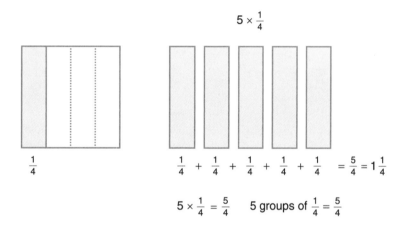

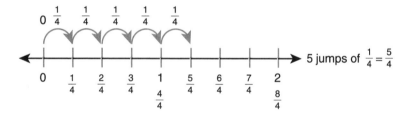

At this point, some students may find a pattern and a more efficient algorithm (procedure) for multiplying a whole number times a fraction (that is, multiply the whole number times the numerator of the fraction) but it is not an expectation for all students. The critical focus of this Standard is to develop an understanding of what is happening when multiplying a whole number times a unit fraction by relating the process to the meaning of multiplication.

Note: The language of this Standard can be confusing. When we multiply a fraction by a whole number we are thinking a whole number of groups of a given fraction (for example, $5 \times \frac{1}{4}$). Students will multiply whole numbers by fractions in grade 5 (for example, $\frac{1}{4} \times 5$).

What the TEACHER does:

- Review the meaning of multiplication of whole numbers as one factor representing the number of "groups" and the other factor representing the number of items in a group using physical representations and the number line.

  - 3 × 4 means I have 3 groups of 4.
  - 3 × 4 means 3 jumps of 4 on the number line.

- Extend this meaning to physical representations of a unit fraction multiplied by a whole number using problem solving contexts.

  I bought 3 boxes of crackers. Each box had $\frac{1}{4}$ lb. What is the total weight of the crackers?

  - $3 \times \frac{1}{4}$ means I have three groups of $\frac{1}{4}$.

  - $3 \times \frac{1}{4}$ means 3 jumps of $\frac{1}{4}$ on the number line.

- Provide students with many experiences to model a whole number times a unit fraction.
- Facilitate student discussions in which students explain their thinking using pictures, words, and numbers.
- Watch for students who see a pattern and may generalize a "rule" for multiplication. Be certain they understand why their rule works.

What the STUDENTS do:

- Model and explain the meaning of whole number multiplication.
- Extend the model to examples in which they multiply a fraction by a whole number.
- Explain their thinking using pictures, words, and numbers.

Addressing Student Misconceptions and Common Errors

Students may see "the rule" without really understanding the connection to the meaning of multiplication. It is especially important to expect these students to model and explain their thinking rather than simply using the rule.

Some students may want to put a denominator on the whole number to relate this work to previous work with addition and subtraction of fractions. These students need additional opportunities to solve problems that provide a context for the meaning of multiplication as it relates to fractions. Once they can model the situation, help them connect the model to a written equation. Ask questions about what is happening and give them opportunities to explain what they are doing.

Notes

b. *Understand a multiple of $\frac{a}{b}$ as a multiple of $\frac{1}{b}$, and use this understanding to multiply a fraction by a whole number.* For example, use a visual fraction model to express $3 \times \frac{2}{5}$ as $6 \times \frac{1}{5}$, recognizing this product as $\frac{6}{5}$. (In general, $n \times \frac{a}{b} = \frac{(n \times a)}{b}$.)

Once students can multiply a whole number times a unit fraction, they extend that understanding to multiplying a whole number times any fraction first with visual models and then connecting those models to numerical representations.

$$3 \times \frac{2}{5}$$

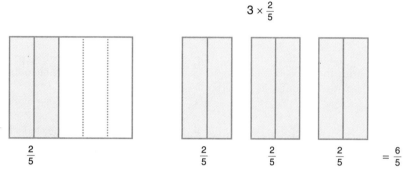

Give enough practice with models and connecting those models to written equations to help students see the structure of multiplication working with fractions. The whole number represents the number of groups and the fraction represents the number of items in each group. Because the numerator gives the count of how many pieces and the denominator describes the pieces, multiplying the number of groups times the count of items in each group (the numerator) will tell the total number of pieces. Because the denominator describes the piece it does not change.

What the TEACHER does:

- Provide a variety of problem contexts for students to model multiplication of any fraction by a whole number.
- Ask questions to facilitate student explanations of their reasoning.

  o How many groups do you have?
  o How many are in each group?
  o What would this look like if you model it with fraction pieces or on the number line?

- Scaffold to problems that include fractions greater than 1 and mixed numbers.
- Help students make explicit connections between models and written equations.
- Watch for students who are able to generalize a rule for multiplying a whole number times any fraction to be certain they understand why it works as well as how it works.

What the STUDENTS do:

- Solve a variety of problems involving multiplication of a fraction by a whole number using models, including area models, fraction strips, and number lines.
- Explain their reasoning using pictures, words, and numbers.

Addressing Student Misconceptions and Common Errors

Watch for students who are rewriting the whole number as a name for 1 (for example, writing 4 as $\frac{4}{4}$ rather than $\frac{4}{1}$). In these situations students should be thinking of the whole number as the number of groups and therefore they do not need to rewrite it as a fraction.

c. *Solve word problems involving multiplication of a fraction by a whole number, e.g., by using visual fraction models and equations to represent the problem.* For example, if each person at a party will eat $\frac{3}{8}$ of a pound of roast beef, and there will be 5 people at the party, how many pounds of roast beef will be needed? Between what two whole numbers does your answer lie?

This Standard should be taught as the same time as parts a and b. Students should have a variety of contexts in which to solve multiplication of whole number and fraction examples so they can estimate, model, and determine whether their answers are reasonable.

What the TEACHER does:

- Provide students with a variety of multiplication problem situations (Table 2, page 256) using multiplication of fractions and mixed numbers by a whole number as contexts.
- Scaffold student experiences.
  - Begin with a fraction times a whole number. $3 \times \frac{4}{5}$
  - Multiply a fraction greater than 1 by a whole number. $3 \times \frac{14}{4}$
  - Multiply a mixed number by a whole number. $9 \times 1\frac{7}{10}$
- Expect students to model and explain their solutions using concrete and pictorial representations, words, and numbers.

What the STUDENTS do:

- Use models to solve a variety of problem situations involving multiplying a whole number times a fraction or mixed number.
- Explain their reasoning using models, pictures, words, and numbers.
- Talk about any patterns they see when multiplying a fraction or mixed number times a whole number in relation to the meaning of the whole number as the number of groups, the numerator and denominator of the fraction, and the meaning of multiplication.

Addressing Student Misconceptions and Common Errors

Students who struggle with identifying and modeling multiplication situations from Table 2 (page 256) need more experience with these situations and using appropriate models. Use fractions of reasonable size so that students can focus both on the situation and why it is a multiplication situation as well as deal with the numbers they need to use to solve the problem. Do not teach students to look for key words (such as *of*) because this does not support making sense of the situation and what is happening with the fractions.

Notes

Number and Operations—Fractions[1]
4.NF.C*

[1] Grade 4 expectations in this domain are limited to fractions with denominators 2, 3, 4, 5, 6, 8, 10, 12, and 100.

Understand decimal notation for fractions, and compare decimal fractions.

STANDARD 5

4.NF.C.5: Express a fraction with denominator 10 as an equivalent fraction with denominator 100, and use this technique to add two fractions with respective denominators 10 and 100.[2] *For example, express $\frac{3}{10}$ as $\frac{30}{100}$, and add $\frac{3}{10} + \frac{4}{100} = \frac{34}{100}$.*

[2] Students who can generate equivalent fractions can develop strategies for adding fractions with unlike denominators in general. But addition and subtraction with unlike denominators in general is not a requirement at this grade.

STANDARD 6

4.NF.C.6: Use decimal notation for fractions with denominators 10 or 100. *For example, rewrite 0.62 as $\frac{62}{100}$; describe a length as 0.62 meters; locate 0.62 on a number line diagram.*

STANDARD 7

4.NF.C.7: Compare two decimals to hundredths by reasoning about their size. Recognize that comparisons are valid only when the two decimals refer to the same whole. Record the results of comparisons with the symbols >, =, or <, and justify the conclusions, e.g., by using a visual model.

*Major cluster

Number and Operations—Fractions[1]   4.NF.C

Cluster C: Understand decimal notation for fractions, and compare decimal fractions.

[1] Grade 4 expectations in this domain are limited to fractions with denominators 2, 3, 4, 5, 6, 8, 10, 12, and 100.

Grade 4 Overview

As students continue to work with fractions, they make explicit connections between building equivalent fractions with tenths and hundredths. They use decimal notation as another way to write these numerical values and build an understanding of tenths and hundredths as an extension of the place value system to numbers less than 1. They compare decimals using physical models. Models for this cluster include base-ten blocks and the number line.

Standards for Mathematical Practice
SFMP 1. Make sense of problems and persevere in solving them.
SFMP 2. Use quantitative reasoning.
SFMP 3. Construct viable arguments and critique the reasoning of others.
SFMP 4. Model with mathematics.
SFMP 5. Use appropriate tools strategically.
SFMP 6. Attend to precision.
SFMP 7. Look for and make use of structure.
SFMP 8. Look for and express regularity in repeated reasoning.

As fourth graders begin to explore decimal notation for a special group of fractions (those with denominators that are powers of 10) and connect decimal numbers to previous experiences with place value, they should have opportunities to find and share examples of where they see decimals used in their everyday life (money, sports statistics). They connect their experiences with equivalent fractions to work with a specific group of fractions, those with denominators that are powers of 10 (tenths and hundredths). They extend their previous work with the structure of our place value system to write these special fractions as decimals, explaining the value of tenths and hundredths as related to the ones place and one whole.

Related Content Standards

3.NF.A.3   4.NF.A.1   4.NF.A.2   5.NBT.A.1   5.NBT.A.3

Express a fraction with denominator 10 as an equivalent fraction with denominator 100, and use this technique to add two fractions with respective denominators 10 and 100.[2] For example, express $\frac{3}{10}$ as $\frac{30}{100}$, and add $\frac{3}{10} + \frac{4}{100} = \frac{34}{100}$.

[2] Students who can generate equivalent fractions can develop strategies for adding fractions with unlike denominators in general. But addition and subtraction with unlike denominators in general is not a requirement at this grade.

Note: Grade 4 expectations in this domain are limited to fractions with denominators 2, 3, 4, 5, 6, 8, 10, 12, and 100.

Students use their previous experience with finding equivalent fractions to change fractions with a denominator of 10 to equivalent fractions with a denominator of 100. This is fourth graders' first and only required experience adding fractions with unlike denominators. They are also preparing for initial work with decimal numbers. Previous experience with building equivalent fractions should support students in the initial stages of working with changing tenths to an equivalent number of hundredths.

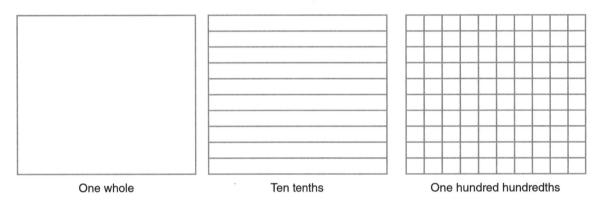

One whole   Ten tenths   One hundred hundredths

What the TEACHER does:

- Provide opportunities for students to find equivalent fractions for tenths.
- Extend activities and instruction to focus on finding equivalent fractions with a denominator of 100. Using base-ten blocks as models will provide a visual model of equivalence and can be used later as students extend this work to decimals.
- Explore adding tenths and hundredths as fractions using models, pictures, words, and numbers. Keep in mind this is exploratory and students' first experience adding fractions with unlike denominators.

What the STUDENTS do:

- Build equivalent fractions that are tenths to fractions that are hundredths using models and pictures.
- Explain their thinking using models, words, and numbers.
- Look for patterns and make generalizations about equivalent fractions that are tenths and hundredths.
- Explore adding and subtracting tenths plus hundredths using models and verbal explanations.

Addressing Student Misconceptions and Common Errors

Remember that at this point students are not expected to develop an algorithm for adding fractions with unlike denominators. This is an important opportunity for students to think about and explore situations in which adding two fractions with unlike denominators necessitates finding a common denominator, and why. Students who add numerators and denominators need more explicit experiences with models and to talk about why the denominator needs to be the same. Experiences should also focus on why they do not add denominators when adding fractions. Reinforcing the meaning of the numerator as the count of the number of pieces and the denominator as a descriptor telling the number of pieces in the whole supports future experiences adding fractions with unlike denominators in Grade 5.

Use decimal notation for fractions with denominators 10 or 100. For example, rewrite 0.62 as $\frac{62}{100}$; describe a length as 0.62 meters; locate 0.62 on a number line diagram.

Note: Grade 4 expectations in this domain are limited to fractions with denominators 2, 3, 4, 5, 6, 8, 10, 12, and 100.

This is the first formal experience with decimals for students. Include models of decimals using base-ten blocks and grid paper (Reproducibles 4 and 3) as students practice visualizing or shading in a number of tenths or hundredths and relate these models to fraction and decimal notation. Their work should focus around understanding that 0.8 and $\frac{8}{10}$ are different representations for the same number. Students extend their work with whole number place value to include decimal places on the place value chart (Reproducible 8). Base-ten blocks, grids, and number lines are primary models for developing conceptual understanding within this Standard. Students should have many opportunities to make connections from previous experiences with whole numbers to showing concrete representations and numerical representations of decimals and reading decimal numbers to hundredths.

Connecting fractions to decimal representations

Base-ten blocks

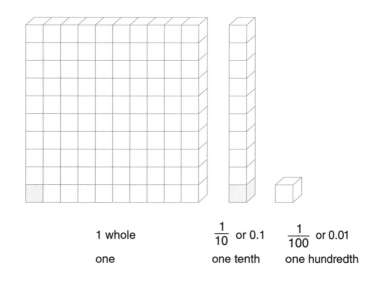

1 whole	$\frac{1}{10}$ or 0.1	$\frac{1}{100}$ or 0.01
one	one tenth	one hundredth

ones	•	tenths	hundredths

| 1 | . | 2 | 7 |

1.27

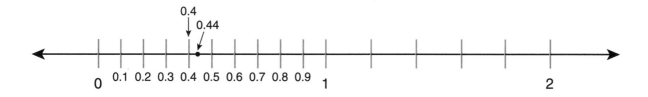

GRADE 4

What the TEACHER does:

- Introduce decimal notation as an extension of whole number place value, emphasizing that as we move one place to the right of 1, the place value is $\frac{1}{10}$ of a whole.
- Connect those experiences to writing a number as a fraction and as a decimal.
- Give students many opportunities to work with tenths using models, pictures, words, and numbers.
- Progress from models to words and written representations of decimal numbers in tenths, emphasizing the meaning of a tenth as one part of ten equal parts in the whole and that $\frac{1}{10}$ and 0.1 are different ways to represent the same number.

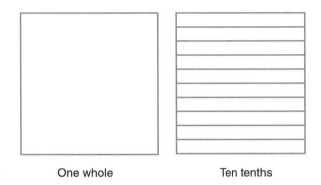

One whole   Ten tenths

- Once students demonstrate understanding of tenths, extend activities to hundredths with models including base-ten blocks (Reproducible 4), grids, and the number line.

  o $\frac{1}{100}$ or 0.01 means one out of one hundred equal pieces that make the whole.

  o $\frac{1}{100}$ also represents dividing one tenth into ten equal pieces.

- Model appropriate reading and writing of decimal numbers to reinforce the meaning of decimals.

  o 0.3 is read as "three tenths" (not as "point three").
  o 0.45 is read as "forty-five hundredths" (not as "point four five").
  o 3.07 is read as "three and seven hundredths" (not as "three point zero seven").

- Facilitate discussions in which students relate decimals to real-life contexts such as money, metric measures, and sports statistics.
- Give students experiences with locating fractions and decimals on a number line to reinforce the fact that they are equivalent values.

What the STUDENTS do:

- Model fractions with denominators of 10 using base-ten blocks and grid paper models.
- Represent fractions in decimal notation and understand that they are two different ways of writing the same quantity. ($\frac{1}{10}$ and 0.1 mean the same amount when referring to the same whole.)
- Model, read, and write decimal numbers in the tenths place using base-ten blocks, extended place value charts, grids, and number lines.
- Model fractions with denominators of 100 using base-ten blocks and grid paper models.
- Model, read, and write decimal numbers to the hundredths place using base-ten blocks, extended place value charts, grids, and number lines.
- Demonstrate understanding that $\frac{1}{100}$ is one of 100 equal pieces in one whole or 1 of ten equal parts of a tenth.
- Explain their reasoning.
- Connect understandings to real life situations that use decimal notation.

Addressing Student Misconceptions and Common Errors

One of the most important understandings of decimal numbers is the relationship of a decimal to one whole as well as a decimal number to other decimal numbers. Just as students need to understand that 100 is the same as 100 ones, they should also understand that it is also the same as 10 tens. Similarly, when working with decimal numbers less than one whole, a foundational understanding that needs to be developed is that 0.01 represents one out of 100 parts of the whole, and it is also one of 10 parts of a tenth (a tenth of a tenth). Student need many activities using concrete models to understand this concept. Similarly one tenth (0.1) is equivalent to ten hundredths (0.10).

Using money as a familiar context will also help to reinforce this understanding.

$.10 is one tenth of a dollar. Ten dimes make 1 dollar.

$.01 is one hundredth of a dollar. One hundred pennies make 1 dollar. Additionally, ten pennies make a dime, so we can think of $.10 as 10 hundredths or one tenth.

Compare two decimals to hundredths by reasoning about their size. Recognize that comparisons are valid only when the two decimals refer to the same whole. Record the results of comparisons with the symbols >, =, or <, and justify the conclusions, e.g., by using a visual model.

Note: Grade 4 expectations in this domain are limited to fractions with denominators 2, 3, 4, 5, 6, 8, 10, 12, and 100.

Students need to understand the relationship among decimal places just as they understand the relationship among places when considering whole number place value. This will support students as they begin to compare decimals that refer to the same whole. Using visual models, including base-ten and grid models as well as number line models, and fractions that are equivalent to the decimals will help students to make sense of this concept rather than learning it by rote rules. Scaffolding examples will help students develop conceptual understanding of decimal place value when comparing numbers. Students should justify their reasoning using models and explanations.

What the TEACHER does:

- Ask students to compare tenths written as fractions with tenths written as decimals to understand that they are different ways to write the same number.
- Give students activities in which they compare two decimals in the tenths place. Expect students to work flexibly among representations (base-ten blocks, grid models, number line, fraction representations) to compare tenths, using representations that make sense to them.

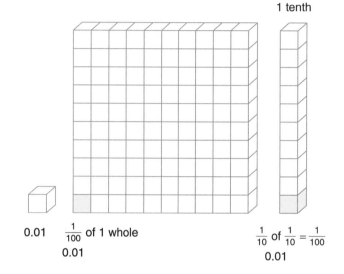

0.01 $\frac{1}{100}$ of 1 whole
0.01

$\frac{1}{10}$ of $\frac{1}{10} = \frac{1}{100}$
0.01

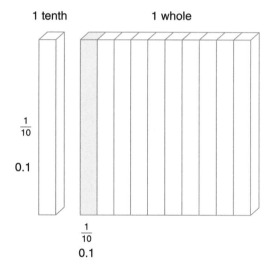

1 tenth   1 whole

$\frac{1}{10}$
0.1

$\frac{1}{10}$
0.1

- Ask students to compare hundredths written as fractions with hundredths written as decimals to understand that they are different ways to write the same number.
- Give students activities in which they compare two decimals in the hundredths place. Expect students to work flexibly among representations (base-ten blocks, grid models, number line, fraction representations) to compare tenths, using representations that make sense to them.

- Provide activities for students to compare tenths and hundredths (for example, compare 0.3 and 0.32) using models and pictures.
- Connect these activities to including numerical representations.
- Ask students to compare decimal numbers in tenths and hundredths and justify their solutions.

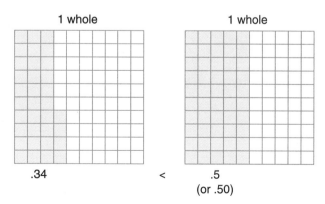

1 whole   1 whole

.34   <   .5
(or .50)

What the STUDENTS do:

- Compare decimals that are tenths using a strategy that makes sense (using fraction numbers, base-ten blocks or the number line).
- Explain their reasoning using models, pictures, numbers, or words.
- Compare decimals that are hundredths using a strategy that makes sense (using fraction numbers, base-ten blocks, or the number line).
- Explain their reasoning using models, pictures, numbers, or words.
- Compare decimals that are hundredths with decimals that are tenths using a strategy that makes sense (using fraction numbers, base-ten blocks, or the number line).
- Explain their reasoning using models, pictures, numbers, or words.

Addressing Student Misconceptions and Common Errors

Watch for students who think that 0.54 is greater than 0.8 because 54 is greater than 8. These students do not understand the relationship between tenths and hundredths and need more experience with modeling decimals. Key to their understanding is the fact that 0.8 is equivalent to 0.80. Writing decimals in terms of equivalent fractions (comparing tenths with tenths and hundredths with hundredths) will help students develop an understanding of the relationship between tenths and hundredths and use this relationship to accurately compare decimals.

Notes

Number and Operations—Fractions

Cluster C: Understand decimal notation for fractions, and compare decimal fractions.

Note: Grade 4 expectations in this domain are limited to fractions with denominators 2, 3, 4, 5, 6, 8, 10, 12, and 100.

Standard: 4.NF.C.6. *Use decimal notation for fractions with denominators 10 or 100. For example, rewrite* 0.62 *as* $\frac{62}{100}$; *describe a length as 0.62 meters; locate 0.62 on a number line diagram.*

Standards for Mathematical Practice:

SFMP 2. Use quantitative reasoning.

Students use reasoning to understand the relationship between tenths and hundredths (0.5 =0 .50).

SFMP 3. Construct viable arguments and critique the reasoning of others.

Students explain their thinking as they describe the value of decimal models and find similarities and differences among their thinking and that of their classmates.

SFMP 4. Model with mathematics.

Students use base-ten blocks to model decimal numbers in order to relate decimal place value to whole number place value and to determine the value of a decimal number.

SFMP 6. Attend to precision.

Students model, read, and write decimal numbers accurately.

SFMP 7. Look for and make use of structure.

Students extend the structure of the place value system with whole numbers to decimal numbers.

SFMP 8. Look for and express regularity in repeated reasoning.

Concrete models provide students with beginning ideas around the relationship among places. Moving a place to the left increased the value of a digit ten times. Moving a place to the right decreased the value of the number by one tenth.

Goal:

Students will model decimal fractions using base-ten blocks.

Planning:

Materials: Decimal place value chart (Reproducible 8), base-ten blocks or cut-outs of base-ten blocks for each student (Reproducible 4)

Sample Activity:

Begin with a discussion identifying the 10 × 10 flat block as one whole. Place it on the place value chart. Ask students to identify the "rod." (tenth) Ask questions that help them to see that 10 rods make a flat, so each rod is $\frac{1}{10}$, also written as 0.1. Place the rod on the place value chart. Continue with the small cube, asking questions that help students identify the 100 small cubes make 1 whole, so it would represent $\frac{1}{100}$, written as 0.01 as a decimal.

Once students demonstrate understanding of the value of each type of block, give them a variety of decimal numbers, first in writing and later orally, for them to model on the place value chart. Then provide them with models and ask them to read and write the decimal.

Questions/Prompts:

Scaffold student experiences so they are progressing from tenths to hundredths. Ask questions that support seeing the relationship between the tenths and hundredths places and between the decimal places and one whole. As students model, reinforce conceptual understanding with questions such as:

- In the decimal 3.42, how many wholes (ones) are there?
- How many tenths?
- How many hundredths?
- Why do we read the decimal as "three and forty-two hundredths" when there are only 2 hundredths?

As students begin work with decimal numbers, be sure they understand that decimals are another way to write fractions with denominators that are powers of ten (10ths, 100ths, 1000ths).

Differentiating Instruction:

Struggling Students: Students who are still shaky on the relationship among places with whole numbers may find decimals more confusing. Give them many concrete experiences modeling ones and tenths before moving to hundredths.

Extension: Include the large block (ten) in the decimals you are modeling. For students who demonstrate understanding, consider extending to thousandths, although that is not a requirement for this grade level.

Notes

Number and Operations—Fractions

Cluster A: Extend understanding of fraction equivalence and ordering.

Note: Grade 4 expectations in this domain are limited to fractions with denominators 2, 3, 4, 5, 6, 8, 10, 12, and 100.

Standard:

Standards for Mathematical Practice:

Goal:

Planning:

Materials:

Sample Activity:

Questions/Prompts:

Differentiating Instruction:

Struggling Students:

Extension:

Number and Operations—Fractions

Cluster B: Build fractions from unit fractions by applying and extending previous understandings of operations on whole numbers.

Note: Grade 4 expectations in this domain are limited to fractions with denominators 2, 3, 4, 5, 6, 8, 10, 12, and 100.

Standard:

Standards for Mathematical Practice:

Goal:

Planning:

Materials:

Sample Activity:

Questions/Prompts:

Differentiating Instruction:

Struggling Students:

Extension:

Number and Operations—Fractions
Cluster C: Understand decimal notation for fractions, and compare decimal fractions.

Note: Grade 4 expectations in this domain are limited to fractions with denominators 2, 3, 4, 5, 6, 8, 10, 12, and 100.

Standard:

Standards for Mathematical Practice:

Goal:

Planning:

Materials:

Sample Activity:

Questions/Prompts:

Differentiating Instruction:

Struggling Students:

Extension:

Number and Operations—Fractions
5.NF.A*

Cluster A

Use equivalent fractions as a strategy to add and subtract fractions.

STANDARD 1 **5.NF.A.1:** Add and subtract fractions with unlike denominators (including mixed numbers) by replacing given fractions with equivalent fractions in such a way as to produce an equivalent sum or difference of fractions with like denominators. *For example,* $\frac{2}{3} + \frac{5}{4} = \frac{8}{12} + \frac{15}{12} = \frac{23}{12}$. *(In general,* $\frac{a}{b} + \frac{c}{d} = \frac{(ad+bc)}{bd}$.)

STANDARD 2 **5.NF.A.2:** Solve word problems involving addition and subtraction of fractions referring to the same whole, including cases of unlike denominators, e.g., by using visual fraction models or equations to represent the problem. Use benchmark fractions and number sense of fractions to estimate mentally and assess the reasonableness of answers. *For example, recognize an incorrect result* $\frac{2}{5} + \frac{1}{2} = \frac{3}{7}$, *by observing that* $\frac{3}{7} < \frac{1}{2}$.

*Major cluster

Number and Operations—Fractions 5.NF.A

Cluster A: Use equivalent fractions as a strategy to add and subtract fractions.
Grade 5 Overview

In fourth grade students added and subtracted fractions with like denominators and began to explore adding tenths plus hundredths in preparation for work with decimals. Students in Grade 5 extend this work to adding and subtracting fractions with unlike denominators using visual representations, reasoning, and equations.

Standards for Mathematical Practice
SFMP 1. Make sense of problems and persevere in solving them.
SFMP 2. Use quantitative reasoning.
SFMP 3. Construct viable arguments and critique the reasoning of others.
SFMP 4. Model with mathematics.
SFMP 5. Use appropriate tools strategically.
SFMP 6. Attend to precision.
SFMP 7. Look for and make use of structure.
SFMP 8. Look for and express regularity in repeated reasoning.

Problem solving provides the context students use to develop conceptual understanding of addition and subtraction of fractions and mixed numbers with unlike denominators. Students use quantitative reasoning to determine whether their answers make sense. Because a common error when adding or subtracting fractions with unlike denominators is to add or subtract the numerators and denominators, using benchmark fractions to reason about the value of the fractions will help students realize that if they add or subtract denominators their answer will not be reasonable. Using appropriate models including area models, fraction bars, and the number line will help students to develop efficient strategies for adding and subtracting fractions and mixed numbers.

Related Content Standards

3.NF.A.2   3.G.A.2   4.NF.B.3

STANDARD 1 (5.NF.A.1)

Add and subtract fractions with unlike denominators (including mixed numbers) by replacing given fractions with equivalent fractions in such a way as to produce an equivalent sum or difference of fractions with like denominators. For example, $\frac{2}{3} + \frac{5}{4} = \frac{8}{12} + \frac{15}{12} = \frac{23}{12}$. (In general, $\frac{a}{b} + \frac{c}{d} = \frac{(ad+bc)}{bd}$.)

As fifth graders begin to add fractions with unlike denominators, they use visual models, including area models, fraction strips, and number lines. They understand the need for like denominators in addition and subtraction by examining situations using concrete models. Students should explore a variety of strategies for finding a common denominator, including examples in which one denominator is a multiple of the other, finding common multiples, and multiplying the denominators. No matter which strategy students use, it is important for students to have many experiences to understand why a strategy works. Note that this Standard does not call for students to use the least common denominator. Once a common denominator is determined, students apply their previous work with equivalent fractions to rewrite the fractions as equivalent fractions with a common denominator.

What the TEACHER does:

- Provide students with opportunities to add fractions with unlike denominators using concrete models, progressing to pictorial models, and making explicit connections to writing it with numerals. Begin with examples in which one denominator is a multiple of the other using visual models.

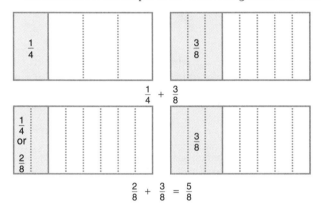

- Facilitate discussions in which students explain why they need to find like denominators to add fractions and their strategies for finding like denominators. Student explanations should include why their strategy works in addition to what they did to find like denominators. Teacher questions should promote student understanding.

  o What makes adding halves and fourths difficult?
  o Why did you choose 4 as a common denominator?

  o How can you show that you can change halves to fourths using models?
  o What patterns do you see in the examples we have solved so far?

- Continue to give students examples with a variety of denominators. Before using any algorithm, give students ample opportunities to work with visual models to see and explain how like denominators are related. Once students understand the need for like denominators and can identify appropriate denominators for addition and subtraction examples, they should apply their understanding of equivalent fractions to rewrite the given fractions so they can add or subtract.
- Expect students to justify their thinking as they use efficient strategies to add and subtract fractions.

What the STUDENTS do:

- Use a variety of visual representations to understand the need for common denominators when adding and subtracting fractions and mixed numbers.
- Practice finding common denominators for a variety of fraction addition and subtraction examples.
- Explain their reasoning as they find like denominators for any given addends.
- Apply their understanding of equivalent fractions to change given fractions in an addition or subtraction example to fractions with like denominators.
- Use reasoning to determine if their answer makes sense.

Addressing Student Misconceptions and Common Errors

Watch for students who have surface understanding of the necessity for finding common denominators when adding and subtracting fractions and mixed numbers. Consistent practice in the form of number talks or using formative assessment tasks coupled with students explaining their thinking and considering the reasonableness of their solutions will help students to see the importance of thinking about the value of the numbers rather than using random calculations (add the numerators, add the denominators). Relating the fractions to benchmark numbers (0, $\frac{1}{2}$, 1) will help students to determine whether their answer is reasonable.

Two areas that should be explicit in providing meaningful situations include considering the size of the piece (that is, how many pieces make one whole or the denominator) and that the fractions must refer to the same size whole. Students must always consider that adding $\frac{1}{2}$ of a small candy bar with $\frac{1}{2}$ of a large candy bar will not produce 1 whole candy bar.

Solve word problems involving addition and subtraction of fractions referring to the same whole, including cases of unlike denominators, e.g., by using visual fraction models or equations to represent the problem. Use benchmark fractions and number sense of fractions to estimate mentally and assess the reasonableness of answers. For example, recognize an incorrect result $\frac{2}{5} + \frac{1}{2} = \frac{3}{7}$, by observing that $\frac{3}{7} < \frac{1}{2}$.

Working with addition and subtraction of fractions should include solving problems with various situations, as shown in the Resources, Table 1 on page 254. Students continue to work with visual representations to understand the need for like denominators in addition and subtraction of fractions. They explain their thinking to classmates as they demonstrate their solution strategies. Important to this Standard is developing number sense with fractions. Using benchmarks $(0, \frac{1}{2}, 1)$ to determine whether an answer is reasonable using comparisons, mental addition, or subtraction will help students to justify their thinking with oral and written explanations.

What the TEACHER does:

- Provide a context for all addition and subtraction of fraction and mixed number problems by using various problem situations with fractions from Table 1 on page 254.
- Facilitate class discussions in which students model and explain their reasoning in finding like denominators and setting up an equation with equivalent fractions using models, pictures, words, and numbers.
- Facilitate class discussions in which students justify why their answer is reasonable—especially when misconceptions such as adding unlike denominators as part of the solution process need to be addressed.

Example:

Anna needs 3 cups of flour for the cookies she is making. She has already measured $\frac{3}{4}$ of a cup of flour. How much more flour does she need?

Note a common error in solving this problem:

Student error   Conceptual model

$$3 - \frac{3}{4} = 2\frac{1}{4}$$

Anna needs $2\frac{1}{4}$ cups of flour.

Using estimation, students should explain that the answer must be somewhere between 2 and 3 cups of flour because she needs 3 cups and has already measured $\frac{3}{4}$ of a cup. So the answer $3\frac{3}{4}$ is not reasonable.

What the STUDENTS do:

- Use visual models including area models, fraction strips, number lines to solve addition and subtraction problems with fractions and mixed numbers.
- Explain their solution process using models, pictures, words, and numbers.
- Analyze results using models and benchmark fractions to determine whether an answer is reasonable.

Example:

Charlie got the following addition problem wrong on his mathematics quiz. Write him a note explaining why the sum doesn't make sense.

$$\frac{3}{5} + \frac{7}{9} = \frac{8}{14}$$

A student could use benchmark fractions to reason that $\frac{3}{5}$ is a little more than $\frac{1}{2}$ and $\frac{7}{9}$ is very close to 1 whole, so the answer should be around $1\frac{1}{2}$. Charlie's answer of $\frac{8}{14}$ is only a little more than $\frac{1}{2}$, so it is not reasonable.

Addressing Student Misconceptions and Common Errors

Students who struggle to determine the appropriate operation to solve a problem need more experience with the problem situations for addition and subtraction (see Table 1 on page 254). They need to use strategies such as act it out, draw a picture, write an equation, or make a model to determine how to best approach a problem. Give students opportunities to explain their thinking as they read the problem and use models to determine the correct operation. Make connections to earlier experiences with whole numbers that will help students to think of addition and subtraction in a particular situation. Once students determine the correct operation, they can use fractions and mixed numbers to solve the problem.

Number and Operations—Fractions
5.NF.B*

Apply and extend previous understandings of multiplication and division to multiply and divide fractions.

STANDARD 3

5.NF.B.3: Interpret a fraction as division of the numerator by the denominator ($\frac{a}{b} = a \div b$). Solve word problems involving division of whole numbers leading to answers in the form of fractions or mixed numbers, e.g., by using visual fraction models or equations to represent the problem. *For example, interpret $\frac{3}{4}$ as the result of dividing 3 by 4, noting that $\frac{3}{4}$ multiplied by 4 equals 3, and that when 3 wholes are shared equally among 4 people each person has a share of size $\frac{3}{4}$. If 9 people want to share a 50-pound sack of rice equally by weight, how many pounds of rice should each person get? Between what two whole numbers does your answer lie?*

STANDARD 4

5.NF.B.4: Apply and extend previous understandings of multiplication to multiply a fraction or whole number by a fraction.

a. Interpret the product $\frac{a}{b} \times q$ as a parts of a partition of q into b equal parts; equivalently, as the result of a sequence of operations $a \times q \div b$. *For example, use a visual fraction model to show $\frac{2}{3} \times 4 = \frac{8}{3}$, and create a story context for this equation. Do the same with $\frac{2}{3} \times \frac{4}{5} = \frac{8}{15}$. (In general, $\frac{a}{b} \times \frac{c}{d} = \frac{ac}{bd}$.)*

b. Find the area of a rectangle with fractional side lengths by tiling it with unit squares of the appropriate unit fraction side lengths, and show that the area is the same as would be found by multiplying the side lengths. Multiply fractional side lengths to find areas of rectangles, and represent fraction products as rectangular areas.

STANDARD 5

5.NF.B.5: Interpret multiplication as scaling (resizing), by:

a. Comparing the size of a product to the size of one factor on the basis of the size of the other factor, without performing the indicated multiplication.

b. Explaining why multiplying a given number by a fraction greater than 1 results in a product greater than the given number (recognizing multiplication by whole numbers greater than 1 as a familiar case); explaining why multiplying a given number by a fraction less than 1 results in a product smaller than the given number; and relating the principle of fraction equivalence $\frac{a}{b} = \frac{(n \times a)}{(n \times b)}$ to the effect of multiplying $\frac{a}{b}$ by 1.

STANDARD 6

5.NF.B.6: Solve real world problems involving multiplication of fractions and mixed numbers, e.g., by using visual fraction models or equations to represent the problem.

STANDARD 7

5.NF.B.7: Apply and extend previous understandings of division to divide unit fractions by whole numbers and whole numbers by unit fractions.[1]

[1] Students able to multiply fractions in general can develop strategies to divide fractions in general, by reasoning about the relationship between multiplication and division. But division of a fraction by a fraction is not a requirement at this grade.

a. Interpret division of a unit fraction by a non-zero whole number, and compute such quotients. *For example, create a story context for $\frac{1}{3} \div 4$, and use a visual fraction model to show the quotient. Use the relationship between multiplication and division to explain that $\frac{1}{3} \div 4 = \frac{1}{12}$ because $\frac{1}{12} \times 4 = \frac{1}{3}$.*

b. Interpret division of a whole number by a unit fraction, and compute such quotients. *For example, create a story context for $4 \div \frac{1}{5}$, and use a visual fraction model to show the quotient. Use the relationship between multiplication and division to explain that $4 \div \frac{1}{5} = 20$ because $20 \times \frac{1}{5} = 4$.*

c. Solve real world problems involving division of unit fractions by non-zero whole numbers and division of whole numbers by unit fractions, e.g., by using visual fraction models and equations to represent the problem. *For example, how much chocolate will each person get if 3 people share $\frac{1}{2}$ lb of chocolate equally? How many $\frac{1}{3}$-cup servings are in 2 cups of raisins?*

*Major cluster

Number and Operations—Fractions   5.NF.B

Cluster B: Apply and extend previous understandings of multiplication and division to multiply and divide fractions.
Grade 5 Overview

Students worked with concrete models for multiplying a fraction by a whole number in Grade 4. They continue to extend this work to additional situations of multiplying a whole number by a fraction. They use area models to connect their understanding of multiplication of whole numbers to multiplication of fractions. Fifth graders make generalizations about multiplying fractions and whole numbers through using scaling as a model for multiplication and reasoning about the size of the product based on the size of the factors. The procedure for multiplying fractions is developed by making sense of what multiplication of fractions means rather than simply presenting students with a rule to follow. They solve a variety of multiplication problems applying their understanding to real-life situations.

Students explore division of a whole number by a fraction and a fraction by a whole number through visual models and contexts in order to make sense of what division fractions entails. They use concrete models and explain their reasoning as they work to apply previous understandings of division to fraction situations.

Standards for Mathematical Practice
SFMP 1. Make sense of problems and persevere in solving them.
SFMP 2. Use quantitative reasoning.
SFMP 3. Construct viable arguments and critique the reasoning of others.
SFMP 4. Model with mathematics.
SFMP 5. Use appropriate tools strategically.
SFMP 6. Attend to precision.
SFMP 7. Look for and make use of structure.
SFMP 8. Look for and express regularity in repeated reasoning.

Students use a variety of problem solving situations to develop understanding of multiplication of fractions and mixed numbers. They solve and write problems that include dividing a fraction by a whole number and a whole number by a fraction using models and verbal explanations. They make connections between the structure of whole number multiplication and division and the structure of multiplication and division of fractions and use these connections to solve problems. Students explain using models and how the meaning of these operations is the same with whole numbers and fractions but the actual procedures are quite different. Following many opportunities to model, explain, and solve problems, students use their experiences to recognize patterns and develop efficient strategies.

Related Content Standards

3.OA.A.1   3.NF.A.2   5.NF.B.4   5.NF.B.5   5.NF.B.6

STANDARD 3 (5.NF.B.3)

Interpret a fraction as division of the numerator by the denominator ($\frac{a}{b} = a \div b$). Solve word problems involving division of whole numbers leading to answers in the form of fractions or mixed numbers, e.g., by using visual fraction models or equations to represent the problem. For example, interpret $\frac{3}{4}$ as the result of dividing 3 by 4, noting that $\frac{3}{4}$ multiplied by 4 equals 3, and that when 3 wholes are shared equally among 4 people each person has a share of size $\frac{3}{4}$. If 9 people want to share a 50-pound sack of rice equally by weight, how many pounds of rice should each person get? Between what two whole numbers does your answer lie?

Students have had some experience considering a fraction as a division situation in Grade 4. They extend their previous work to expressing the quotient of a division problem as a fraction or mixed number. Real-life problems present situations and contexts in which expressing the remainder as a fraction makes sense. Using concrete materials such as fraction pieces and area models will help students to understand what the "leftover" fraction represents.

Division examples with the remainder expressed as a fraction:

Example 1:

Josh and Jean are packing bags of cookies for the bake sale. They have 152 cookies and want to put one dozen cookies in each bag. How many bags can they fill? What part of a bag will be left?

$$
\begin{array}{r}
12 \\
12\overline{)152} \\
\underline{12} \\
32 \\
\underline{24} \\
8
\end{array}
$$

They can fill 12 bags and they will have 8 out of the 12 cookies they need to fill another bag, so they will fill 12 bags. There will be $\frac{8}{12}$ (or $\frac{2}{3}$) of a bag left.

Example 2:

Liz has 4 candy bars. She wants to split them among 5 friends: Suzie, Joe, Fred, Marta, and Julieta. If each person should get the same amount, what part of a candy bar will each friend get?

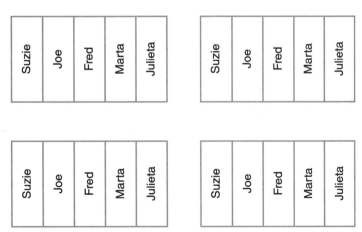

Liz can break each candy bar into five parts and give each friend one of those parts. So each friend will receive $\frac{4}{5}$ of a candy bar, because they get 4 out of the 5 pieces (or $\frac{4}{5}$) of the whole candy bar.

What the TEACHER does:

- Provide students with a variety of division problems to model interpreting the remainder as a fraction.
- Give students the opportunity to model problems and determine the meaning of the remainder when it is expressed as a fraction. It is important for students to understand that the fraction tells what part of a whole is left over.
- Facilitate student discussions about the meaning of the remainder and why a fraction makes sense in given situations.
- Combine a variety of division problems and ask students to determine what to do with the remainder.

  o The remainder is the answer.
  o Drop the remainder.
  o Add one to the quotient and drop the remainder.
  o Express the remainder as a fraction.

- Provide students with a variety of division problems in which the divisor is greater than the dividend, so that the quotient will be a fraction. Give students time to explore using various representations including concrete and pictorial models.
- Facilitate classroom discussions in which students explain their thinking and the meaning of their solutions given the constraints of the problem.

What the STUDENTS do:

- Model and solve division problems in which they interpret the remainder as a fraction and explain their thinking.
- Explain their reasoning for interpreting the remainder as a fraction.
- Solve a variety of division problems determining what to do with the remainder. Explain their thinking.
- Model problems in which the divisor is greater than the dividend and share their thinking about the quotient being a fraction.
- Explain their reasoning, connecting to a generalization that a fraction is a type of division problem.

Addressing Student Misconceptions and Common Errors

Students may initially think that you cannot divide a "smaller number by a bigger number" since this will be a new situation for them to consider. Provide them with good problems to solve and give them many opportunities to explore with models so that they are developing conceptual understanding. It is important that they understand this concept in a way that makes sense to them rather than be shown how to do it. The role of the teacher is to provide sensible problem situations, ask supporting questions, and facilitate conversations in which the students are making sense of the situation and why their answers make sense.

Students who struggle with interpreting the remainder of division examples need more experience solving problems using concrete models so they understand that the remainder tells what part of a group is left over. Asking questions such as "How many are left?" and "How many would it take to make another full group?" and modeling what part of a full group is left over will help them to understand the meaning of the remainder when it is expressed as a fraction.

Notes

STANDARD 4 (5.NF.B.4)

Apply and extend previous understandings of multiplication to multiply a fraction or whole number by a fraction.

a. *Interpret the product $\frac{a}{b} \times q$ as a parts of a partition of q into b equal parts; equivalently, as the result of a sequence of operations $a \times q \div b$. For example, use a visual fraction model to show $\frac{2}{3} \times 4 = \frac{8}{3}$, and create a story context for this equation. Do the same with $\frac{2}{3} \times \frac{4}{5} = \frac{8}{15}$. (In general, $\frac{a}{b} \times \frac{c}{d} = \frac{ac}{bd}$.)*

In Grade 4, students used models to multiply a fraction by a whole number (for example, $4 \times \frac{3}{5}$), connecting to the meaning of whole number multiplication. Fifth grade students extend this concept by using models to represent situations in which they need to multiply a whole number by a fraction ($\frac{3}{5} \times 4$) or a fraction by a fraction ($\frac{1}{4} \times \frac{3}{5}$). Provide students with real-life contexts and situations to model in order to give them experiences they need to develop understanding of what is happening when they multiply a fraction by a fraction.

What the TEACHER does:

- Explicitly connect multiplication of whole numbers to multiplication with fractions by giving students connected situations that they can model.
- Scaffold problems beginning with unit fraction factors and build to multiplying with other fractions and mixed numbers.

Example 1:

Frank baked 3 pans of brownies. He cut 6 brownies in each pan. How many brownies did Frank bake? (3 groups of 6)

$3 \times 6 = 18$
3 groups of 6 = 18

Example 2:

Marcella made 4 gallons of punch. One-fifth of the punch was orange juice. How much orange juice did she use in the punch?

A student might think of this as $\frac{1}{5}$ of each gallon being orange juice. Because there are 4 gallons that would show that $\frac{4}{5}$ of a gallon is orange juice.

$\frac{1}{5} \times 4$

1 whole   1 whole   1 whole   1 whole

$\frac{1}{5} \times 4$ means $\frac{1}{5}$ of each group of 4 $= \frac{4}{5}$

Example 3:

The distance from Elsa's house to her grandmothers is $\frac{3}{4}$ of a mile. She biked $\frac{1}{3}$ of the way there and stopped to rest. How far did Elsa travel before her rest stop?

A student might say, because I wanted one-third of the distance, I divided each fourth into 3 sections since I thought $\frac{1}{3}$ of the way would be the same as $\frac{1}{3}$ of each fourth. When I put them together, the total distance she biked before resting would be $\frac{3}{12}$ of a mile.

$\frac{1}{3} \times \frac{3}{4}$

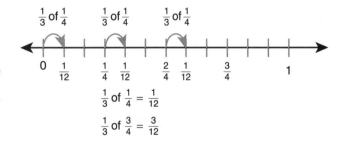

$\frac{1}{3}$ of $\frac{1}{4} = \frac{1}{12}$

$\frac{1}{3}$ of $\frac{3}{4} = \frac{3}{12}$

- Give students time to work in groups to explore solutions using models, including area models, fraction bars, and number lines.
- Monitor group work by noting what students are doing and asking supporting questions.
- Facilitate class discussions in which students model and explain their thinking.

(continued)

What the TEACHER does (continued):

- Use formative assessment tasks to determine whether students understand what is happening when they multiply two fractions and why the product is smaller than the factors. Students need to understand that because each factor represents a part of the whole, when they multiply a fraction times a fraction, they are taking part of a part.

  For example, given the example $\frac{1}{2} \times \frac{1}{4}$, students should understand that they are taking a part $(\frac{1}{2})$ of a part $(\frac{1}{4})$ and the result $(\frac{1}{8})$ will be smaller than the part they had at the beginning.

- As students demonstrate conceptual understanding of what happens when they multiply fractions using models, pictures, words, and numbers, encourage students to look for patterns so they can generalize a procedure for multiplying fractions and justify why that procedure works. Why can you multiply numerators and multiply denominators to get the product of two fractions?

What the STUDENTS do:

- Explore what happens when multiplying a whole number by a fraction by solving a variety of word problem contexts using models, pictures, words, and numbers.
- Explain their reasoning to partners, groups, and to the class. Compare different strategies focusing on how strategies are similar and how they are different.
- Explore multiplication of a fraction by a fraction by solving a variety of word problem contexts using models, pictures, words, and numbers.
- Explain their reasoning to partners, groups, and to the class. Compare different strategies focusing on how strategies are similar and how they are different.
- Look for patterns when multiplying fractions. Explain why those patterns work using models, pictures, words, and numbers.
- Apply the patterns to determine a procedure for multiplying fractions.

Addressing Student Misconceptions and Common Errors

Students may see the pattern and see that to multiply fractions you "simply" multiply the numerators and multiply the denominators. This is the correct algorithm or procedure. However, only references to real-life situations and using models and visual representations will help students develop a conceptual understanding of what is actually happening when they multiply fractions.

Notes

> b. *Find the area of a rectangle with fractional side lengths by tiling it with unit squares of the appropriate unit fraction side lengths, and show that the area is the same as would be found by multiplying the side lengths. Multiply fractional side lengths to find areas of rectangles, and represent fraction products as rectangular areas.*

Using area models was a focus of work with multiplication of whole numbers in grades 3 and 4. Fifth graders extend this work to examples with area models that have fractional side lengths. Students should have a variety of problems to solve using area models. This Standard can be taught in conjunction with earlier exploration of multiplication of whole numbers by a fraction, fractions by fractions, and mixed numbers.

What the TEACHER does:

- Provide students with problem contexts in which they find the area of a rectangle with one side that is a fraction and the other side a whole number.
- Facilitate a discussion in which students determine the part of the unit square used to tile the rectangle based on the dimensions of the side.
- Have students work in pairs or groups using grid paper to model the problem and discuss how to find the area of the rectangle.

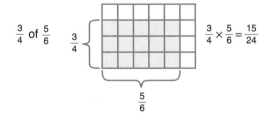

- Ask students to explain their thinking using pictures, words, and numbers.
- Extend the problem to situations finding the area of a rectangle with both sides as fractions or mixed numbers.
- Have students work in pairs or groups using grid paper to model the problem and discuss how to find the area of the rectangle when one or both sides include a fraction.

$\frac{3}{4}$ of $\frac{5}{6}$ $\quad \frac{3}{4} \Big\{ \quad \quad \quad \frac{3}{4} \times \frac{5}{6} = \frac{15}{24}$

$\frac{5}{6}$

- Facilitate classroom discussions in which students explain their reasoning and strategies to solve the problems using pictures, words, and numbers.
- Ask students to compare previous work and generalizations with multiplying fractions and mixed numbers to the solutions of these problems. What is similar? What is different?

What the STUDENTS do:

- Work in groups to solve the area problems using pictures and models.
- Explain the measures of the pieces they use to tile the rectangle, determining what part of a unit square each piece represents.
- Share the strategies and reasoning they use to solve each problem using models, pictures, words, and numbers.
- Compare the process and results of solving these problems with the previous work involving multiplication of fractions.

Addressing Student Misconceptions and Common Errors

Watch for students who have difficulty determining the part of the unit square. Thinking in terms of the whole rectangle will help them define the number of parts when the dimensions are fractional parts of the whole. Reinforcing when they multiply a fraction by a fraction they are taking part of a part will help students to see that the "overlap" is the number of pieces (or numerator), and the total number of pieces in the whole is the denominator.

STANDARD 5 (5.NF.B.5)

Interpret multiplication as scaling (resizing), by:

   a. Comparing the size of a product to the size of one factor on the basis of the size of the other factor, without performing the indicated multiplication.

Students explore a variety of multiplication situations in which they resize one of the factors and consider what happens to the size of the product. This Standard gives students the opportunity to reason about the size of the product when one of the factors is scaled or resized. Ample class time should be spent on giving students the opportunity to justify their thinking by creating mathematical arguments, comparing their thinking and strategies with those of their classmates, and thinking about similarities and differences in the various strategies.

Charlie's room is 15 feet by 12 feet. He has an awesome closet that is 3 feet by 12 feet. He wants to carpet the bedroom but tile the closet. How does the amount of carpet he needs to buy compare with the amount of tile he needs?

Molly's garden is 10 feet by 8 feet. Anna's garden is twice as long as half as wide. Without multiplying, compare the areas of their gardens and explain your reasoning.

Mark's garden is twice as long as Molly's and twice as wide. Without multiplying, compare the areas of their gardens and explain your thinking.

What the TEACHER does:

- Provide students with a variety of multiplication examples and problems in which one or both of the factors is scaled (resized)
- Give students time to discuss the impact of scaling factor(s) on the size of the product and justify their reasoning.

What the STUDENTS do:

- Reason about the impact of scaling one or both factors on the size of a product before multiplying.
- Justify their thinking using pictures and models.
- Compare their strategies with that of classmates to find similarities and differences in reasoning.

Addressing Student Misconceptions and Common Errors

Students will likely have many misconceptions about what happens to the product when one or both factors are scaled. For example, if both the length and width of a rectangle are doubled, some students will assume the product (area) is doubled. When they test their conjecture by drawing a picture, they will see that the product is actually four times greater. Allow students to explore a variety of multiplication scaling situations by drawing pictures and making models that will help them to make conjectures as to *why* the results are true, which is less likely to happen if they simply multiply.

Notes

b. *Explaining why multiplying a given number by a fraction greater than 1 results in a product greater than the given number (recognizing multiplication by whole numbers greater than 1 as a familiar case); explaining why multiplying a given number by a fraction less than 1 results in a product smaller than the given number; and relating the principle of fraction equivalence $\frac{a}{b} = \frac{(n \times a)}{(n \times b)}$ to the effect of multiplying $\frac{a}{b}$ by 1.*

As students work with various models for multiplication of whole numbers, fractions, and mixed numbers, visual representations will help them to understand the size of the product when they multiply a fraction by a whole number, a whole number times a fraction, or a fraction by a fraction. This Standard also revisits building sets of equivalent fractions to extend previous work with equivalent fractions to generalizing that as they build sets of equivalent fractions they are multiplying the original fraction by names for 1. This Standard should not be taught as a standalone topic; these understandings should be incorporated into all student discussions about multiplication of fractions when appropriate.

What the TEACHER does:

- Give students explicit opportunities to examine and predict the size of a product when they multiply

  o a given whole number by a fraction;
  o a given fraction by a whole number;
  o a fraction by a fraction;
  o multiplication with mixed numbers by whole numbers, fractions, and mixed numbers.

- Ask questions that provide students with opportunities to share ideas, clarify their understanding, develop mathematical arguments, and make generalizations about the products of multiplication with fractions.

What the STUDENTS do:

- Explain that when multiplying a whole number greater than 1 by a fraction, the size of the product will be less that the whole number (because they are taking a part of the whole number) and greater than the fraction (because they have more than 1 group of the fraction).
- Use visual representations including area models, fraction strips, and number lines to support their thinking.

Addressing Student Misconceptions and Common Errors

Students are often puzzled when they find that the product is less than one or both of the factors. In previous work with multiplication of whole numbers, the product was always greater than both factors. Give students many opportunities to use visual models to "see" what is happening when they multiply with fractions. Discussions in which students explain their thinking will also help to identify and address misconceptions.

Notes

Solve real world problems involving multiplication of fractions and mixed numbers, e.g., by using visual fraction models or equations to represent the problem.

This Standard should be incorporated throughout this cluster. Problems provide a context for thinking about what is happening when students multiply fractions and mixed numbers.

What the TEACHER does:

- Provide a wide variety of multiplication problems with fractions and mixed numbers using the situations described in Table 2, page 256.

Example 1:

Louise ate $\frac{1}{2}$ of the bunch of grapes that were in the fruit bowl. Her brother ate $\frac{1}{4}$ of the grapes that were left. What part of the bunch of grapes did Louise and her brother eat?

Example 2:

Marty is training for the swim team. On Monday he swam 16 laps. On Tuesday he swam $1\frac{1}{2}$ times as many laps. On Wednesday he swam $1\frac{1}{2}$ as many laps as Tuesday. How many laps did Marty swim on those 3 days?

- Give students opportunities to work with partners, in small groups, and individually to solve problems using visual models and determining whether their answers make sense.

What the STUDENTS do:

- Use a variety of strategies, including make a model, draw a picture, make a table, look for a pattern, and guess and check, to solve problems that provide a context for multiplying fractions and mixed numbers.
- Think about the reasonableness of their solutions in terms of the context and the numbers.
- Explain their solution process using models, pictures, words, and numbers.

Addressing Student Misconceptions and Common Errors

Watch for misconceptions from previous multiplication standards. Students who struggle understanding why they should multiply in these problems need more experience using visual representations. It is helpful to have them break the problem into smaller parts and explain their thinking as they complete each part of the problem.

Notes

Apply and extend previous understandings of division to divide unit fractions by whole numbers and whole numbers by unit fractions.[1]

[1] Students able to multiply fractions in general can develop strategies to divide fractions in general, by reasoning about the relationship between multiplication and division. But division of a fraction by a fraction is not a requirement at this grade.

This is students' first experience with division of fractions. They use their understanding of whole number division to visualize what happens when they are dividing whole numbers by fractions and fractions by whole numbers. Beginning with a review of division of whole number situations will help students to apply their understanding to fraction situations. (See Grade 3, Operations and Algebraic Thinking, Clusters A and B.)

a. *Interpret division of a unit fraction by a non-zero whole number, and compute such quotients.* For example, create a story context for $\frac{1}{3} \div 4$, and use a visual fraction model to show the quotient. Use the relationship between multiplication and division to explain that $\frac{1}{3} \div 4 = \frac{1}{12}$ because $\frac{1}{12} \times 4 = \frac{1}{3}$.

Start with problem situations and visual representations for what is happening when dividing a fraction by a whole number. This may be confusing to some students, and they will need many concrete experiences to develop understanding. After students can visualize situations and connect those experiences to writing division equations, they can talk about the equations in terms of a missing factor and make generalizations. It is important that students be given opportunities to make sense of this and not be given a rule ("invert and multiply") that makes no sense to them and can cause misconceptions and errors.

Example (Partitive division: Knowing how many groups and finding the number of items in a group):

I have $\frac{1}{2}$ lb. of chocolate raisins and I want to divide it up to put the same amount of chocolate in each of 3 small bags. How much should each small bag of chocolate raisins weigh?

(Students ask themselves, "If I divide $\frac{1}{2}$ into 3 groups, how much will be in each group?")

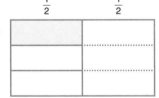

$\frac{1}{6}$ of the whole

$\frac{1}{2} \div 3 = \frac{1}{6}$

What the TEACHER does:

- Review partitive model of division of whole numbers. Give students problems to solve and have them explain their thinking.

  Whole number example:

  My mom gave my four sisters and me 100 quarters to spend at the arcade. If we each get the same number of quarters, how many do we each have to spend?

- Relate this work to division of a fraction by a whole number. Ask how it is similar and how it is different.

  Fraction example:

  The snow plow has $\frac{1}{4}$ of a ton salt that must be spread on 3 streets. If the driver wants to use the same amount of salt on each street, how much salt will he spread on each?

- Pose a variety of problems in which students model dividing a unit fraction by a whole number.

- Facilitate conversations in which students explain their work.
- Following multiple experiences modeling, connect that work to written equations.
- Discuss patterns students see in written equations and connect those equations to the relationship between multiplication and division.

  $\frac{1}{2} \div 3 = \underline{\hspace{1cm}}$ $3 \times \underline{\hspace{1cm}} = \frac{1}{2}$

What the STUDENTS do:

- Solve problems involving division of a unit fraction by a whole number using models and pictures.
- Explain their work using pictures, words, and numbers.
- Connect visual representations to writing division equations.
- Look for connections between division with fractions and multiplication with fractions using previous experiences with the relationship between multiplication and division.

Dividing a fraction by a whole number is likely to cause students initial confusion around understanding how you can possibly divide a fraction (part of a whole) by a whole number. One misconception is that you always have to "divide the bigger number by the smaller number." Connect to work with earlier standards in this domain in which students interpreted a fraction such as $\frac{3}{4}$ to also mean 3 divided by 4. It is important to give students many opportunities to solve problems with visual representations to develop understanding that this is the same as the sharing situations they used when dividing whole numbers. Do not rush students into writing equations. Allow students to write their own problems modeled after those you have given. This will help them to think about the situation and when it makes sense to divide a fraction by a whole number. Do not give them the traditional rule for division of fractions. Rather, take time for classroom discussions in which students explain their thinking and work to make sense out of the solution process and to determine the reasonableness of their answers. The role of the teacher is to clarify student thinking by posing good questions.

Notes

b. *Interpret division of a whole number by a unit fraction, and compute such quotients.* For example, create a story context for $4 \div \frac{1}{5}$, and use a visual fraction model to show the quotient. Use the relationship between multiplication and division to explain that $4 \div \frac{1}{5} = 20$ because $20 \times \frac{1}{5} = 4$.

This Standard extends the ideas in the previous Standard to situations that call for dividing a whole number by a fraction. Using the measurement meaning of division (looking for the number of groups that can be made when the total and the number of items in a group are known) will help students to visualize and model what is happening when dividing a whole number by a fraction.

Example:

I have 3 quarts of lemonade. Each cup holds $\frac{1}{4}$ of a quart. How many cups can I fill?

(Students ask themselves, "How many groups of $\frac{1}{4}$ can I make out of 3?")

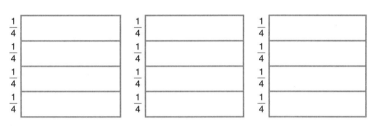

$3 \div \frac{1}{4}$ How many $\frac{1}{4}$s are in 3 wholes?

I can fill 12 cups.

What the TEACHER does:

- Review the measurement model of division of whole numbers. Give students problems with whole numbers to solve and have them explain their thinking.
- Relate this work to division of a whole number by a fraction. Ask how it is similar and how it is different.
- Pose a variety of problems in which students model dividing a whole number by a unit fraction.
- Facilitate conversations in which students explain their work.
- Model questions that students can ask themselves to help interpret the problem.

  o How many groups of $\frac{1}{4}$ can I make out of 3?

  o Relate this question to the visual representations students use to solve the problem.

- Following multiple experiences modeling, connect that work to written equations.

- Discuss patterns students see in written equations and connect those equations to the relationship between multiplication and division.

  $3 \div \frac{1}{4} = \underline{\qquad}$ $\frac{1}{4} \times \underline{\qquad} = 3$

What the STUDENTS do:

- Solve problems involving division of a whole number by a unit fraction using models and pictures.
- Explain their work using pictures, words, and numbers.
- Ask themselves appropriate questions to relate the meaning of the problem to the action needed to solve the problem. ("How many groups of ____ can I make out of ____?")
- Connect visual representations to writing division equations.
- Look for connections between division with fractions and multiplication with fractions using previous experiences with the relationship between multiplication and division.

Addressing Student Misconceptions and Common Errors

Watch for students who are having difficulty identifying what operation to use in solving problems with fractions. Using key words is not helpful and removes making sense from the process. Rather, have students model the problem using pictures and ask supporting questions, such as "What do you know? What do you want to find out? How can you show that in your picture?" As students solve mixed problems, adapt your questions to help students think about the meaning of the operations and how it can help them determine which operation to use.

Give students a variety of problems and ask them to model and write an expression they would use to solve the problem. Ask them to explain their model and expression.

Solve real world problems involving division of unit fractions by non-zero whole numbers and division of whole numbers by unit fractions, e.g., by using visual fraction models and equations to represent the problem.

For example, how much chocolate will each person **get if 3 people share** $\frac{1}{2}$ lb of chocolate equally? How many $\frac{1}{3}$-cup servings are in 2 cups of raisins?

Solving real-world problems should be included throughout this Standard. Once students have had experiences with dividing a fraction by a whole number and a whole number by a fraction, they can solve mixed problems that involve both situations. At some point students should solve problems with fractions and mixed numbers that include all four operations.

What the TEACHER does:

- Pose a variety of problems in which students divide a whole number by a unit fraction or a unit fraction divided by a whole number.
- Facilitate conversations in which students explain their work.
- Following multiple experiences modeling expect students to connect their models to written equations.
- Discuss patterns students see in written equations and link patterns and problems to the relationship between multiplication and division (Table 2, page 256).

What the STUDENTS do:

- Solve problems involving division of a whole number by a unit fraction or a unit fraction divided by a whole number.
- Explain their work using pictures, words, and numbers.
- Ask themselves appropriate questions to relate the meaning of the problem to the action needed to solve the problem.
- Connect visual representations to writing division equations.
- Look for connections between division with fractions and multiplication with fractions using previous experiences with the relationship between multiplication and division.

Addressing Student Misconceptions and Common Errors

Students may struggle determining which number goes where in the division problem. "Am I dividing the fraction by the whole number or the whole number by the fraction?" Drawing a picture using the information in the problem and focusing on what they want to find out will help. Model asking questions and encourage them to ask themselves similar questions, such as

- What is being divided or broken up?
- Am I trying to determine how much in a group or how many groups?
- What visual representations can I use to show the actions of the problem?

Notes

Number and Operations—Fractions
Cluster A: Use equivalent fractions as a strategy to add and subtract fractions.

Standard: 5.NF.A.2. *Solve word problems involving addition and subtraction of fractions referring to the same whole, including cases of unlike denominators, e.g., by using visual fraction models or equations to represent the problem. Use benchmark fractions and number sense of fractions to estimate mentally and assess the reasonableness of answers.* For example, recognize an incorrect result $\frac{2}{5} + \frac{1}{2} = \frac{3}{7}$, by observing that $\frac{3}{7} < \frac{1}{2}$.

Standards for Mathematical Practice:

SFMP 2. Reason abstractly and quantitatively.

Students will use previous understanding of fractions to determine whether a fraction is closest to 0, $\frac{1}{2}$, or 1 whole.

SFMP 3. Construct viable arguments and critique the reasoning of others.

Students justify their reasoning with clearly stated arguments.

SFMP 4. Model with mathematics.

Students use fraction models to help them determine benchmark fractions.

SFMP 8. Look for and express regularity in repeated reasoning.

Students look for patterns and explore how to determine a benchmark fraction without the use of models.

Goal:

Students use models, patterns, and reasoning to determine if a fraction is closest to 0, $\frac{1}{2}$, or 1 whole in preparation for estimating with benchmark fractions.

Planning:

Materials: Fraction models including area models, fraction strips, and number lines. A variety of fractions written on index cards gathered into a deck.

Sample Activity:

Make a table with 3 columns on the blackboard. Label the columns "0 $\frac{1}{2}$ 1."

Choose an index card from the deck. Ask students to determine whether that fraction is closest to 0, $\frac{1}{2}$, or 1

whole, justifying their response using any of their fraction models. If the class agrees, the fraction is written in the correct column on the table. Continue with a variety of fractions monitoring when students seem less reliant on the models. Discuss patterns they see on the table. Continue with additional fractions and ask students to determine the closest benchmark fractions, reasoning with the patterns they found rather than using the models.

Notes

Questions/Prompts:

- How did you know $\frac{7}{8}$ is closest to 1 whole?

- What do you notice about the fractions that are closest to zero? Why do you think that is true?

- What do you notice about the fractions that are closest to one-half? Why do you think that is true?

- What do you notice about the fractions that are closest to one whole? Why do you think that is true?

- Are there any fractions that do not fit the pattern?

- Add some more fractions to each of the columns.

- How can benchmark fractions help you to determine if your answer to an addition or subtraction problem is reasonable?

Differentiating Instruction:

Struggling Students: Struggling students may need more experience with models. They should compare each fraction to each of the benchmarks and determine which is the closest.

Use simpler fractions to begin with and ask explicit questions that will help students make generalizations, such as fractions that are close to 0 have numerators and denominators that are far apart. Fractions close to $\frac{1}{2}$ have a numerator that is close to half of the denominator. Fractions close to 1 have a numerator that is very close to the denominator.

Extension: Extend this work to identifying benchmarks with mixed numbers.

Notes

Number and Operations—Fractions

Cluster A: Use equivalent fractions as a strategy to add and subtract fractions.

Standard:

Standards for Mathematical Practice:

Goal:

Planning:

Materials:

Sample Activity:

Questions/Prompts:

Differentiating Instruction:

Struggling Students:

Extension:

Number and Operations—Fractions

Cluster B: Apply and extend previous understandings of multiplication and division to multiply and divide fractions.

Standard:

Standards for Mathematical Practice:

Goal:

Planning:

Materials:

Sample Activity:

Questions/Prompts:

Differentiating Instruction:

Struggling Students:

Extension:

Reflection Questions: Number and Operations—Fractions

1. How do unit fractions form the foundations part for developing the concept of equivalence in Grade 3 and with fractional number operations in 4 and 5? Give an example of how unit fractions build conceptual understanding at your grade level.

2. How does understanding the meaning of the denominator and the meaning of the numerator affect conceptual understanding of addition and subtraction of fractions? How are addition and subtraction of whole numbers the same as addition and subtraction of fractions? How are they different?

3. How does understanding of the meaning of multiplication and division of whole numbers relate to understanding the meaning of multiplication and division of fractions? How can this relationship help to build conceptual understanding when multiplying and dividing fractions and mixed numbers?

4. Look at the Related Content Standards listed in each cluster overview for this domain. Make a chart with a sequence of Standards across grades 3–5. From this work describe how fraction concepts grow from one grade to the next as well as within a specific grade level.

Part 4

Measurement and Data

Measurement and Data

Domain Overview

GRADE 3
The study of measurement in third grade will apply directly to students' daily lives. Students will learn to tell time by the minute, solve story problems with elapsed time, and become proficient in using measurement tools as they work with volume, mass, and weight. Experiences provided at this level will help students formulate questions that can be answered using data. Third graders will also connect multiplication to the area of a rectangle.

GRADE 4
Fourth graders will focus their learning on understanding the relationship between units within one system of measurement. Emphasis will be placed on solving problems involving distances, intervals of time, liquid volumes, masses of objects, money, and area and perimeter. Students will also learn to use a protractor to measure angles and will interpret data using line plots they created.

GRADE 5
Fifth graders will convert like measurement units within a given measurement system and continue to represent and interpret data. In this domain, students will center their learning on geometric measurement with a spotlight on understanding the concept of volume.

SUGGESTED MATERIALS FOR THIS DOMAIN

3	4	5	
✓	✓	✓	A variety of classroom objects to weigh and/or measure, such as paper clips, pencils, crayons, books, paper, plants, scissors, erasers
✓		✓	A variety of containers to fill, such as cups, beakers, boxes, liters
	✓		Brass fastener and cardboard paper strips (for angles)
✓		✓	Color tiles and color cubes (both cm and inch)
		✓	Dot paper (Reproducible 10)
✓	✓	✓	Geoboards, geobands (rubber bands) (Reproducible 9)
		✓	Grid paper (Reproducible 3)
✓	✓		Individual student clocks to manipulate with both small and big hands
✓	✓	✓	Individual student whiteboards/markers and paper
✓	✓	✓	Measurement tools such as rulers, yardsticks, meter sticks, balances, protractors
✓	✓	✓	Number lines (predetermined/premade) and empty/open number lines
	✓		*Spaghetti and Meatballs for All* by Marilyn Burns

KEY VOCABULARY

3	4	5	
✓	✓	✓	**analyze data or interpret data** process of assigning meaning to the collected information and determining conclusions
	✓		**angle** a shape, formed by two lines or rays diverging from a point (the vertex)
✓	✓	✓	**area** the size of a surface
		✓	**area of base** the bottom of a shape, solid, or three-dimensional object found by multiplying length times width
✓		✓	**array** an arrangement of objects, pictures, or numbers in columns and rows
✓	✓	✓	**attributes** characteristic of an object, such as color, size, thickness, or number of sides
✓			**bar graph** a graph with rectangular bars showing how large each value is. The bars can be horizontal or vertical.
✓			**capacity** the amount a container can hold when filled
✓	✓	✓	**classify** categorize

(Continued)

(Continued)

3	4	5	
✓	✓	✓	**conversion** change in the units or form of a measurement, different units, without a change in the size or amount
✓	✓	✓	**customary** (also called standard) U.S. measurement system for length in inches, feet, yards, and miles; capacity in cups, pints, quarts
✓	✓	✓	**data** information in numerical form that can be processed
✓	✓		**data display** a visual of data in graphic form
	✓		**decomposing** breaking apart
	✓		**degree** a unit for measuring angles and temperature
	✓		**diagram** a drawing used to describe
✓	✓	✓	**distributive property** property stating that multiplying a sum by a number is the same as multiplying each addend by the number and then adding the products
✓	✓		**elapsed time** the amount of time passed since an event started
✓	✓	✓	**estimate** roughly determine the size
✓	✓	✓	**formula** an equation that shows the relationship between variables such as $V = l \times w \times h$
✓		✓	**gap/overlap** gap = unfilled space; overlap = cover up a part of
✓	✓	✓	**gram** a metric unit of mass
✓	✓	✓	**height** a measure of a polygon or solid figure taken as a perpendicular from the base of the figure
✓	✓	✓	**inches, foot, centimeter, meter, yards** units used to measure length in the customary or measurement system. There are 12 inches in a foot, and 36 inches in a yard. Centimeters and meters are units used to measure length in the metric measurement system. There are 100 centimeters in a meter.
✓	✓		**intervals** distance between one number and the next on the scale of a graph
✓			**key** part of a graph used to identify the number of categories present in a graph, also called a legend
✓	✓	✓	**kilogram** a metric measure of mass
✓	✓	✓	**length** the distance from end to end
✓	✓	✓	**line plot** a number line with an × placed above the corresponding value on the line for each piece of data
✓	✓	✓	**liter** a metric unit of volume, usually to measure liquid
✓	✓	✓	**mass/weight** a measure of how much matter is in an object

3	4	5		
✓	✓	✓	**metric system**	measurement system that measures length in millimeters, centimeters, meters, and kilometers; capacity in liters and milliliters; mass in grams and kilograms; and temperature in degrees Celsius
✓	✓	✓	**number line**	a model or representation with whole counting numbers or fractions, used to show the position of a number in relation to zero and other numbers
✓	✓	✓	**perimeter**	distance around a figure or object
✓			**picture graph**	a type of graph using pictures to represent data
✓	✓	✓	**plane figure**	two-dimensional shapes
✓			**point**	an exact position or location on a plane surface
	✓		**protractor**	tool for measuring angles
✓	✓	✓	**polygon**	many-sided shape whose sides are the same length and interior angles are the same measure
	✓		**ray**	a line that starts at a point and goes off in a particular direction to infinity
	✓		**rectangular prism**	a solid (three-dimensional) object that has six rectangular faces and the same cross-section along a length, which makes it a prism
✓			**rectilinear**	a figure whose edges meet at right angles
✓			**scale (graphs)**	the horizontal scale across the bottom and the vertical scale along the side of a graph that tell how much/many
	✓		**solid figure**	a three-dimensional object with depth, width, and height
✓	✓	✓	**square unit**	the area of a square whose sides measures 1 unit used to measure area
✓	✓	✓	**standard**	(also called customary measurement) U.S. measurement system of length in inches, feet, yards, and miles; capacity in cups, pints, quarts
	✓		**three-dimensional figures**	figures with three dimensions: length, width, and height
✓		✓	**tiling**	a collection of subsets of the plane, that is, tiles that cover the plane without gaps or overlaps
✓	✓	✓	**two-dimensional figures**	figures with two dimensions: length and width
✓	✓		**vertex**	the common endpoint of two or more rays or line segments
✓		✓	**volume**	the measure of the amount of space inside of a solid figure, like a cube, ball, cylinder, or pyramid, measured with cubic units
✓	✓	✓	**weight**	the total number of substance present in an object. Customary and metric units can be used to calculate the mass (weight).

Measurement and Data
3.MD.A*

Cluster A

Solve problems involving measurement and estimation of intervals of time, liquid volumes, and masses of objects.

STANDARD 1   **3.MD.A.1:** Tell and write time to the nearest minute and measure time intervals in minutes. Solve word problems involving addition and subtraction of time intervals in minutes, e.g., by representing the problem on a number line diagram.

STANDARD 2   **3.MD.A.2:** Measure and estimate liquid volumes and masses of objects using standard units of grams (g), kilograms (kg), and liters (l).[1] Add, subtract, multiply, or divide to solve one-step word problems involving masses or volumes that are given in the same units, e.g., by using drawings (such as a beaker with a measurement scale) to represent the problem.[2]

[1] Excludes compound units such as cm3 and finding the geometric volume of a container.

[2] Excludes multiplicative comparison problems (problems involving notions of "times as much"; see Table 2 in the Resources, page 256).

*Major cluster

Measurement and Data   3.MD.A

Cluster A: Solve problems involving measurement and estimation of intervals of time, liquid volumes, and masses of objects.
Grade 3 Overview

This cluster focuses on two Standards. First, students will learn to tell time to the minute and solve elapsed-time word problems with the use of clock models or number lines. Second, students will estimate and weigh objects by filling containers to understand the size and weight of a liter, gram, and kilogram. Third graders will also solve problems involving mass and volume.

Standards for Mathematical Practice
SFMP 1. Make sense of problems and persevere in solving them.

Students will interpret, analyze, and solve word problems involving elapsed time, volume, and mass.

SFMP 4. Model with mathematics.

Students will apply the mathematics they know to solve measurement word problems.

SFMP 5. Use appropriate tools strategically.

Students will use estimation and measurement tools as they solve elapsed time, volume, and mass word problems.

SFMP 6. Attend to precision.

Students will attend to precision by using appropriate mathematical language.

Related Content Standard

2.MD.C.7

Notes

STANDARD 1 (3.MD.A.1)

Tell and write time to the nearest minute and measure time intervals in minutes. Solve word problems involving addition and subtraction of time intervals in minutes, e.g., by representing the problem on a number line diagram.

What the TEACHER does:

- Provide learning opportunities for students to use clock models and number lines to tell, record, and solve problems with elapsed time. Elapsed time is the time that has passed from one point to another. It is an important skill as we continually need to determine starting and ending times of events or how much time is needed to get something done or to get somewhere. Finding elapsed time includes knowing the starting and ending time of an event, then determining how much time has passed. Before teaching elapsed time, use analog clocks to give students experiences moving the minute hand to tell time. Ask students to set the clock to show various times, such as 8:14, 10:21, 3:54, and so on. Include numerous experiences representing time from a digital clock to an analog clock and vice versa.

- Demonstrate the use of a predetermined number line and ask students to show the "jumps." Prepare addition and subtraction problems such as, "It is 7:45 a.m. School will begin in 15 minutes. What time will it be? Use the number line to show the time." In the following example, students will find 7:45 and "jump" 15 minutes to show 8:00.

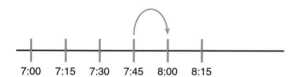

7:00   7:15   7:30   7:45   8:00   8:15

- Create a variety of word problems involving addition and subtraction of time intervals in minutes for students to read and represent on a number line. For example, "I get home from school at 4:30. I can play outside for 45 minutes and play on my computer inside for 25 minutes. Then, Mom calls me for dinner. What time is it?" Another example is "I am at the shopping mall. I notice the time is 1:30 p.m. I have been at the mall for 90 minutes. What time did I arrive at the shopping mall?" Invite students to create their own elapsed-time word problems for the class to solve.

- Allow students to use open or empty number lines to determine their own intervals and sizes of jumps to solve the problems. An open or empty number line is simply a number line with no numbers or markers used as a visual representation for recording students' thinking.

- Model measurement vocabulary. Use the terms *estimate, time, time intervals, minute, hour,* and *elapsed time.*

- Ensure students have opportunities to talk with the teacher and each other to make sense of what they are learning about elapsed time. Be sure to provide numerous experiences during the school day to look at a real clock and tell the time to the minute. Tape an index card numbered 1 to 10 on the desk of each student. At various times during the day, ask students to look at the clock and record the current time on the index card. Then, give students simple problems like "It is 2:05 p.m. What time will it be in fifteen minutes?"

What the STUDENTS do:

- Tell and record time to the nearest minute using a clock.
- Determine elapsed time by using a number line.
- Solve simple word problems using elapsed time.

Addressing Student Misconceptions and Common Errors

Some third graders may have difficulty simply reading a clock to tell time. Before teaching elapsed time, make sure students can tell time to the minute. Allow students to use a clock with movable hands, but keep in mind that numerous ongoing practices telling time to the minute using a clock or number line to show elapsed time will help students become proficient.

Notes

Measure and estimate liquid volumes and masses of objects using standard units of grams (g), kilograms (kg), and liters (l).[1] Add, subtract, multiply, or divide to solve one-step word problems involving masses or volumes that are given in the same units, e.g., by using drawings (such as a beaker with a measurement scale) to represent the problem.[2]

[1] Excludes compound units such as cm3 and finding the geometric volume of a container.

[2] Excludes multiplicative comparison problems (problems involving notions of "times as much"; see Table 2 in the Resources, page 256).

What the TEACHER does:

- Provide numerous hands-on experiences for students to develop an understanding about mass and volume. Students will be working with capacity, discovering the amount a container holds, and will be weighing objects to tell how heavy the objects are. Allow students to explore by estimating and weighing all kinds of objects and by filling containers to help them comprehend the size and weight of a liter, a gram, and a kilogram. Use milliliters to show amounts that are less than a liter.
- Plan a scavenger hunt to find classroom items that weigh close to a gram or kilogram and have students locate things that will that hold about a liter. Allow students to touch and feel the objects. Ask students to estimate and then record their findings.
- Use the vocabulary terms *measure, liquid volume, mass, standard units, metric, gram (g), kilogram (kg), liter (L)* as students are studying this Standard. Expect students to use the terms as they estimate, measure, weigh, and communicate their understandings.
- Help students learn to solve mass and volume word problems that include adding, subtracting, multiplying, or dividing to solve one-step word problems given in the same unit. For example, "Mandy has ten paper clips that have a mass of 5 grams each. What is the mass of the paper clips?" Or, "Each carton of grape juice I bought holds 250ml of juice. How much juice did I buy in all?" Be sure to help student learn to use drawings to represent the problems. Ongoing daily word problem solving will be a key to students' success as students must experience a variety of word problems before becoming proficient.
- Ensure students have opportunities to talk with the teacher and each other to make sense of mass and volume.

What the STUDENTS do:

- Estimate and find the capacity of objects to the nearest liter.
- Measure liquids using liters.
- Estimate and determine the mass of objects to the nearest gram or kilogram.
- Measure mass using grams and kilograms.
- Choose appropriate units of measure for specific word problems.
- Understand the concept of mass in relationship to weight.
- Understand the concept when a liquid takes up space it is measured by volume.
- Understand units of metric capacity (liter, gram, and kilogram).
- Solve word problems about metric capacity and mass.

Addressing Student Misconceptions and Common Errors

Students may incorrectly think about size as they determine estimates for mass. To avoid this common error, allow students to handle and touch all objects before they give an estimate.

Notes

Measurement and Data
3.MD.B*

Represent and interpret data.

| STANDARD 3 | **3.MD.B.3:** Draw a scaled picture graph and a scaled bar graph to represent a data set with several categories. Solve one- and two-step "how many more" and "how many less" problems using information presented in scaled bar graphs. *For example, draw a bar graph in which each square in the bar graph might represent 5 pets.* |

| STANDARD 4 | **3.MD.B.4:** Generate measurement data by measuring lengths using rulers marked with halves and fourths of an inch. Show the data by making a line plot, where the horizontal scale is marked off in appropriate units—whole numbers, halves, or quarters. |

*Supporting cluster

Measurement and Data   3.MD.B

Cluster B: Represent and interpret data.
Grade 3 Overview

At this level, third graders will not only construct, read, and interpret bar and pictographs but will solve one- and two-step word problems using information presented in the bar graphs. Students will also learn to generate measurement data and show it on a line plot marked with halves and fourths of an inch.

Standards for Mathematical Practice
SFMP 1. Make sense of problems and persevere in solving them.

Third graders will solve one- and two-step problems using information presented in the graphs.

SFMP 4. Model with mathematics.

Students will apply addition and subtraction to solve problems with graphs.

SFMP 6. Attend to precision.

Students will attend to precision with appropriate vocabulary to describe bar graphs, picture graphs, and line plots.

Related Content Standards
2.MD.D.9   2.MD.D.10

Notes

STANDARD 3 (3.MD.B.3)

Draw a scaled picture graph and a scaled bar graph to represent a data set with several categories. Solve one- and two-step "how many more" and "how many less" problems using information presented in scaled bar graphs. For example, draw a bar graph in which each square in the bar graph might represent 5 pets.

What the TEACHER does:

- Provide numerous experiences for students to categorize and collect data, such as lunch counts (students who buy school lunch versus bring a bag lunch from home), ways to get to school (car, bus, walk), or kinds of favorites such as colors, ice cream, toys, or movies.

- Show students how to display information they collect by graphically using a scaled picture graph or scaled bar graph. For the picture graph, pick a topic and demonstrate gathering data by surveying each third grader in the classroom. Create the outline of the graph by drawing a rectangle and writing the title of the graph above the rectangle. For example, if the graph displays information about school lunches, the title can be *Types of Lunches We Eat at School*. Next, students will label the outside of the picture graph with the categories *school lunch* and *bag lunch* as shown in the following illustration. Students will then choose a symbol to represent the number of students for each symbol and assign a value to the symbol. For example, a ☺ can be used to represent one, two, or five students. Make a key near the graph to show exactly what the happy face represents, such as ☺ = 2 students. Finish the graph by putting the designated symbol horizontally within the rectangle next to the category with which it corresponds.

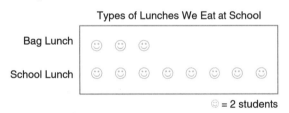

Types of Lunches We Eat at School

- Teach students to analyze and interpret data. Ask questions such as, "How many of our third grade students eat school lunches? How many eat bag lunches from home? How many more students eat a school lunch than a bag lunch from home? How many students eat lunches altogether?"

- Show students how to collect information to create horizontal and vertical bar graphs. Model creating a graph, including a title, scale, scale label, categories, category label, and data.

- Ensure that each student has the opportunity to explain, analyze, and interpret both the picture and bar graphs he or she creates.

- Model and promote student usage of the following vocabulary terms: *scale*, *scaled picture graph*, *scaled bar graph*, *line plot*, *key*, and *data*.

What the STUDENTS do:

- Collect and categorize data to display graphically.
- Draw a scaled picture graph to represent a data set with several categories.
- Draw a scaled bar graph to represent a data set with several categories.
- Analyze and interpret data on picture and bar graphs they create.
- Solve one- and two-step "how many more" and "how many less" problems using information presented in scaled bar graphs.

Addressing Student Misconceptions and Common Errors

Some students may be challenged by interpreting a graph because we read from left to right. Reading a graph requires students to interpret the information both horizontally and vertically. Pointing this out to students may help. Often, intervals on a bar graph may confuse students. Although intervals are not in single units, students may count each square as one unit. To address this misconception, have students pencil in tick marks between each interval, beginning each scale with zero to skip count when thinking about the value of a bar.

STANDARD 4 (3.MD.B.4)

Generate measurement data by measuring lengths using rulers marked with halves and fourths of an inch. Show the data by making a line plot, where the horizontal scale is marked off in appropriate units—whole numbers, halves, or quarters.

What the TEACHER does:

- Begin by discussing students' previously acquired second grade measurement skills. Remind students they learned to measure and record lengths of objects to the nearest whole inch. Tell students third graders will learn to measure to the nearest half and quarter inch.
- Plan an activity for students to make a twelve-inch paper ruler. Discuss and connect their understanding of fractions to the ruler and linear measurement. Have students fold the ruler to find the half and quarter marks between the inches.
- Model measuring to the nearest one-half and one-quarter inch. Allow students to practice measuring the length of a variety of things found in the classroom such as pencils, paper, books, desks, bulletin board, book shelves, plants, scissors, and so on. Ask students to choose and record eight items they measured to the nearest half or quarter of an inch.
- Review line plots by reminding students line plots can be described as plotting data on a number line. First, students will draw the number line along with a horizontal numerical scale marked in whole, half, and quarter units. To show data on a line plot, students place an x above the corresponding value on the line that represents each piece of data. Next, model data collection and a line plot display. Finally, demonstrate how to analyze data and interpret the results.
- Discuss vocabulary used with line plots and the measurement of objects to the nearest half and quarter inch.
- Using the eight items each student measured, have them display the data they collected by creating their own line plots. For example, Martin collected the following data for

eight objects: crayon, $3\frac{1}{2}$ inches; pencil eraser, $3\frac{1}{2}$ inches; scissors, $6\frac{1}{4}$ inches; marker, $4\frac{1}{2}$ inches; used pencil, $4\frac{1}{2}$ inches; book, $6\frac{1}{4}$ inches; flash card, $3\frac{1}{2}$ inches; and pencil sharpener, $3\frac{1}{2}$ inches.

Martin's Objects Measured in Half and Quarter Inches

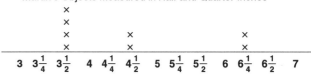

- Ask students to talk about and share the data collected for their line plots. In the previous example, Martin may say that four objects in the room each measured $3\frac{1}{2}$ inches, two objects measured $4\frac{1}{2}$ inches, and two more objects measured $6\frac{1}{4}$ inches. Twice as many objects measured $3\frac{1}{2}$ inches as did $4\frac{1}{2}$ inches. A total of 8 objects were measured.

What the STUDENTS do:

- Measure objects to the nearest whole, half, and quarter inch.
- Create a line plot to display the data of the objects they measured.
- Share the data on a line plot they created.

Addressing Student Misconceptions and Common Errors

Some students may mark Xs on the line plot as different sizes, some small and some large. Talk with students to help them discover that different sizes of Xs on the plot may make it difficult to analyze and interpret. A common error made in measuring is that some students do not accurately line up the object to be measured. Instead of starting with the zero point on the ruler, students often start measuring at the one-inch marking on the ruler. To address this, discuss how this affects the measurement of an object. Draw a chalk number line on the playground for students to walk. Remind students that a space is covered before they step on the number one, and it is the same idea for measuring with a ruler. Another common error students may make is not knowing what measurement to use if the object measures between $\frac{1}{4}$ and $\frac{1}{2}$ inch. Help students understand that measuring is approximate and that items will not exactly measure to $\frac{1}{4}$, $\frac{1}{2}$, or one whole inch.

Notes

Measurement and Data
3.MD.C*

Cluster C

Geometric measurement: Understand concepts of area and relate area to multiplication and to addition.

STANDARD 5 **3.MD.C.5:** Recognize area as an attribute of plane figures and understand concepts of area measurement.

a. A square with side length 1 unit, called "a unit square," is said to have "one square unit" of area, and can be used to measure area.

b. A plane figure which can be covered without gaps or overlaps by *n* unit squares is said to have an area of *n* square units.

STANDARD 6 **3.MD.C.6:** Measure areas by counting unit squares (square cm, square m, square in, square ft., and improvised units).

STANDARD 7 **3.MD.C.7:** Relate area to the operations of multiplication and addition.

a. Find the area of a rectangle with whole-number side lengths by tiling it, and show that the area is the same as would be found by multiplying the side lengths.

b. Multiply side lengths to find areas of rectangles with whole-number side lengths in the context of solving real world and mathematical problems, and represent whole-number products as rectangular areas in mathematical reasoning.

c. Use tiling to show in a concrete case that the area of a rectangle with whole-number side lengths *a* and *b* + *c* is the sum of *a* × *b* and *a* × *c*. Use area models to represent the distributive property in mathematical reasoning.

d. Recognize area as additive. Find areas of rectilinear figures by decomposing them into non-overlapping rectangles and adding the areas of the non-overlapping parts, applying this technique to solve real world problems.

*Major cluster

Measurement and Data 3.MD.C

Cluster C: Geometric measurement: Understand concepts of area and relate area to multiplication and to addition.
Grade 3 Overview

At this level, third graders will recognize area as an attribute of two-dimensional regions. Students will measure the area of a shape by finding the number of square units needed to cover the shape. Students will learn that rectangular arrays can be decomposed into identical rows or into identical columns. Students will also connect the concept of area to multiplication by decomposing rectangles into rectangular arrays of squares.

Standards for Mathematical Practice
SFMP 1. Make sense of problems and persevere in solving them.

Third graders will solve word problems involving rectilinear figures.

SFMP 4. Model with mathematics.

Students will apply multiplication and addition to solve area problems.

SFMP 6. Attend to precision.

Students will attend to precision with appropriate vocabulary to describe decomposing rectilinear figures.

Related Content Standards

2.MD.A.1.4   2.MD.B.5   2.MD.B6

186 The Common Core Mathematics Companion: The Standards Decoded, Grades 3–5

STANDARD 5 (3.MD.C.5)

Recognize area as an attribute of plane figures and understand concepts of area measurement.

> a. *A square with side length 1 unit, called "a unit square," is said to have "one square unit" of area, and can be used to measure area.*
>
> b. *A plane figure which can be covered without gaps or overlaps by n unit squares is said to have an area of n square units.*

STANDARD 6 (3.MD.C.6)

Measure areas by counting unit squares (square cm, square m, square in, square ft., and improvised units).

STANDARD 7 (3.MD.C.7)

Relate area to the operations of multiplication and addition.

What the TEACHER does:

- Provide numerous experiences for students to explore the concept of covering a region with "unit squares." Start by supplying students with a variety of rectangles in different sizes. Using one-inch color tiles (unit squares), have students cover the rectangles, measuring the area or space inside each rectangle in square inches. Talk about the idea that area is a measure of covering. Explain that area describes the size of an object that is two-dimensional. Ask students to count and record the number of tiles for each rectangle.

- Try an activity with geoboards and rubber geobands. Each student should create a rectangle with a large geoband.

Next the student will use smaller geobands to explore the area of the rectangle he or she created by finding all the square units within the rectangle. The unit of area on the geoboard is the smallest square that can be made by connecting four nails with the geoband.

In the example, students will count the square units and describe the rectangle as having an area of six square units.

- After various experiences with the color tiles and geoboards, have students shade rectangles and other shapes using grid

or graph paper. With a pencil and one-inch graph paper, the teacher traces around students' shoes. Focus on the idea of graph paper unit squares to measure the area of the shoes. Have students count the square units and describe the area of their shoes as *n* square units. Also, experiment with finding the area in square units of the students' face profiles drawn or copied to graph paper.

- Model and promote student usage of the following vocabulary terms: *measuring, covering, area, square unit, plane figure, gap, overlap, square inches.*

- Ensure students have opportunities to talk with the teacher and each other to make sense of the concept of area measurement with square units. Students need to develop the meaning for determining the area of a rectangle. The teacher should talk about the connection between the number of squares it takes to cover a rectangle and the dimensions of the rectangle. Ask students to discuss questions such as, "What does the length of a rectangle describe about the squares covering it? What does the width of a rectangle describe about the squares covering it?" Students will need to make a connection of the area of a rectangle to the area model used to represent multiplication. This connection justifies the formula for the area of a rectangle.

What the STUDENTS do:

- Experience hands on manipulatives to recognize area as an attribute of plane figures and understand concepts of area measurement via square units used to cover a shape.

- Use appropriate measurement vocabulary to describe area of measurement with square units.

- Connect the area of a rectangle to the area model used to represent multiplication.

Students may incorrectly miscount the unit squares covered to determine the area of a shape using graph paper. To avoid an incorrect count, students can put the numbers of the counting sequence in each square as they count them.

When students use geoboards to create very unusual shapes, they may not be able to determine the area with square units. Help students visualize square units as they use geobands to find the area.

Notes

a. *Find the area of a rectangle with whole-number side lengths by tiling it, and show that the area is the same as would be found by multiplying the side length.*

b. *Multiply side lengths to find areas of rectangles with whole-number side lengths in the context of solving real world and mathematical problems, and represent whole-number products as rectangular areas in mathematical reasoning.*

What the TEACHER does:

- Have students create a rectangle with 3 rows of 5 squares. Point to

  1 row of 5 squares

  2 rows of 5 squares

  3 rows of 5 squares

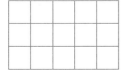

Show students how to multiply length measurements to find the area of a rectangular region by stating: "3 rows of 5 squares = 5 + 5 + 5 = 3 × 5 = 15 squares." This will help students figure out the measurement of rectangular regions as a multiplicative relationship of the number of square units in a row and the number of rows.

- Invite students to draw several rectangles. Demonstrate how to partition a rectangle into identical squares to make an array of squares formed from rows and columns. Show students how to find the number of squares by multiplying the number in each row by the number of rows. Guide students in a discussion to connect the area of a rectangle to the area model used to represent multiplication. As learned in the previous measurement Standards, this connection will help students justify the formula for the area of a rectangle.

- Provide real-world and mathematical problems for student to solve. For example:

  ○ A rectangular sheet of paper is 10 inches long and 8 inches wide. What is its area?

  ○ Each side of my bedroom is 8 feet long. What is its area?

  ○ My book is 7 inches long and 5 inches wide. What is the area?

- Model and promote student usage of the following vocabulary terms: *measuring, covering, area, square unit, plane figure, gap,* and *overlap*.

What the STUDENTS do:

- Find the area of a rectangle with whole number side lengths by tiling it or partitioning rectangles into identical squares to make an array of squares formed from rows or columns.
- Understand and explain why multiplying the side lengths of a rectangle yields the same measurement of area.
- Solve word problems by multiplying side lengths to find areas of rectangles with whole number side lengths involving area measurement.

Addressing Student Misconceptions and Common Errors

Instead of multiplying, some students may merely count unit squares to determine the area. Applying multiplication facts may be an issue. To address this, have them sketch a rectangle with rows of squares and ask them to write a number sentence instead of counting, such as "4 rows of 5 squares = 5 + 5 + 5 + 5 = 4 × 5 = 20 squares."

c.   *Use tiling to show in a concrete case that the area of a rectangle with whole-number side lengths* a *and* b + c *is the sum of* a × b *and* a × c. *Use area models to represent the distributive property in mathematical reasoning.*

What the TEACHER does:

- Provide numerous examples for students to experience the distributive property (*a* and *b* + *c* is the sum of: *a* × *b* and *a* × *c*) using an area model. Start with two colors of one-inch square tiles to show the area of an 8 × 6 figure. The following figure illustrates the distributive property with an 8 × 6 figure as 5 × 6 (blue tiles) and 3 × 6 (white tiles). To find the area, students will multiply 5 × 6 = 30 square units added to 3 × 6 = 18 square units, or a total of 48 square units.

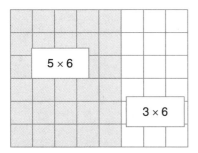

- Allow students to explore by creating tile areas of rectangles using two different colors of tiles. Have them record the length and width of the rectangle and investigate patterns in the numbers. Help students discover that area can be found by multiplying length times width.
- Model and promote student usage of the following vocabulary terms: *distributive property, area, square unit, tiling, length,* and *width*.
- Ensure students have opportunities to talk with the teacher and each other to make sense of the concept of the distributive property using tiles to find the area.

What the STUDENTS do:

- Use an area model to represent the distributive property (*a* and *b* + *c* is the sum of *a* × *b* and *a* × *c*).
- Create a rectangular figure to explore the concept of area and investigate patterns in the numbers.
- Discover area can be found by multiplying length times width.

Addressing Student Misconceptions and Common Errors

Some students may count unit squares to determine the area without realizing that the distributive property with multiplication may make the area of a rectangular region easier to find. To address this, teachers can create additional experiences with tiles to determine area using the distributive property. Students should describe and explain how they found the area.

Notes

d. Recognize area as additive. Find areas of rectilinear figures by decomposing them into non-overlapping rectangles and adding the areas of the non-overlapping parts, applying this technique to solve real world problems.

What the TEACHER does:

- Begin by having students find the area of a figure that is made by adjoining two rectangles, such as:

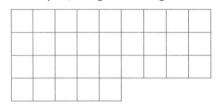

- Allow third graders to explore and determine that the area of figure above is the sum of the areas of the two rectangles and is found by multiplying the side lengths of each rectangle, and then adding the products.
  $5 \times 4 = 20$. $4 \times 3 = 12$. So, $20 + 12$ or 32 square units is the area of the figure.

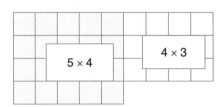

- Explain to students they have just discovered that area is additive because they *added* the area of two decomposed rectangular areas to find a total area of the entire figure.
- Help students apply the technique of decomposing a rectangular figure, then adding the areas of the decomposed figures to find the total area. Provide word problems for students to use the technique, such as:

My mom created side-by-side gardens for both flowers and vegetables without any space between the gardens. Mom's flower garden is 6 feet long by 4 feet wide. Her vegetable garden is 3 feet long by 3 feet wide. What is the total area of her gardens?

Use pictures, words, and numbers to explain your understanding of the distributive property for the problem.

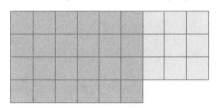

- Model and promote student usage of the following vocabulary terms: *distributive property, area, square unit, tiling, length, width,* and *rectilinear*. A rectilinear figure is a polygon that has all right angles.
- Ensure that students have opportunities to talk with the teacher and each other to make sense of the concept of the distributive property using rectilinear figures.

What the STUDENTS do:

- Apply the technique of decomposing a rectangular figure, then adding the areas of the decomposed figures to find the total area.
- Solve word problems with rectilinear figures.

Addressing Student Misconceptions and Common Errors

Some students may be challenged by simply visualizing and finding the rectangles in the figures. Provide additional experiences for these students to locate the rectangles before finding the area.

Notes

Measurement and Data
3.MD.D*

Cluster D

Geometric measurement: Recognize perimeter as an attribute of plane figures and distinguish between linear and area measures.

STANDARD 8 **3.MD.D.8:** Solve real world and mathematical problems involving perimeters of polygons, including finding the perimeter given the side lengths, finding an unknown side length, and exhibiting rectangles with the same perimeter and different areas or with the same area and different perimeters.

*Additional cluster

Measurement and Data 3.MD.D

Cluster D: Geometric measurement: Recognize perimeter as an attribute of plane figures and distinguish between linear and area measures.
Grade 3 Overview

At this level, third graders will learn about perimeter as the distance around the outside of an object. They will find the perimeter by measuring all the sides of an object and then adding the measurements together. Students will also discover the difference between perimeter and area.

Standards for Mathematical Practice
SFMP 1. Make sense of problems and persevere in solving them.

Third graders will solve one and two step problems using information presented in the graphs.

SFMP 4. Model with mathematics.

Students will apply addition and subtraction to solve problems with graphs.

SFMP 6. Attend to precision.

Students will attend to precision with appropriate vocabulary to describe bar graphs, picture graphs, and line plots.

Related Content Standards

2.MD.D.9 2.MD.D.10

Notes

STANDARD 8 (3.MD.D.8)

Solve real world and mathematical problems involving perimeters of polygons, including finding the perimeter given the side lengths, finding an unknown side length, and exhibiting rectangles with the same perimeter and different areas or with the same area and different perimeters.

What the TEACHER does:

- Provide experiences for third graders to develop an understanding of the concept of perimeter. Start by having children walk around the perimeter of the school gym, cafeteria, or playground. Tell students the dimensions of the place they walked. Upon returning to the classroom, have students sketch a rectangle to represent the place they walked and show them how to write the measurement above each side. To find the perimeter, students will write an addition equation. (FYI, a typical school gymnasium has a perimeter of 320 feet.)

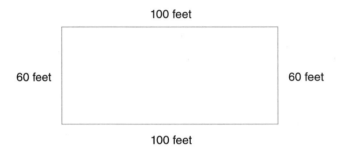

- Continue learning about perimeter with a hands-on experience using geoboards and geobands to find the perimeter of a plane figure on a geoboard. Ask students to create several different shapes on their geoboard with a perimeter of fourteen units and record each shape on dot paper.

- Since third graders have learned to measure objects, have them find the perimeter of objects such as books, sheets of paper, bulletin boards, desks, and so on. Ask them to keep a record of both the objects measured and their perimeters.
- Provide opportunities for third graders to find the side lengths of rectangles given only the perimeter and one side length, as well as rectangles with the same perimeter and different area, or rectangles with the same area and different perimeters.
- Ensure students have opportunities to explain how they can find the perimeter of objects and a pattern they will notice with rectangular shapes. Ask third graders to talk about, use written words, diagrams, pictures, and numbers to find the perimeter given a length or width to find the missing length or width.
- Model and promote student usage of the term *perimeter*.

What the STUDENTS do:

- Measure to find the perimeter shapes on a geoboard.
- Measure to find the perimeter of real world objects.
- Sketch a picture or diagram to explain how to find the perimeter of an unknown side.
- Use the term *perimeter* appropriately and know the difference between area and perimeter.

Addressing Student Misconceptions and Common Errors

Some third graders may be confused when given a rectangle with only two of the side lengths shown or a problem situation with only two of the side lengths provided. The students may add only the dimensions shown to find the perimeter. To avoid this misconception, have student write the dimension on the other sides of the rectangle.

Students are often confused between the concepts of perimeter and area. To address this, provide additional experience for students to discover that the concept of an object's perimeter as a one-dimensional attribute and area as two-dimensional. Students should talk about the fact that area is expressed with square units.

Measurement and Data

Cluster A: Solve problems involving measurement and estimation of intervals of time, liquid volumes, and masses of objects.

Standard: 3.MD.A1. *Tell and write time to the nearest minute and measure time intervals in minutes. Solve word problems involving addition and subtraction of time intervals in minutes, e.g., by representing the problem on a number line diagram.*

Standards for Mathematical Practice:

SFMP 1. Make sense of problems and persevere in solving them.
Students will interpret, analyze, and solve word problems involving elapsed time.

SFMP 4. Model with mathematics.
Students will apply the mathematics they know to solve measurement word problems.

SFMP 5. Use appropriate tools strategically.
Students will use estimation and measurement tools as they solve elapsed time, volume, and mass word problems.

Goal:
Students will learn to tell elapsed time using a number line.

Planning:

Materials: Pencil and paper, analog clocks, number lines

Sample Activity:
- Start by talking about the time students arrive at school and the time they go to lunch in the cafeteria. Ask, "How much time will pass?" Allow students to share their thinking with one another. After listening to several responses, model the elapsed time on an analog clock.
- Next, demonstrate elapsed time using a prepared, predetermined number line. Also model the time that passes with an empty or open number line.
- Prepare problems such as, "It is 10:05 a.m. Recess will begin in fifteen minutes. What time will it be? Use a number line to show the time."
- Throughout the day, ask students to look at the clock in the classroom to tell the time. Ask questions like, "It is 11:20 a.m. What time was it three hours ago?"

Questions/Prompts:

- Can students tell time to the nearest hour, half-hour, quarter-hour, five minutes, and nearest minute? Have students demonstrate various time on an analog clock.
- Can students explain time intervals and what elapsed time means?
- Can students show elapsed time on an analog clock and on a number line?
- Can students solve word problems involving elapsed time?

Differentiating Instruction:

Struggling Students: Some third graders may not be able to tell time to the minute. Make sure they can do this prior to teaching elapsed time. Provide a variety of experiences for students to tell time to the nearest minute, five minutes, quarter-hour, half-hour, and hour during the day. Use individual hands–on clocks to practice.

Extension: Allow students to create word problems involving elapsed time for other students to solve. Give them prompts to use with their word problems, such as the start and ending time of a favorite movie or the time it takes them to get dressed and ready for school, and so on.

Measurement and Data

Cluster A: Solve problems involving measurement and estimation of intervals of time time, liquid volumes, and masses of objects.

Standard:

Standards for Mathematical Practice:

Goal:

Planning:

Materials:

Sample Activity:

Questions/Prompts:

Differentiating Instruction:

Struggling Students:

Extension:

Measurement and Data
Cluster B: Represent and interpret data.

Standard:

Standards for Mathematical Practice:

Goal:

Planning:

Materials:

Sample Activity:

Questions/Prompts:

Differentiating Instruction:

Struggling Students:

Extension:

Measurement and Data
Cluster C: Geometric measurement: Understand concepts of area and relate area to multiplication
and to addition.

Standard:

Standards for Mathematical Practice:

Goal:

Planning:

Materials:

Sample Activity:

Questions/Prompts:

Differentiating Instruction:

Struggling Students:

Extension:

Measurement and Data

Cluster D: Geometric measurement: Recognize perimeter as an attribute of plane figures and distinguish between linear and area measures.

Standard:

Standards for Mathematical Practice:

Goal:

Planning:

Materials:

Sample Activity:

Questions/Prompts:

Differentiating Instruction:

Struggling Students:

Extension:

Measurement and Data
4.MD.A*

Solve problems involving measurement and conversion of measurements from a larger unit to a smaller unit.

STANDARD 1

4.MD.A.1: Know relative sizes of measurement units within one system of units including km, m, cm; kg, g; lb, oz.; l, ml; hr, min, sec. Within a single system of measurement, express measurements in a larger unit in terms of a smaller unit. Record measurement equivalents in a two-column table. *For example, know that 1 ft is 12 times as long as 1 in. Express the length of a 4 ft snake as 48 in. Generate a conversion table for feet and inches listing the number pairs (1, 12), (2, 24), (3, 36), . . .*

STANDARD 2

4.MD.A.2: Use the four operations to solve word problems involving distances, intervals of time, liquid volumes, masses of objects, and money, including problems involving simple fractions or decimals, and problems that require expressing measurements given in a larger unit in terms of a smaller unit. Represent measurement quantities using diagrams such as number line diagrams that feature a measurement scale.

STANDARD 3

4.MD.A.3: Apply the area and perimeter formulas for rectangles in real world and mathematical problems. *For example, find the width of a rectangular room given the area of the flooring and the length, by viewing the area formula as a multiplication equation with an unknown factor.*

*Supporting cluster

Measurement and Data   4.MD.A

Cluster A: Solve problems involving measurement and conversion of measurements from a larger unit to a smaller unit.
Grade 4 Overview

Fourth graders will focus their learning on understanding the relationship between units within one system of measurement. Emphasis will be placed on solving word problems involving distances, intervals of time, liquid volumes, masses of objects, money, and area and perimeter.

Standards for Mathematical Practice
SFMP 1. Make sense of problems and persevere in solving them.

Students will solve problems involving measurement and the conversion of measurements from a larger unit to a smaller unit.

SFMP 2. Reason abstractly and quantitatively.

Students will recognize angle measure as additive.

SFMP 3. Construct viable arguments and critique the reasoning of others.

Students will construct and critique arguments relating to relative size of measurement units with everyday objects.

SFMP 4. Model with mathematics.

Students will construct line plots to display data of measurements in fractions of a unit.

SFMP 5. Use appropriate tools strategically.

Students will select and use rulers, balances, graduated cylinders, angle rulers, and protractors to measure.

SFMP 6. Attend to precision.

Students will specify units of measure and state the meaning of the symbols used.

Related Content Standard

5.MD.A.1

Know relative sizes of measurement units within one system of units including km, m, cm; kg, g; lb., oz.; l, ml; hr., min, sec. Within a single system of measurement, express measurements in a larger unit in terms of a smaller unit. Record measurement equivalents in a two-column table. For example, know that 1 ft. is 12 times as long as 1 in. Express the length of a 4 ft. snake as 48 in. Generate a conversion table for feet and inches listing the number pairs (1, 12), (2, 24), (3, 36), . . .

What the TEACHER does:

- Begin by teaching students to understand relative sizes of measurement units within one system, including km, m, cm; kg, g; lb., oz.; l, ml; hr., min, and sec. Students should touch real objects and use measurement tools to measure, then think about and make a connection for measurement units. For example, a cm is about the width of a large paper clip, a meter is a little more than a yard, and a kilometer is three times the walking distance around a football field. A gram can be thought of as the mass of a small paper clip and a kilogram as the mass of an average mathematics textbook or a little more than two pounds. A liter is about the size of a small pitcher, and a milliliter is about a drop from an eye dropper. Relating and thinking about the relative sizes helps students develop a benchmark for the units.
- Plan experiences for students to discover hands-on measurement relationships before they create tables to express measurements in a larger unit to a smaller unit. For example, have students use a twelve-inch ruler to discover that 3 twelve-inch rulers or thirty-six inches is equivalent to one yard.
- Provide activities for students to create tables to show measurements equivalents with larger units expressed as smaller units within the metric system. Students can also make tables or charts to show equivalent measurements for pounds and ounces and for hours/minutes/seconds. Note that fourth graders will need numerous experiences to explore the patterns and see the relationships with these units of measure.

- Model and promote student usage of the measurement vocabulary terms: *measure, metric, customary, convert/ conversion, relative size, liquid volume, mass, length, distance, kilometer (km), meter (m), centimeter (cm), kilogram (kg), gram (g), liter (L), milliliter (mL), inch (in), foot (ft.), yard (yd.), mile (mi), ounce (oz.), pound (lb.), cup (c), pint (pt.), quart (qt.), gallon (gal), time, hour, minute, second,* and *equivalent*.
- Ensure students have opportunities to talk with their teacher and each other as they experience measurement conversions and measurement equivalents. Allow students to make statements such as "If one foot is 12 inches, then 3 feet has to be 36 inches because there are 3 groups of 12."

What the STUDENTS do:

- Learn to visually *see* and think about benchmark measurements such as a cm is about the size of the width of a small paperclip.
- Express measurements in a larger unit in terms of a smaller unit by recording measurement equivalents in a two-column table.
- Use both metric and standard measurement vocabulary.

Measurement Equivalents

1 ft.	12 in.
2 ft.	24 in.
3 ft.	36 in.
4 ft.	
5 ft.	

Addressing Student Misconceptions and Common Errors

Some students misunderstand that the larger the unit, the smaller the number you get when you measure. Student may incorrectly think that larger units will give larger measures. To correct this common misconception, provide addition experiences for students to measure the same object with two different measuring units, such as rulers and yardsticks. Help students learn that it takes fewer yardsticks to measure a hallway than it takes rulers.

STANDARD 2 (4.MD.A.2)

Use the four operations to solve word problems involving distances, intervals of time, liquid volumes, masses of objects, and money, including problems involving simple fractions or decimals, and problems that require expressing measurements given in a larger unit in terms of a smaller unit. Represent measurement quantities using diagrams such as number line diagrams that feature a measurement scale.

What the TEACHER does:

- Provide numerous word problems for students to experience and solve. Encourage students to explain their thinking and demonstrate how they solved the problems. Problems should include examples like the following:

  Addition: Molly practiced piano for 45 minutes on Monday, 25 minutes on Tuesday, and 30 minutes on Wednesday. How much time did she practice before the concert on Thursday?

  Subtraction: A cake is taken out of an oven at 2:10 p.m. The cake took 65 minutes to bake. What time did the cake go into the oven?

  Multiplication: Roberto is making hot chocolate for his Cub Scout Troop of 16 boys. Each boy will drink 2 cups of hot chocolate. How many quarts of hot chocolate will he make?

  Division: LaShanda cut two and one half yards of yarn into 3 equal lengths for her art project. How many inches long is each piece of yarn?

  Multiplication: Sam wants to convert 12 feet to inches. Use a number line to show how he can solve the problem.

What the STUDENTS do:

- Solve measurement word problems including the operations of addition, subtraction, multiplication, and division.
- Represent measurement quantities using diagrams such as number line diagrams that feature a measurement scale.

Addressing Student Misconceptions and Common Errors

Some students may have difficulty converting a word problem into the necessary mathematical form needed to solve the problem. To address this, teachers need to provide multiple experiences with measurement problems on an ongoing basis.

Notes

Apply the area and perimeter formulas for rectangles in real world and mathematical problems. For example, find the width of a rectangular room given the area of the flooring and the length, by viewing the area formula as a multiplication equation with an unknown factor.

What the TEACHER does:

- Begin by reminding students what they previously learned about perimeter and area as third graders. Model several examples and have students practice finding both area and perimeter. This Standard will extend students' learning and invites fourth graders to generalize their understanding of area and perimeter by connecting the concepts to mathematical formulas.
- Provide numerous experiences for students to apply simple area and perimeter formulas such as

  ○ **Dad will purchase carpet for our tree house floor. Find the area of the carpet we need by looking at the dimensions below.**

12 ft.

6 ft.

  ○ **Or, Maria has a rectangular garden as shown below. What length of fencing will she need to fence her garden?**

5 ft.

3 ft.

- Next, fourth graders find the width of a rectangular room given the area of the flooring and the length by viewing the area formula as a multiplication equation with an unknown factor. The formula is a generalization of students' understanding, for example, if they know a unit of length, then a rectangle whose sides have width units and length units can be partitioned into width rows of unit squares with length squares in each row. The product $l \times w$ tells the number of unit squares in the partition, so the area measurement is $l \times w$ square units. Students can

think about and discuss advantages and disadvantages of different formulas for the perimeter length of a rectangle that is l units by w units. For example, $P = 2l + 2w$ has two multiplications and one addition, but $P = 2(l + w)$ has one addition and one multiplication with fewer calculations. Try problems such as *A rectangular hallway has an area of sixty square feet. The hallway is five feet wide. How long is the hallway?* Providing students with the area and the width creates an unknown factor problem. Students can also solve perimeter problems that give the perimeter and the length of one side and ask the length of the adjacent side.

- Encourage students to share their thinking with one another and use the appropriate terminology for this Standard, including *perimeter, area, length, width, side, cm, mm, m, ft., yard, inches, add, multiply, divide,* and *subtract.*

What the STUDENTS do:

- Apply the area and perimeter formulas with both real-world and mathematical problems.
- Find the width of a rectangular room given the area of the flooring and length by using an area formula as a multiplication equation with an unknown factor.
- Use appropriate vocabulary for the concepts of perimeter and area.

Addressing Student Misconceptions and Common Errors

Some fourth graders may be confused when given a rectangle with only two of the side lengths shown or a problem situation with only two of the side lengths provided. The students may add only the dimensions shown to find the perimeter. To avoid this misconception, have students write the dimension on the other sides of the rectangle.

Students are often confused between the concepts of perimeter and area. The formulas fourth graders learn must be developed through experience not just memorization. To address this, provide additional experiences for students to discover both area and perimeter. Help students notice that the formula for area is $l \times w = a$. The answer for area will always be in square units. The formula for perimeter can be $2l + 2w = p$, and the answer will always be in linear units.

Measurement and Data
4.MD.B*

Represent and interpret data.

STANDARD 4	**4.MD.B.4:** Make a line plot to display a data set of measurements in fractions of a unit ($\frac{1}{2}, \frac{1}{4}, \frac{1}{8}$). Solve problems involving addition and subtraction of fractions by using information presented in line plots. *For example, from a line plot find and interpret the difference in length between the longest and shortest specimens in an insect collection.*

*Supporting cluster

Measurement and Data   4.MD.B

Cluster B: Represent and interpret data.
Grade 4 Overview

This cluster is about creating line plots to display a data set of objects measured in fractional units of $\frac{1}{2}$, $\frac{1}{4}$, and $\frac{1}{8}$. Students will solve problems using the data they collected.

Standards for Mathematical Practice
SFMP 2. Reason abstractly and quantitatively.

Students will attend to the meaning of the measured objects and plots on the number line.

SFMP 4. Model with mathematics.

Students will use line plots to display data of objects measured in fractional units.

SFMP 5. Use appropriate tools strategically.

Students will use a ruler to measure objects to the nearest $\frac{1}{8}$, $\frac{1}{4}$, and $\frac{1}{2}$ inch.

SFMP 6. Attend to precision.

Students will attend to precision with specific vocabulary to describe and analyze data of objects measured and displayed on line plots.

Related Content Standards

3.NF.A.2   3.NF.A.3   3.NF.A.3d

> *Notes*

Make a line plot to display a data set of measurements in fractions of a unit ($\frac{1}{2}, \frac{1}{4}, \frac{5}{8}$). Solve problems involving addition and subtraction of fractions by using information presented in line plots. For example, from a line plot find and interpret the difference in length between the longest and shortest specimens in an insect collection.

What the TEACHER does:

- Start with a discussion of how students have previously represented fractions on a number line, how they measured objects to the nearest quarter- and half-inch, and how they displayed the data on a line plot. Ask students to explain the benefits for using a line plot to show the data collected.
- Next, provide students with experiences to display data on line plots with fractional units including halves, fourths, and eighths to plot multiple data points for each fraction. Measure twelve objects found in the classroom, such as a *used* pencil, a *used* crayon, a small straw, an eraser, and so on. Have students create a number line to display the measurement of the items. Ask students to analyze and interpret their data. Then, begin solving simple problems involving addition and subtraction of fractions by using information presented in the line plots. For example, "What is the difference in length between the smallest fraction and the largest fraction shown on your line plot?" Students may create their own problems using their own line plots.
- Encourage students to share their thinking with one another and use the appropriate terminology for this Standard, including *data*, *line plot*, *length*, and *fractions*.

What the STUDENTS do:

- Create line plots to show a data set of objects with fractional measurements of $\frac{1}{2}$, $\frac{1}{4}$, and $\frac{1}{8}$.
- Solve simple word problems involving addition and subtraction of the fractions found in their line plots.
- Use appropriate vocabulary when working with line plots and fractional measurements.

Addressing Student Misconceptions and Common Errors

Some students may not know what measurement to use if the object measures between $\frac{1}{8}$ and $\frac{1}{4}$ inch. To address this, help students understand that measuring is approximate and items will not exactly measure to $\frac{1}{8}$, $\frac{1}{4}$, $\frac{1}{2}$, or one whole inch. Another error occurs when students use whole number names when counting fractional parts on a number line. To address this, remind students that the fraction name should be used instead. For example, if two-eighths is displayed on the line plot three times, then there would be six-eighths.

Notes

Measurement and Data
4.MD.C*

Geometric measurement: Understand concepts of angle and measure angles.

STANDARD 5

4.MD.C.5: Recognize angles as geometric shapes that are formed wherever two rays share a common endpoint, and understand concepts of angle measurement:

a. An angle is measured with reference to a circle with its center at the common endpoint of the rays, by considering the fraction of the circular arc between the points where the two rays intersect the circle. An angle that turns through $\frac{1}{360}$ of a circle is called a "one-degree angle," and can be used to measure angles.

b. An angle that turns through n one-degree angles is said to have an angle measure of n degrees.

STANDARD 6

4.MD.C.6: Measure angles in whole-number degrees using a protractor. Sketch angles of specified measure.

STANDARD 7

4.MD.C.7: Recognize angle measure as additive. When an angle is decomposed into non-overlapping parts, the angle measure of the whole is the sum of the angle measures of the parts. Solve addition and subtraction problems to find unknown angles on a diagram in real world and mathematical problems, e.g., by using an equation with a symbol for the unknown angle measure.

*Additional cluster

Measurement and Data   4.MD.C

Cluster C: Geometric measurement: Understand concepts of angle and measure angles.
Grade 4 Overview

This cluster engages fourth graders with activities to measure angles using a protractor. Students will recognize angles as geometric shapes formed wherever two rays share a common endpoint and sketch angles of specified measure.

Standards for Mathematical Practice
SFMP 1. Make sense of problems and persevere in solving them.

Students will solve word problems involving measurement of angles.

SFMP 2. Reason abstractly and quantitatively.

Students will recognize angle measurement as additive in relation to the reference to a circle.

SFMP 6. Attend to precision.

Students will attend to precision with specific vocabulary to describe the measurement of angles.

Related Content Standard

4.G.A.1

Notes

Recognize angles as geometric shapes that are formed wherever two rays share a common endpoint, and understand concepts of angle measurement:

    a. An angle is measured with reference to a circle with its center at the common endpoint of the rays, by considering the fraction of the circular arc between the points where the two rays intersect the circle. An angle that turns through $\frac{1}{360}$ of a circle is called a "one-degree angle," and can be used to measure angles.

    b. An angle that turns through n one-degree angles is said to have an angle measure of n degrees.

What the TEACHER does:

- Begin by discussing angles. Angles are geometric shapes made of two rays that are infinite in length. To help understand this, students can create angles by joining two strips of heavy paper or cardboard attached together with a brass fastener. The cardboard will represent the rays of an angle. Ask students to move the cardboard rays to create a right angle.

- Explain that if the rays are less than the measure of a right angle, the angle is called an acute angle. Have students demonstrate an acute angle as shown below.

  Students can also model an obtuse angle, which is greater than the measure of a right angle.

- Ask students to draw and explain the three types of angles. Each student can have a piece of paper and create a paper foldable that will help them visualize each angle. To do this, students may use a sheet of paper folded horizontally like a letter can be folded before it is put into an envelope. Next, fold the paper in half vertically. Unfold. Then, in each of the sections, students can draw the picture of the angle, label it, and describe it.

Right angle	An angle that equals one quarter of a full rotation of a circle
Acute angle	An angle that is less than a right angle
Obtuse angle	An angle that is more than a right angle

- Allow students to explore and compare angles to determine whether an angle is acute or obtuse. Provide five or six illustrations of angles and allow student to determine the type of angle each one is. This will be a valuable experience as students will have a benchmark reference for what an angle measure should be.
- Next, ask students to find, identify, and discover classroom examples of angles in two-dimensional figures.
- Explore the connection between angles (measure of rotation) and circular measurement (360 degrees). Discuss how an angle is measured with reference to a circle with its center at the common endpoint of the rays by considering the fraction of the circular arc between the points where the two rays intersect the circle. Explain that an angle that turns through $\frac{1}{360}$ of a circle is called a "one-degree angle" and can be used to measure angles. An angle that turns through *n* one-degree angles is said to have an angle measure of *n* degrees. Talk about a water sprinkler's rotation with one degree at each interval. Make the connection with a protractor and a sprinkler that rotates a total of 80°.
- Ensure students have opportunities to talk with the teacher and each other to make sense of what they are learning about angles.
- Promote the appropriate terminology for this Standard, including *measure, point, end point, geometric shapes, ray, angle, circle, degree,* and *protractor.*

What the STUDENTS do:

- Construct angles using cardboard and a fastener to recognize angles as geometric shapes that are formed wherever two rays share a common endpoint.
- Understand concepts of angle measurement.
- Demonstrate an acute, obtuse, and right angle using cardboard and fasteners.
- Use correct vocabulary when describing angles.

Addressing Student Misconceptions and Common Errors

Some students may have difficulty visualizing both obtuse and acute angles. To address this, the students may need to compare two angles by using a transparency to trace an angle and place it over another angle. This can help them notice the rays of the angles.

STANDARD 6 (4.MD.C.6)

Measure angles in whole-number degrees using a protractor. Sketch angles of specified measure.

What the TEACHER does:

- Start by introducing a protractor. If students can articulate and show the difference between an acute and an obtuse angle, they can learn to use a protractor. If they understand the two angle types, students will be able to determine whether a measure of an angle is reasonable based on the relationship of the angle to the right angle. Talk with fourth graders about how angles are measured in degrees. Remind students there is a relationship between the number of degrees in an angle and circle, which has a measure of 360 degrees. Recap the connection with a water sprinkler's rotation found in Standard 4.MD.C.5.
- Demonstrate how to use a protractor by placing the origin of the protractor over the point or vertex of the angle to be measured. Next, align the bottom line of the angle with the base line and follow the top line of the angle up to the measurements on the protractor's arc. Remember that smaller angles will be less than 90 degrees and wider angles will be more than 90 degrees.
- Direct students to make sketches of angles of specified measure. To do this, begin by drawing a ray that is the line of reference for the angle. The other ray of the angle will be drawn from this one. Place the origin of the protractor at a point on the ray. The point will become the vertex. Align the base line of the protractor with the ray just created. Mark a spot on the paper at the degree of measurement, such as 65 degrees, and draw the ray past the protractor's arc. Students will need numerous examples to be able to make sketches of angles.
- Ensure students have opportunities to talk with the teacher and each other to make sense with what they are learning about angles.
- Promote the appropriate terminology for this Standard, including *measure, point, end point, vertex, geometric shapes, ray, angle, circle, degree,* and *protractor.*

What the STUDENTS do:

- Understand how angles are measured in degrees.
- Measure angles in whole-number degrees using a protractor.
- Make sketches of specified angle measures.
- Use measurement vocabulary as they measure and draw angles.

Addressing Student Misconceptions and Common Errors

Some students may look at a protractor with a set of double numbers and not know the number to use when finding the measure of an angle. To address this misconception, students should think about the size of an angle. If the angle is less than a 90 degree right angle, it is an acute angle with a measurement of 0 to 89 degrees. If the angle is greater than 90 degrees, it will be an obtuse angle and will be between 91 and 179 degrees.

Some students' angle measurements are incorrect because some protractors have an edge along the bottom. Students are incorrectly lining up the protractor as zero degrees begins about $\frac{1}{4}$ of an inch above the bottom edge. To address this common error, point this out to students. Show students how they can get inaccurate angle measures if they do not correctly line up the protractor.

GRADE 4

STANDARD 7 (4.MD.C.7)

Recognize angle measure as additive. When an angle is decomposed into non-overlapping parts, the angle measure of the whole is the sum of the angle measures of the parts. Solve addition and subtraction problems to find unknown angles on a diagram in real world and mathematical problems, e.g., by using an equation with a symbol for the unknown angle measure.

What the TEACHER does:

- Begin by explaining that when an angle is decomposed into non-overlapping parts, the angle measure of the whole is the sum of the angle measures of the parts. For example, a lawn water sprinkler rotates 55 degrees and then pauses. It then rotates an additional 35 degrees. What is the total degree of the water sprinkler rotation? By adding the two angle measures together, students can recognize angle measure as additive. With this knowledge, students can solve addition and subtraction problems to find the measurements of unknown angles on a diagram in real-world and mathematical problems.
- Provide word problems for students to practice, such as:

  I am scanning a photograph on my computer printer. I rotate the photo 90 degrees the first time and another 90 degrees the second time. How many more degrees would I need to rotate my photo to make a complete 360-degree turn?

  Look at the angles below. Angles are not exact. Do not use a protractor for this problem.

  Angle A = $\frac{1}{3}$ of the straight angle. What is the value of angle B? Explain how you know.

- Ensure students have opportunities to talk with the teacher and each other to make sense of what they are learning about angles that are decomposed and the recognition of angle measure as additive.
- Promote the appropriate terminology for this Standard, including *measure, point, end point, vertex, geometric shapes, ray, angle, circle, degree, protractor, decompose,* and *additive.*

What the STUDENTS do:

- Recognize angles as additive.
- Solve addition and subtraction problems to find unknown angles on a diagram in real world and mathematical problems.
- Use measurement vocabulary for angles.

Addressing Student Misconceptions and Common Errors

Some students may be able to understand and recognize angle measure as additive but may not be able to solve word problems. To address this, provide multiple experiences and activities for students to solve word problems on an ongoing basis.

Notes

Measurement and Data

Cluster A: Solve problems involving measurement and conversion of measurements from a larger unit to a smaller unit.

Standard: 4.MD.A.3. *Apply the area and perimeter formulas for rectangles in real world and mathematical problems.* For example, find the width of a rectangular room given the area of the flooring and the length, by viewing the area formula as a multiplication equation with an unknown factor.

Standards for Mathematical Practice:

SFMP 1. Make sense of problems and persevere in solving them.

Students will solve problems involving area and perimeter.

Goal:

Using the book *Spaghetti and Meatballs for All* by Marilyn Burns, students will explore the concepts of area and perimeter by arranging eight dinner tables to seat various numbers of guests.

Planning:

Materials: *Spaghetti and Meatballs for All* by Marilyn Burns, pencil and paper or individual student whiteboard and marker, 1-inch tiles for tables and paper clips for chairs

Sample Activity:

- Begin by reading aloud *Spaghetti and Meatballs for All.* The book tells the story about Mr. and Mrs. Comfort, who are preparing a feast and arranging eight tables and thirty-two chairs for all their guests to sit at the tables. As the guests arrive, families do not want to sit separately at different tables and ask to sit together. The guests want to eat at one big table so they can be closer to everyone else. However, that creates a major problem. As the guests push tables together they find out there are not enough sides for the chairs. The Comforts have to rearrange the tables.
- Using the scenario, students can explore the concepts of area and perimeter. Using tiles for tables and paper clips for chairs, students explore with table arrangements to find the perimeter for each arrangement. Explain that only one chair can be on an edge, and the number of edges equals the perimeter of the table.

Questions/Prompts:

- Are the students able to understand the difference between perimeter and area? Ask, "What is the process for finding the perimeter? What is the process for finding area?"
- Are the students able to apply the formulas for area and perimeter?

Differentiating Instruction:

Struggling Students: Students are often confused between the concepts of perimeter and area. The formulas fourth graders learn must be developed through experience, not just memorization. To address this, provide additional experiences for students to discover both area and perimeter. Help students notice that the formula for area is $l \times w = a$. The answer for area will always be in square units. The formula for perimeter can be $2l + 2w = p$. The answer will always be in linear units.

Extension: For an extension of learning, ask students to figure the arrangements for thirty-six and forty-eight guests or another number of guests they choose. Have students sketch a solution, show their drawings, and explain their thinking of how the problem can be solved.

Measurement and Data

Cluster A: Solve problems involving measurement and conversion of measurements from a larger unit to a smaller unit.

Standard:

Standards for Mathematical Practice:

Goal:

Planning:

Materials:

Sample Activity:

Questions/Prompts:

Differentiating Instruction:

Struggling Students:

Extension:

Measurement and Data
Cluster B: Represent and interpret data.

Standard:

Standards for Mathematical Practice:

Goal:

Planning:

Materials:

Sample Activity:

Questions/Prompts:

Differentiating Instruction:

Struggling Students:

Extension:

Measurement and Data
Cluster C: Geometric measurement: Understand concepts of angle and measure angles.

Standard:

Standards for Mathematical Practice:

Goal:

Planning:

Materials:

Sample Activity:

Questions/Prompts:

Differentiating Instruction:

Struggling Students:

Extension:

Measurement and Data
5.MD.A*

Convert like measurement units within a given measurement system.

STANDARD 1 **5.MD.A.1:** Convert among different-sized standard measurement units within a given measurement system (e.g., convert 5 cm to 0.05 m), and use these conversions in solving multi-step, real world problems.

*Supporting cluster

Measurement and Data   5.MD.A

Cluster A: Convert like measurement units within a given measurement system.
Grade 5 Overview

In this cluster, students will convert both customary and standard measurements within the same system of measurement and solve multistep word problems. Fifth graders will discover base-ten conversions within the metric system, that is, 1 kilometer = 1,000 meters.

Standards for Mathematical Practice
SFMP 1. Make sense of problems and persevere in solving them.

Students will interpret and make sense of the word problems they solve involving customary and standard measurement conversions.

SFMP 2. Reason abstractly and quantitatively.

Students will make sense of the number of units in relationship to the size of the unit when converting.

SFMP 6. Attend to precision.

Students will use specific vocabulary to convert measurements.

SFMP 7. Look for and make use of structure.

Students will discover the relationship of base-ten conversions within the metric system.

Related Content Standards

3.MD.A.1   3.MD.A.2   4.MD.A.1   4.MD.A.2

Notes

Convert among different-sized standard measurement units within a given measurement system (e.g., convert 5 cm to 0.05 m), and use these conversion in solving multi-step, real world problems.

What the TEACHER does:

- Start with review activities from previously covered third and fourth grade customary and metric conversions. Remind the students of the charts they previously created such as:

Measurement Equivalents

1 ft.	12 in.
2 ft.	24 in.
3 ft.	36 in.

Explain that measurement in fifth grade focuses on the *relationship* between the units. To have a better knowledge of relationships between units, more hands-on measuring is necessary. Provide activities for students to measure with all kinds of tools, including rulers, yardsticks, tape measures, scales, cups, quarts, beakers, and so on. Students must experience hands-on measuring again at this grade level because they need to understand that the *number* of units relates to the *size* of the unit. For example, there are 12 inches in 1 foot and 3 feet in 1 yard. This understanding is critical when converting inches to yards. Using 12-inch rulers and yardsticks, students can see that three of the 12-inch rulers are the same as one yardstick (3×12 inches = 36 inches; 36 inches = 1 yard). With this understanding, students will be able to determine whether they need to multiply or divide when making conversions.

- Focus on helping students convert measurements into larger or smaller units within a measurement system by reinforcing place value for whole numbers and decimals and then focus on the connection between fractions and decimals (for example, $1\frac{1}{2}$ centimeters can be expressed as 1.5 centimeters or 250 millimeters). Before converting, students should think about the units to be converted and be able to explain whether the converted amount will be more or less than the original unit.

- Promote student practice with the use of conversions in solving multistep, real-world problems. This should occur only after students understand the relationship between units and how to do the conversions. Begin the problem solving with simple problems that focus on renaming units to *represent* the solution before experiencing problems that require renaming to *find* the solution.

- Model vocabulary usage with measurement terms, including *conversion/convert*, *metric* and *customary measurement*, and from previous grades, *relative size*, *liquid volume*, *mass*, *length*, *kilometer (km)*, *meter (m)*, *centimeter (cm)*, *kilogram (kg)*, *gram (g)*, *liter (L)*, *milliliter (mL)*, *inch (in)*, *foot (ft.)*, *yard (yd.)*, *mile (mi)*, *ounce (oz.)*, *pound (lb.)*, *cup (c)*, *pint (pt.)*, *quart (qt.)*, *gallon (gal)*, *hour*, *minute*, and *second*.

- Provide time for student discussion about measurement tools and the ideas they are learning.

What the STUDENTS do:

- Convert different-sized standard measurement units within the same measurement system.
- Solve word problems involving conversions of metric and customary units.
- Use the vocabulary associated with the metric and customary conversions.

Addressing Student Misconceptions and Common Errors

Some students may not pay attention to the unit of measurement when subtracting. For example, when subtracting 5 inches from 2 feet (2 ft. – 5 in.), students may incorrectly think the answer is l ft. and 5 inches instead of 1 feet and 7 inches. To address this misconception, talk about and show the example using 2 twelve-inch rulers, then subtract.

Notes

Measurement and Data
5.MD.B*

Represent and interpret data.

STANDARD 2   **5.MD.B.2:** Make a line plot to display a data set of measurements in fractions of a unit ($\frac{1}{2}$, $\frac{1}{4}$, $\frac{1}{8}$). Use operations on fractions for this grade to solve problems involving information presented in line plots. *For example, given different measurements of liquid in identical beakers, find the amount of liquid each beaker would contain if the total amount in all the beakers were distributed equally.*

*Supporting cluster

Measurement and Data   5.MD.B

Cluster B: Represent and interpret data.
Grade 5 Overview

This cluster focuses on solving problems using line plots created to display measurement data in fractions of a unit.

Standards for Mathematical Practice
SFMP 1. Make sense of problems and persevere in solving them.

Students will interpret and make sense of word problems involving information presented in line plots.

SFMP 2. Reason abstractly and quantitatively.

Students will attend to the meaning of the measured objects and plots on the number line and will use operations involving fractions.

SFMP 4. Model with mathematics.

Students will use line plots to display data of objects measured in fractional units.

SFMP 5. Use appropriate tools strategically.

Students will use a ruler to measure objects to the nearest $\frac{1}{8}$, $\frac{1}{4}$, and $\frac{1}{2}$ inch.

SFMP 6. Attend to precision.

Students will attend to precision with specific vocabulary to describe and analyze data of objects measured and displayed on line plots.

Related Content Standards

4.MD.B.4   5.NF.A1-2   5.NF.B.4   5.NF.B.7

Notes

Make a line plot to display a data set of measurements in fractions of a unit ($\frac{1}{2}, \frac{1}{4}, \frac{1}{8}$). Use operations on fractions for this grade to solve problems involving information presented in line plots. For example, given different measurements of liquid in identical beakers, find the amount of liquid each beaker would contain if the total amount in all the beakers were distributed equally.

What the TEACHER does:

- Start by providing a ruler and allowing students to measure ten objects found in their desks and classroom to the nearest one-eighth of an inch. Direct students to record by displaying the measurement of the objects on a line plot. Remind students that a line plot is a visual, graphic representation that shows the frequency of data using x's along a number line.
- When finished, have students analyze and interpret the data. Ask questions such as, "How many objects measured $\frac{7}{8}$, or if you put all the objects end to end, what would their total length be?"
- Next, have students measure with liquids. Ask students to partially fill ten beakers with water. Tell them to fill two of the beakers one-half way full, three of the beakers one-fourth of the way full, two of the beakers one-eighth full, and finally estimate and fill the remaining beakers about $\frac{5}{8}$ full. After filling the beakers, ask the students to each create a line plot to show the data collected from filling the beakers. When finished, have students analyze and interpret the data. Ask students questions such as, "If the liquid is redistributed equally, how much liquid would each beaker have?"
- After students experience measurement with length and liquid volume, provide balance scales for students to measure mass by weighing a variety of objects. Have students record by displaying the measurements of the objects they weighted on a line plot.

What the STUDENTS do:

- Measure objects to one-eighth of a unit, including length, mass, and liquid volume.
- Construct a line plot with information gathered and will display, analyze, and interpret their own line plots.
- Solve problems using operations on fractions from information presented in the line plot.
- Use appropriate vocabulary when working with line plots and fractional measurements.

Addressing Student Misconceptions and Common Errors

Some students may not know what measurement to use if the object measures between $\frac{1}{8}$ and $\frac{1}{4}$ inch. To address this, help students understand that approximations can be used to measure to the closest $\frac{1}{8}$ inch and $\frac{1}{4}$ inch.

Notes

Measurement and Data
5.MD.C*

Geometric measurement: Understand concepts of volume and relate volume to multiplication and to addition.

STANDARD 3 **5.MD.C.3:** Recognize volume as an attribute of solid figures and understand concepts of volume measurement.

    a. A cube with side length 1 unit, called a "unit cube," is said to have "one cubic unit" of volume, and can be used to measure volume.

    b. A solid figure which can be packed without gaps or overlaps using n unit cubes is said to have a volume of n cubic units.

STANDARD 4 **5.MD.C.4:** Measure volumes by counting unit cubes, using cubic cm, cubic in, cubic ft, and improvised units.

STANDARD 5 **5.MD.C.5:** Relate volume to the operations of multiplication and addition and solve real world and mathematical problems involving volume.

    a. Find the volume of a right rectangular prism with whole-number side lengths by packing it with unit cubes, and show that the volume is the same as would be found by multiplying the edge lengths, equivalently by multiplying the height by the area of the base. Represent threefold whole-number products as volumes, e.g., to represent the associative property of multiplication.

    b. Apply the formulas $V = l \times w \times h$ and $V = b \times h$ for rectangular prisms to find volumes of right rectangular prisms with whole-number edge lengths in the context of solving real world and mathematical problems.

    c. Recognize volume as additive. Find volumes of solid figures composed of two non-overlapping right rectangular prisms by adding the volumes of the non-overlapping parts, applying this technique to solve real world problems.

*Major cluster

Measurement and Data   5.MD.C

Cluster C: Geometric measurement: Understand concepts of volume and relate volume to multiplication and to addition.
Grade 5 Overview

This cluster focuses on recognizing volume as an attribute of solid figures and zero in on the understanding of volume measurement. Students will learn that a 1-unit by 1-unit by 1-unit cube is the standard unit for measuring volume. Fifth graders will select appropriate units, strategies, and tools for solving problems that involve estimating and measuring volume.

Standards for Mathematical Practice
SFMP 1. Make sense of problems and persevere in solving them.

Students will solve real-world and mathematical problems involving volume.

SFMP 4. Model with mathematics.

Students will apply the formulas $V = l \times w \times h$ and $V = b \times h$ for rectangular prisms to find volumes of right rectangular prisms with whole-number edge lengths.

SFMP 5. Use appropriate tools strategically.

Students will use manipulatives to build cubes and rectangular prisms to discover the formula for the volume of rectangular prisms.

SFMP 6. Attend to precision.

Students will attend to precision with specific vocabulary to describe the measurement of volume.

SFMP 7. Look for and make use of structure.

Students will use their knowledge of the mathematical structure of area and apply that knowledge to volume.

Related Content Standard

4.MD.A.3

Notes

STANDARD 3 (5.MD.C.3)

Recognize volume as an attribute of solid figures and understand concepts of volume measurement:

    a. *A cube with side length 1unit, called a "unit cube," is said to have "one cubic unit" of volume, and can be used to measure volume.*

    b. *A solid figure which can be packed without gaps or overlaps using n unit cubes is said to have a volume of n cubic units.*

STANDARD 4 (5.MD.C.4)

Measure volumes by counting unit cubes, using cubic cm, cubic in, cubic ft, and improvised units.

STANDARD 5 (5.MD.C.5)

Relate volume to the operations of multiplication and addition and solve real world and mathematical problems involving volume.

    a. *Find the volume of a right rectangular prism with whole-number side lengths by packing it with unit cubes, and show that the volume is the same as would be found by multiplying the edge lengths, equivalently by multiplying the height by the area of the base. Represent threefold whole-number products as volumes, e.g., to represent the associative property of multiplication.*

    b. *Apply the formulas V = l × w × h and V = b × h for rectangular prisms to find volumes of right rectangular prisms with whole-number edge lengths in the context of solving real world and mathematical problems.*

    c. *Recognize volume as additive. Find volumes of solid figures composed of two non-overlapping right rectangular prisms by adding the volumes of the non-overlapping parts, applying this technique to solve real world problems.*

What the TEACHER does:

- Plan several activities for fifth graders to experience finding the volume of a rectangular prism by counting cubes. Finding the volume by counting cubes means figuring out the amount of space or cubes a rectangular prism takes up. Give student partner pairs of one-inch cubes and a rectangular prism such as a shoe box. Ask them to cover the bottom layer of the prism with the cubes and then determine how many additional layers of cubes should be added to fill the box. As students are beginning to understand volume, explain that volume is measured in cubic units, that is, cubic inches or cubic centimeters. Student should note that a 1-unit by 1-unit by 1-unit cube is the standard unit for measuring volume. The cube has a length of 1 unit, a width of 1 unit, and a height of 1 unit. It is called a *cubic unit* and is written with an exponent of 3 (for example, in³). Explain to the students that *a solid figure packed without gaps or overlaps using* n *unit cubes is said to have a volume of* n *cubic units.* Ask the students to describe how they found the volume and what the volume in cubic units is for their rectangular prisms. For example, a partner pair of students may say that their rectangular prism has a bottom layer of 10 cubes for the length and 5 cubes for the width or 50 cubes for their bottom layer. The students may say there are 4 layers of 50 cubes or 200 cubes in all or 200 cubic inches or that the volume of their prism is 200 in³.

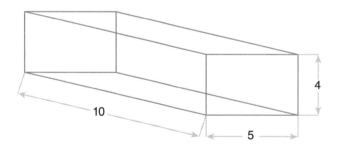

- Provide additional manipulative experiences for students to find the volume of different sizes of rectangular boxes with the cube method before moving to pictorial representations. For one of the additional experiences, give each student only one cubic inch block and a small rectangular box or prism. Direct the students to find the volume of the prism in cubic inches. Ask students to explain their thinking and how they found the volume using only one cube. Then, have students check their answers by filling the box with multiple cubes. With numerous experiences, fifth graders will likely begin to develop an understanding of the volume formula ($V = l \times w \times h$).

(continued)

What the TEACHER does (continued):

- Allow students to apply the formulas ($V = l \times w \times h$ and $V = b \times h$) to find volumes of rectangular prisms with whole-number edge lengths in the context of solving real-world and mathematical problems *only* when they have developed the conceptual understanding. Fifth graders should have experiences to describe and reason about why the formula works before using it abstractly. Try problems such as, "The length of my cereal box is 25 cm, the width of the box is 9 cm, and the height is 30 cm. What is the volume of my cereal box in cubic centimeters?"
- Model measurement vocabulary with terms such as *measurement, attribute, volume, solid figure, rectangular prism, unit, unit cube, gap, overlap, cubic units (cubic cm, cubic in., cubic ft.), multiplication, addition, edge lengths, height,* and *area of base.*
- Plan time for dialogue and discussion to solidify the learning for the concept of volume.

What the STUDENTS do:

- Recognize volume as an attribute of three-dimensional space.
- Understand that volume can be measured by finding the total number of same-sized units of volume required to fill the space without gaps or overlaps.
- Measure volume by counting unit cubes, using cubic cm, cubic in., and cubic ft.
- Find the volume of a rectangular prism with whole-number side lengths by packing it with unit cubes, and demonstrate that the volume is the same as multiplying the height by the area of the base.
- Apply the formulas $V = l \times w \times h$ and $V = b \times h$ for rectangular prisms to find volumes of rectangular prisms with whole-number edge lengths as they solve real-world and mathematical problems.
- Use measurement vocabulary associated with the concept of volume.

Addressing Student Misconceptions and Common Errors

Some students may think only about one of the dimensions needed to find volume. Some students may believe that because an object is tall, it will have lots of volume, ignoring the other two dimensions. Provide additional experiences for students to measure and compare a variety of objects by using all three dimensions to address this misconception.

Notes

Measurement and Data
Cluster C: Geometric measurement: Understand concepts of volume and relate volume to multiplication and to addition.

Standard: 5.MD.C.5. *Relate volume to the operations of multiplication and addition and solve real world and mathematical problems involving volume.*

b. *Apply the formulas* $V = l \times w \times h$ *and* $V = b \times h$ *for rectangular prisms to find volumes of right rectangular prisms with whole-number edge lengths in the context of solving real world and mathematical problems.*

Standards for Mathematical Practice:
SFMP 7. **Look for and make use of structure.**
Students will use their knowledge of the mathematical structure of area and apply that knowledge to volume.

Goal:
Students will apply the volume formula within the context of solving real-world and mathematical problems.

Planning:

Materials: A variety of empty boxes children bring from home, measuring tapes, and paper and pencil for each pair of students

Sample Activity:
- Provide experiences for partner pairs of students to estimate what they think the volume of three different boxes, such as a detergent box, a cereal box, and a tissue box, will be. Ask students to arrange the boxes from the least volume to the greatest volume.
- Using the tape measure, have the students measure the dimensions of each box in inches. Ask the students to find the volume by using the formula $V = l \times w \times h$ and record the answer in cubic units. Students will then compare the estimated volumes to the actual results.
- Try the activity again with different boxes. Ask students to share their findings.

Questions/Prompts:

- Within reason, can students estimate the volume of each box?
- Can students accurately measure the objects to the nearest inch?
- Can students correctly multiply $l \times w \times h$?
- Can students correctly apply the formula for finding volume?
- Did students record their answers in cubic inches?

Differentiating Instruction:

Struggling Students: Some student may think that because an object is tall, or skinny, it will have lots of volume, ignoring the other two dimensions. Numerous experiences finding volume with different sizes of boxes will help students make sense of the concept of volume.

Extension: Try problems such as, "What is the volume of a cube with an edge that measures 5 cm?" Or, "What is the volume of a cube with an edge that measures 10 cm?"

Measurement and Data
Cluster A: Convert like measurement units within a given measurement system.

Standard:

Standards for Mathematical Practice:

Goal:

Planning:

Materials:

Sample Activity:

Questions/Prompts:

Differentiating Instruction:

Struggling Students:

Extension:

Measurement and Data
Cluster B: Represent and interpret data.

Standard:

Standards for Mathematical Practice:

Goal:

Planning:

Materials:

Sample Activity:

Questions/Prompts:

Differentiating Instruction:

Struggling Students:

Extension:

Measurement and Data

Cluster C: Geometric measurement: Understand concepts of volume and relate volume to multiplication and to addition.

Standard:

Standards for Mathematical Practice:

Goal:

Planning:

Materials:

Sample Activity:

Questions/Prompts:

Differentiating Instruction:

Struggling Students:

Extension:

Reflection Questions: Measurement and Data

1. Discuss how the study of measurement will apply directly to students' lives.

2. Why are hands-on measurement tools and manipulatives a must for student success in grades 3–5?

3. Explain how to develop the concept of area using a geoboard.

4. Why must teachers provide numerous experiences for students to collect data and organize it?

5. Explain how open or empty number lines will help students solve word problems with elapsed time.

Part 5

Geometry

Geometry

Domain Overview

GRADE 3

The study of geometry in third grade builds upon previous experiences from Grade 2. Students have been exposed to numerous shapes as they play, draw, color, build, and explore with toys and technology. These experiences help to develop spatial reasoning, which is important in daily life for interpreting and making drawings, forming mental images, visualizing changes, and generalizing about perceptions in the environment. At this level students will identify and draw triangles, pentagons, and hexagons and specifically concentrate on quadrilaterals. Third graders will also focus on fractions by partitioning a whole shape such as a circle or rectangle into equal parts.

GRADE 4

At the fourth grade level, the study of geometry features descriptions, analysis, comparisons, and classification of two-dimensional shapes. Students will learn three important concepts and skills. First, students will draw points, lines, line segments, rays, angles, and perpendicular and parallel lines. Second, two-dimensional figures based on the presence or absence of parallel or perpendicular lines or the presence or absence of angles of a specified size will be classified. Third, students will recognize and draw a line of symmetry for a two-dimensional shape. By building, drawing, and analyzing two-dimensional shapes, students expand their knowledge of properties of two-dimensional objects and the use of them to solve problems involving symmetry.

GRADE 5

In fifth grade, students will be thinking about the underlying structure of the coordinate system and learning how axes make it possible to locate points anywhere on a coordinate plane. At this grade level, students will also represent real-world and mathematical problems by graphing and interpreting points in the first quadrant of the coordinate plane. Students will also make a connection that attributes belonging to a category of two-dimensional shapes that belong to all subcategories of that category. As a result of this learning, students will develop a foundational understanding for future concepts with the coordinate system and also be able to classify and better understand geometric shapes.

SUGGESTED MATERIALS FOR THIS DOMAIN

3	4	5	
✓	✓	✓	Geoboards and geobands (rubber bands)
✓			Straws, toothpicks, pipe cleaners, Popsicle sticks to create quadrilaterals
✓	✓	✓	Paper and pencil for drawing shapes (or individual whiteboards and markers)
	✓		Construction paper die-cut alphabet letters (used to find symmetry)
	✓		Miras or mirrors to show reflections of symmetry
✓	✓		A variety of cut-out paper shapes, including circles, triangles, pentagons, hexagons
✓	✓		Pattern blocks (Reproducible 11)
✓			Scissors
	✓		Tangrams (Reproducible 12)
	✓		*The Greedy Triangle* by Marilyn Burns

KEY VOCABULARY

3	4	5	
	✓		**acute angle** an angle smaller than a right angle (less than 90 degrees)
✓	✓		**angles** two rays (<) that share an endpoint
✓	✓	✓	**attributes** sides, angles, color, shape, size, girth
		✓	**axis (axes = plural)** the horizontal number line (*x*-axis) and the vertical number line (*y*-axis) on the coordinate plane. Axes are also the lines at the side and bottom of a graph.
	✓	✓	**classify** put things into groups (classes) based on a property
		✓	**congruent** equal in size and shape
		✓	**coordinate** a number in an ordered pair that names the location of a point on the coordinate plane
✓	✓	✓	**closed figure** a shape that begins and ends at the same point; for example, a triangle
✓	✓	✓	**edge** sides
	✓		**eighth** one eighth, one of eight equal parts
✓			**equal shares** equal sizes, the same amount
✓	✓	✓	**figure** a closed shape in two or three dimensions

(Continued)

(Continued)

3	4	5		
✓	✓	✓	**fraction**	a part of a whole number
✓	✓	✓	**geometry**	the study of properties, measurement, and relationships of points, lines, angles, surfaces, and solids
		✓	**grid**	a coordinate grid that locates a point by its distance from the intersection of two straight lines
✓	✓	✓	**half**	one of two parts
✓	✓	✓	**line**	the shortest distance between any two points on a plane
		✓	**line plot**	a graph that shows frequency of data along a number line, usually plotted with an x
	✓	✓	**horizontal**	a straight line on a coordinate plane where all points on the line have the same y coordinate
✓	✓	✓	**line segment**	a part of a line that connects two points
		✓	**obtuse**	an angle measuring more than 90 degrees but less than 180 degrees
✓	✓	✓	**open figure**	a shape made up of line segments with at least one line segment that isn't connected to anything at one of its endpoints
		✓	**ordered pairs**	pair of numbers used to locate a point on a coordinate plane; the first number tells how far to move horizontally and the second number tells how far to move vertically
		✓	**origin**	the starting point on a coordinate grid
	✓	✓	**parallel**	two lines in a plane that do not intersect
✓	✓	✓	**partition**	equal dividing
	✓	✓	**perpendicular**	lines that are at right angles (90 degrees) to each other
	✓	✓	**plane**	a flat two-dimensional surface
	✓	✓	**plot**	used to pinpoint where places on a line are located to show data
	✓	✓	**point**	an exact position or location on a plane surface
		✓	**prism**	three-dimensional figure with two congruent and parallel faces that are polygons; the rest of the faces are parallelograms
✓	✓	✓	**properties**	a quality that something has, such as color, size, height, and so on
		✓	**quadrant**	a graph divided into four sections
✓	✓	✓	**quarter**	one of four parts
	✓	✓	**ray**	a line that starts at a point and goes off in a particular direction to infinity
		✓	**reflection**	a mirror image of a geometric figure

3	4	5		
✓	✓		**regular hexagon**	a polygon with six equal sides and six equal angles
✓	✓	✓	**regular polygon**	a closed plane figure having three or more sides
	✓	✓	**right angle**	an angle that measures exactly 90 degrees
✓	✓	✓	**side**	a line segment of a many-sided figure
	✓		**straight angle**	an angle that measures exactly 180 degrees
✓	✓	✓	**surface**	area of faces and cured surfaces of a three-dimensional figure
	✓		**symmetry**	an object is symmetrical when one half is a mirror image of the other half.
✓	✓	✓	**triangle**	a three-sided polygon

       scalene   triangle with none of the sides the same length

       isosceles   a triangle with two equal sides; the angles opposite the equal sides are also equal

       equilateral   triangle with three equal sides and three equal angles

3	4	5		
✓	✓	✓	**two-dimensional shapes**	shapes with two dimensions: length and width

- circle
- square
- triangle
- rectangle
- hexagon
- trapezoid
- quadrilateral
- rhombus
- parallelogram

3	4	5		
✓			**Venn diagram**	a graphic organizer for comparison and contrast
✓	✓	✓	**vertex/corner**	point at which two line segments meet to form an angle
	✓	✓	**vertical**	an up/down position

Geometry
3.G.A*

Reason with shapes and their attributes.

STANDARD 1 **3.G.A.1:** Understand that shapes in different categories (e.g., rhombuses, rectangles, and others) may share attributes (e.g., having four sides), and that the shared attributes can define a larger category (e.g., quadrilaterals). Recognize rhombuses, rectangles, and squares as examples of quadrilaterals, and draw examples of quadrilaterals that do not belong to any of these subcategories.

STANDARD 2 **3.G.A.2:** Partition shapes into parts with equal areas. Express the area of each part as a unit fraction of the whole. *For example, partition a shape into 4 parts with equal area, and describe the area of each part as $\frac{1}{4}$ of the area of the shape.*

*Supporting cluster

Geometry   3.G.A

Cluster A: Reason with shapes and their attributes.
Grade 3 Overview

At the third grade level, students will describe, analyze, and compare properties of two-dimensional shapes. A variety of experiences must be provided for students to compare and classify shapes by their sides and angles. Third graders will also connect fractions to geometry by understanding that the area of part of a circle, square, or rectangle is a unit fraction of a whole and can be partitioned into equal parts.

Standards for Mathematical Practice
SFMP 6. Attend to precision.

Third graders will use clear, precise language to describe quadrilaterals in discussions with others.

SFMP 7. Look for and make use of structure.

The students will conceptualize a quadrilateral as a closed figure with four straight sides and notice characteristics of the angles and the relationship between opposite sides. The experience of discussing and thinking about attributes of shapes will help third graders understand geometric structure.

Related Content Standards

2.G.A.1   3.G.A.2

Notes

STANDARD 1 (3.G.A.1)

Understand that shapes in different categories (e.g., rhombuses, rectangles, and others) may share attributes (e.g., having four sides), and that the shared attributes can define a larger category (e.g., quadrilaterals). Recognize rhombuses, rectangles, and squares as examples of quadrilaterals, and draw examples of quadrilaterals that do not belong to any of these subcategories.

What the TEACHER does:

- Begin by providing a variety of experiences for students to investigate quadrilaterals. Students can create the shapes with straws, toothpicks, Popsicle sticks, pipe cleaners; use geoboard and geobands; draw the shapes; look at pictures of the shapes; or use technology to investigate quadrilaterals. Remind students that quadrilateral means *four sides* and every four-sided shape is a quadrilateral. There are many different kinds of quadrilaterals, but all have several things in common: all of them have four sides (edges) and four vertices (corners). Have students discuss and explain how quadrilateral shapes are alike and what makes them different. Ask questions such as, "Is a quadrilateral a rhombus? Is a rhombus a quadrilateral? Explain your thinking."
- Model vocabulary with numerous examples and encourage students to use geometric terms such as *properties, attributes, quadrilateral, open figure, closed figure, rhombus, rectangle,* and *square.*
- Try a sorting activity for students to sort geometric shapes with the focus on recognizing shapes that are and are not quadrilaterals. Third graders should be able to understand that a quadrilateral is a closed figure with four straight sides, should observe characteristics of the angles and the relationship between opposite sides, and should use the correct terminology when describing the properties of quadrilaterals.
- Help students use the geometry concepts learned with real-world applications appropriate to third grade. Try having students locate shapes in their classrooms and school building such as, "The bulletin boards are quadrilaterals we call rectangles," or "The reading table is a special quadrilateral we call a trapezoid."
- Ensure students have opportunities to talk with the teacher and each other to make sense of what they are learning. If students are not talking about the mathematics, they may not be actively engaged in their learning of third grade geometry.

What the STUDENTS do:

- Describe, analyze, and compare properties of two-dimensional shapes.
- Recognize shapes that are and are not quadrilaterals by examining the properties of the geometric shapes.
- Conceptualize a quadrilateral as a closed figure with four straight sides, and notice characteristics of the angles and the relationship between opposite sides.
- Draw rhombuses, rectangles, and squares as examples of quadrilaterals, and draw examples of quadrilaterals that do not belong to any of these subcategories.
- Use geometric terms when describing quadrilaterals.

Addressing Student Misconceptions and Common Errors

Some third graders may identify a square as a "non-rectangle" or a "non-rhombus" and may not understand that a square is a rectangle because it has all of the properties of a rectangle. Some children may be able to tell the properties of each shape separately, but may not figure out the relationships between the shapes. For example, students may not notice the properties of a square that are characteristic of other shapes too. To address this misconception, provide toothpicks or straws to create shapes. To help students visually see the relationship between a rhombus and a square, ask students to change the angles. Have students talk about the relationship they noticed as they moved the angles. As students develop definitions for specific shapes, relationships between the properties will make sense to them.

Partition shapes into parts with equal areas. Express the area of each part as a unit fraction of the whole. For example, partition a shape into 4 parts with equal area, and describe the area of each part as $\frac{1}{4}$ of the area of the shape.

What the TEACHER does:

- Provide students with a variety of cut-out circle, square, rectangle, regular hexagon, and equilateral triangle shapes in many different sizes, or have students draw the shapes with pencil and paper. Ask students to find all the ways they can partition the shapes into parts with equal area.
- Help students begin developing sophisticated levels of thinking and communication. Help children learn to describe how a shape can be partitioned into four parts with equal area. Talk about the area of each part as $\frac{1}{4}$ of the area of the shape. Show students how to express partitions of shapes in writing with the symbols used for fractions.
- Always model correct terminology third graders need to express the area of each part as a unit fraction of the whole.
- Ensure that students have opportunities to talk with the teacher and each other to make sense of what they are learning about partitioning shapes.

What the STUDENTS do:

- Draw different shapes and find how many ways the shapes can be partitioned or divided into parts with equal area.
- Given a shape, partition it into equal parts, recognizing that these parts all have the same area.
- Identify and describe the fractional name of the area of the shape. For example, students will say, "This rectangle divided into four equal parts. Each part is $\frac{1}{4}$ of the total area of the rectangle."

Addressing Student Misconceptions and Common Errors

Some third graders are confused with the concept that equal shares of identical wholes may not have the same shape. Some students may not understand an area model represents one out of two or three or four fractional parts without understanding the parts are equal shares. Additional experiences and discussions about equal shares with different shapes will help students begin to understand this confusing concept.

Fourths

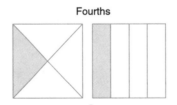

Notes

Geometry
Cluster A: Reason with shapes and their attributes.

Standard: 3.G.A.1. *Understand that shapes in different categories (e.g., rhombuses, rectangles, and others) may share attributes (e.g., having four sides), and that the shared attributes can define a larger category (e.g., quadrilaterals). Recognize rhombuses, rectangles, and squares as examples of quadrilaterals, and draw examples of quadrilaterals that do not belong to any of these subcategories.*

Standards for Mathematical Practice:
SFMP 6. Attend to precision.
Third graders will use clear, precise language to describe quadrilaterals in discussions with others.

SFMP 7. Look for and make use of structure.
Experiences of discussing/thinking about attributes of shapes helps third graders understand geometric structure.

Goal:
Students will create, identify, and draw triangles, pentagons, hexagons, and specifically concentrate on quadrilaterals. Recognize rhombuses, rectangles, and squares as examples of quadrilaterals.

Planning:

Materials: Geoboards/geobands for each student, paper and pencil to record shapes, toothpicks or straws, *The Greedy Triangle* by Marilyn Burns.

Sample Activity:
- Read Marilyn Burns's *The Greedy Triangle* to students. The story tells of a triangle character dissatisfied with its shape that decides to take on new identities with the help of a Shapeshifter. The triangle continues to add one more side to itself to change from a triangle to a quadrilateral. As the story is read, students can create the shapes with geoboards and geobands. After reading the book, focus on creating quadrilaterals with the geoboards. Talk about rhombuses, rectangles, and squares as examples of quadrilaterals. Create quadrilaterals and sort the geoboards into two groups, such as quadrilaterals that are not rectangles.
- Draw examples of quadrilaterals with paper/pencil not belonging to the subcategories of rhombuses, squares, or rectangles.

Questions/Prompts:

- Ask students "What is the difference between a rhombus and a rectangle?"
- Ask students "All squares are rectangles, but not all rectangles are squares. Why?"
- Ask students "All squares are rhombuses, but not all rhombuses are squares. Why?"
- Ask students to create and draw a quadrilateral with given attributes, such as two sets of parallel lines.

Differentiating Instruction:

Struggling Students: Some children may be able to tell the properties of each shape separately but may not figure out the relationships between the shapes. For example, students may not notice the properties of a square that are characteristic of other shapes too. To help struggling students, provide toothpicks or straws to create shapes. To help students see the relationship between a rhombus and a square, ask students to change the angles. Talk about the relationship students noticed as they moved the angles. As students develop definitions for shapes, relationships between the properties begin to make sense.

Extension: Students can choose two quadrilateral shapes (square, rectangle, rhombus, parallelogram, or trapezoid) to compare and contrast using a Venn diagram.

Geometry
Cluster A: Reason with shapes and their attributes.

Standard:

Standards for Mathematical Practice:

Goal:

Planning:

Materials:

Sample Activity:

Questions/Prompts:

Differentiating Instruction:

Struggling Students:

Extension:

Geometry
4.G.A*

Draw and identify lines and angles, and classify shapes by properties of their lines and angles.

STANDARD 1   **4.G.A.1:** Draw points, lines, line segments, rays, angles (right, acute, obtuse), and perpendicular and parallel lines. Identify these in two-dimensional figures.

STANDARD 2   **4.G.A.2:** Classify two-dimensional figures based on the presence or absence of parallel or perpendicular lines, or the presence or absence of angles of a specified size. Recognize right triangles as a category, and identify right triangles.

STANDARD 3   **4.G.A.3:** Recognize a line of symmetry for a two-dimensional figure as a line across the figure such that the figure can be folded along the line into matching parts. Identify line-symmetric figures and draw lines of symmetry.

*Additional cluster

Geometry   4.G.A

Cluster A: Draw and identify lines and angles, and classify shapes by properties of their lines and angles.
Grade 4 Overview

In this cluster, students not only identify, describe, and draw points, lines, line segments, rays, angles, and perpendicular and parallel lines but also identify these in two-dimensional shapes. Through building, drawing, and analyzing shapes, students expand their knowledge of properties of two-dimensional objects and the use of them to solve problems involving symmetry.

Standards for Mathematical Practice
SFMP 4. Model with mathematics.

Students will use two-dimensional shapes and spatial reasoning to solve problems involving symmetry.

SFMP 5. Use appropriate tools strategically.

Fourth graders will draw lines, point, segments, angles, and perpendicular and parallel lines using both technological and hands on tools to deepen their understanding of geometry.

SFMP 6. Attend to precision.

Students will talk about and use geometric vocabulary to analyze and describe lines, angles, and symmetrical shapes.

Related Content Standards

4.G.A.1   4.G.A.3   4.MD.C.5   4.MD.C.6

Notes

Draw points, lines, line segments, rays, angles (right, acute, obtuse), and perpendicular and parallel lines. Identify these in two-dimensional figures.

What the TEACHER does:

- Ask students to create a point on a sheet of paper by drawing a dot with a pencil. Have students label the dot with the vocabulary term *point*. Create another point in another location on the same paper. Tell students to connect the two points by drawing a *line segment* with a ruler's straight edge. Explain that a line segment is part of a line and always has two endpoints (beginning and end points) and may be labeled with a letter to describe each point. On another part of the paper, draw a line that will contain an infinite number of points and has no endpoints and goes on and on forever. This is a line. Label *line* on the paper. Make a *ray* on paper and label it. A ray is part of a line that has one endpoint and extends forever in only one direction. Create and label *parallel lines* that are lines that never cross and are the same distance apart. Draw and label *perpendicular lines* intersect to form *right angles*. Talk about right, obtuse, acute, and straight angles. Draw and label these on the paper. Help students identify angles without measuring or mentioning degrees. Angles can be classified in comparison to right angles, such as greater than, less than, or the same size as a right angle. Students should use the corner of a sheet of paper as a benchmark for a right angle and use it to determine relationships of other angles.
- Provide geoboards and geobands for every student. Have students use the geoboards to find different ways to make line segments that touch exactly seven pins. Ask the students to discuss the parallel line segments, intersecting line segments, and perpendicular line segments they created.
- Direct students to observe classroom examples of points, lines, line segments, rays, angles, and perpendicular and parallel lines, that is, a student may find a pencil to show as an example of point, or the hands on a clock to show angles, and so on. Expect students to use the appropriate terminology as they locate real-world examples.
- Remind students that mathematical terms are not only useful in communicating geometric ideas but for constructing examples, such as drawing angles and lines. Analyzing the shapes to be able to construct them requires students to think about the shapes. For example, when thinking about a square, how many degrees are the angles? Fourth graders should not only be able to think about how many angles or the degrees are in a shape but should be able to think about the properties of each shape. Students should also be able to compare and contrast how shapes are alike and different.

What the STUDENTS do:

- Draw points, lines, line segments, rays, angles (right, acute, obtuse), and perpendicular and parallel lines.
- Identify points, lines, line segments, rays, angles (right, acute, obtuse), and perpendicular and parallel lines in two-dimensional figures.
- Use the correct geometric terminology when drawing the shapes.

Addressing Student Misconceptions and Common Errors

Students may incorrectly think a wide angle with short sides is smaller than a narrow angle with long sides. To address this misconception, help fourth graders compare two angles by tracing one and placing it over the other, which will help them understand the length of the sides does not determine whether one angle is larger or smaller than another angle. The measure of the angle does not change.

Classify two-dimensional figures based on the presence or absence of parallel or perpendicular lines, or the presence or absence of angles of a specified size. Recognize right triangles as a category, and identify right triangles.

What the TEACHER does:

- Ensure that students understand parallel and perpendicular lines. Two lines are parallel if they never intersect and are an equal distance apart. Two lines are perpendicular if they are at right angles to each other. Students should be able to identify parallel and perpendicular sides in the shapes below.

- Remind students there are many different types of quadrilaterals, but all have 4 sides and 2 diagonals. Explore many different examples and models of each type of quadrilateral (squares, rectangles, trapezoids, rhombuses/ rhombi, and parallelograms) to discover specific properties for each shape.
- Discuss the relationship among the various quadrilaterals based on the number of sides, opposite sides, side lengths, and angle measures.
- Create a diagram to classify and sort quadrilaterals. This will help fourth graders make sense of the types of quadrilaterals.

Quadrilaterals		
No pairs of parallel sides	**1 pair of parallel sides**	**2 pairs of parallel sides**
↓	↓	↓
Kites	Trapezoids	Parallelogram Rectangle Rhombi Squares

From the diagram, students can determine that a trapezoid is not a parallelogram. A trapezoid only has one pair of parallel lines. Students should notice that a square, a parallelogram, a rectangle, and a rhombus are quadrilaterals.

- To help students classify angles, first plan experiences for drawing and identifying right, acute, and obtuse angles. Explain that two-dimensional figures are classified based on specified angle measurements. The benchmark angles of 90°, 180°, and 360° can be used to estimate an angle's measure, and right triangles can be used as a category for classification.
- Expect students to use correct geometrical vocabulary as they talk about and classify shapes including the terms *classify, properties, shapes, point, line, line segment, ray, angle, vertex/vertices, right angle, acute, obtuse, perpendicular, parallel, right triangle, isosceles triangle, equilateral triangle, scalene triangle, line of symmetry, symmetrical figures, two dimensional, polygon, rhombus, rectangle, square, triangle, quadrilateral, pentagon, hexagon,* and *trapezoid.*
- Create numerous shape examples on card stock for students to sort by categories. For example, sort the shapes by parallel lines/no perpendicular lines.

What the STUDENTS do:

- Classify two-dimensional figures based on the presence or absence of parallel or perpendicular lines, or the presence or absence of angles of a specified size.
- Discuss the relationship among various quadrilaterals based on the number of sides, opposite sides, side lengths, and angle measurement.
- Use geometrical terminology as they talk about, classify, and sort shapes.

Addressing Student Misconceptions and Common Errors

Some students may confuse the name of a square with the term *diamond*. To address the misconception, remind students that there is no geometric shape named a diamond. The shape is a square or a rhombus. Remind students to draw a square right-angled in an upright position.

Another common difficulty for fourth graders is comprehending how and why many of the shapes are called quadrilaterals but have different names based upon the properties. To address this, listen to students' thinking as they begin sorting with concrete objects and describing the properties. Help the students rediscover the specific properties of each shape.

GRADE 4

Recognize a line of symmetry for a two-dimensional figure as a line across the figure such that the figure can be folded along the line into matching parts. Identify line-symmetric figures and draw lines of symmetry.

What the TEACHER does:

- Start by providing one geoboard per student. Have each student create a shape using one geoband, then a second geoband to divide the shape into two equal parts. Note that some of the shapes students create cannot be divided into equal parts. As students attempt to divide shapes, find examples of shapes with a line of symmetry and ask students to share their example with the class. A line of symmetry divides a shape into two halves that are mirror images of each other. A shape can have more than one line of symmetry; for example, a square has four lines of symmetry. Also discuss students' examples that do not have a line of symmetry and have students explain why not.
- Provide additional activities for students to find lines of symmetry by folding paper shapes that have been cut out. Explain that a line of symmetry divides a shape into two congruent parts that can be matched by folding the cut-out shape in half. Also direct students to fold paper in half and then cut shapes such as hearts, trees, shamrocks, snowflakes, leaves, and so on leaving the fold in place. Ask students to open the folded shape to notice that both sides are equal and are a reflection of each other. Draw the line of symmetry with a pencil. If miras or mirrors are available, fourth graders can determine how dividing a shape with a line of symmetry creates a mirror image of the opposite side.

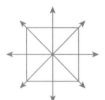 

- Continue by using both symmetrical and nonsymmetrical shapes and both regular and nonregular polygons. Point out that shapes can have more than one line of symmetry. Use die-cut block alphabet letters to fold. Ask students to find and show the line(s) of symmetry. This activity engages students in problem solving that requires spatial and visual thinking.

- Experiment by using hands-on pattern blocks or tangram shapes to help students find lines of symmetry. To record, use paper to trace around each piece and then draw a line(s) of symmetry.
- Use miras or mirrors to show reflections that will help students discover and draw symmetrical lines.
- Focus on vocabulary by asking students to name the following two-dimensional shapes as they demonstrate, fold, and draw lines of symmetry: *polygon, rhombus, rectangle, square, triangle, quadrilateral, pentagon, hexagon,* and *trapezoid.*
- Ensure that students have opportunities to talk with the teacher and each other to make sense of what they are learning.

What the STUDENTS do:

- Experiment with two-dimensional shapes to discover and draw lines of symmetry.
- Use geometric terminology to describe the shapes used to draw lines of symmetry.

Addressing Student Misconceptions and Student Errors

Some students may incorrectly believe there is only one line of symmetry for each shape or object. Instead of merely drawing a line of symmetry while looking at a picture or worksheet, provide multiple paper copies of multiple shapes. Ask students to fold shapes in more than one way. The misconception will be addressed through numerous paper-shape-folding experiences to find the lines of symmetry.

Geometry
Cluster A: Draw and identify lines and angles, and classify shapes by properties of their lines and angles.

Standard: 4.G.A.3. *Recognize a line of symmetry for a two-dimensional figure as a line across the figure such that the figure can be folded along the line into matching parts. Identify line-symmetric figures and draw lines of symmetry.*

Standards for Mathematical Practice:
SFMP 4. Model with mathematics.
Students will use two-dimensional shapes and spatial reasoning to solve problems involving symmetry.

SFMP 6. Attend to precision.
Students will talk about/use geometric vocabulary to analyze and describe lines, angles, and symmetrical shapes.

Goal:
Students will discover which alphabet letters are symmetrical.

Planning:

Materials: Paper/pencil to draw alphabet letters and create a recording chart. Die-cut letters for students who are struggling who may need to fold the letters to find the symmetry.

Sample Activity:
Write all letters of the alphabet as capital letters. Ask students to find the line(s) of symmetry for each letter by drawing lines. As students analyze their work, have them create a chart to record which letters have 1, 2, more than 2 lines, or no lines of symmetry.

Questions/Prompts:

- Can students accurately draw lines of symmetry with alphabet letters? Ask, "How did you know you found all the lines of symmetry for each letter? Which letters have more than one line of symmetry?"
- Were students able to explain strategies for finding symmetry? Ask, "What strategies did you use to make sure you are correct?"
- Can the students find nonsymmetrical letters? Ask, "Which letters are nonsymmetrical?"

Differentiating Instruction:

Struggling Students: Some students may incorrectly believe there is only one line of symmetry for each letter. Help them by creating die-cut letters that can be folded to discover the symmetry.

Extension: Students can find real-world applications of symmetry in the classroom. Ask them to show an imaginary line "drawn" to show the symmetry of objects.

Geometry
Cluster A: Draw and identify lines and angles, and classify shapes by properties of their lines and angles.

Standard:

Standards for Mathematical Practice:

Goal:

Planning:

Materials:

Sample Activity:

Questions/Prompts:

Differentiating Instruction:

Struggling Students:

Extension:

Geometry
5.G.A*

Graph points on the coordinate plane to solve real-world and mathematical problems.

STANDARD 1   **5.G.A.1:** Use a pair of perpendicular number lines, called axes, to define a coordinate system, with the intersection of the lines (the origin) arranged to coincide with the 0 on each line and a given point in the plane located by using an ordered pair of numbers, called its coordinates. Understand that the first number indicates how far to travel from the origin in the direction of one axis, and the second number indicates how far to travel in the direction of the second axis, with the convention that the names of the two axes and the coordinates correspond (e.g., *x*-axis and *x*-coordinate, *y*-axis and *y*-coordinate).

STANDARD 2   **5.G.A.2:** Represent real world and mathematical problems by graphing points in the first quadrant of the coordinate plane, and interpret coordinate values of points in the context of the situation.

*Additional cluster

GRADE 5

Geometry   5.G.A

Cluster A: Graph points on the coordinate plane to solve real-world and mathematical problems.
Grade 5 Overview

At the fifth grade level, students learn to graph ordered pairs in the first quadrant of the coordinate plane. A variety of opportunities should be provided for students to apply these experiences to real-world map location skills or *Battleship*™ types of games. Students also classify two-dimensional shapes and figures based on their properties.

Standards for Mathematical Practice
SFMP 1. Make sense of problems and persevere in solving them.

Students will solve and analyze problems through the use of coordinate plane.

SFMP 4. Model with mathematics.

Students will use coordinate planes to represent real world problems by graphing points in the first quadrant.

SFMP 6. Attend to precision.

Students will use clear, specific directions, attending to precision as points are plotted on the coordinate plane.

SFMP 7. Look for and make use of structure.

Students will notice a pattern that may be generalized as real world problems are represented on the coordinate plane.

Related Content Standards

5.G.A.1   5.GA.2

Notes

Use a pair of perpendicular number lines, called axes, to define a coordinate system, with the intersection of the lines (the origin) arranged to coincide with the 0 on each line and a given point in the plane located by using an ordered pair of numbers, called its coordinates. Understand that the first number indicates how far to travel from the origin in the direction of one axis, and the second number indicates how far to travel in the direction of the second axis, with the convention that the names of the two axes and the coordinates correspond (e.g., x-axis and x-coordinate, y-axis and y-coordinate).

What the TEACHER does:

- Explain the structure of the coordinate system and how to locate points in the first quadrant (positive numbers) on the coordinate plane. The plane includes a horizontal number line, called the *x*-axis, and a vertical number line, called the *y*-axis, intersecting at a point called the origin. Points in the coordinate plane can be located by an ordered pair of numbers (x,y). When an ordered pair is used to locate a point on a grid, the two numbers are called the coordinates of the point.

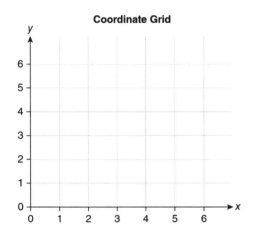

- Construct a classroom coordinate system using tape on the floor to create a coordinate grid. Allow the students to physically locate coordinate points. For example, starting at the origin point $(0,0)$ students should first walk along the *x*-axis to find the first number in an ordered pair such as $(3,2)$ and then walk up two units for the second number in the pair.
- Provide activities for students to construct their own coordinate grid and locate points. For example, plot $(1,1)$, $(2,4)$, and $(3,1)$ on the grid and direct students to connect the points with line segments. Remind students to begin with the *x* or horizontal axis. Ask students to connect the points with line segments. Allow students to create their own simple shapes on the coordinate grid and write a set of directions explaining how to get to the locations to create the shapes. For example, plot a point starting at $(0,1)$. Plot a second point at $(1,3)$. Connect both points with a line segment. Plot another point at $(3,3)$. Connect $(1,3)$ and $(3,3)$ with a line segment. Plot $(4,1)$. Connect $(3,3)$ and $(4,1)$ with a line segment. End by connecting $(4,1)$ and $(0,1)$ with a line segment.
- Include motivational games such as *Battleship*™ to practice finding coordinate locations.
- Focus on vocabulary for this standard because it plays an integral role in the understanding and learning of the coordinate plane system, including *coordinate system, coordinate plane, first quadrant, points, lines, axis/axes, x-axis, y-axis, horizontal, vertical, intersection of lines, origin, ordered pairs, coordinates, x-coordinate,* and *y-coordinate*.
- Ensure that students have opportunities to talk with the teacher and each other to make sense of what they are learning about coordinate geometry and ordered pairs.

What the STUDENTS do:

- Locate coordinates on a coordinate grid by using an ordered pair of numbers.
- Understand the first number of an ordered pair indicates how far to travel from the origin in the direction of one axis and the second number indicates how far to travel in the direction of the second axis.
- Use specific vocabulary and directions to explain ordered pair locations.

Addressing Student Misconceptions and Common Errors

The *x* and *y* axes may confuse students, because this is the first time they are working with coordinates using the first quadrant of a coordinate grid. Some students may not understand the first number of the ordered pair (*x*-axis) indicates how far to move *horizontally* from the origin and must occur first. Some students may not think the order is critical. To address the misconception, students can plot points so that the position of the coordinates is switched. For example, have students plot $(4,5)$ and $(5,4)$ and ask them to explain and discuss the importance of order used to plot the points.

STANDARD 2 (5.G.A.2)

Represent real world and mathematical problems by graphing points in the first quadrant of the coordinate plane, and interpret coordinate values of points in the context of the situation.

What the TEACHER does:

- Remind students that coordinate graphs show relationships between numbers on a coordinate grid. A coordinate grid includes two perpendicular lines, called the *x* and *y* axes, and are labeled like number lines. The horizontal axis is called the *x*-axis and the vertical axis is called the *y*-axis. The point where the *x*-axis and *y*-axis intersect is called the origin. Numbers on a coordinate grid locate points. Each point is an ordered pair of numbers, for example, a number on the *x*-axis is called an *x*-coordinate. A number on the *y*-axis is called a *y*-coordinate. Ordered pairs are always written in parentheses (*x*-coordinate, *y*-coordinate) with the origin located at (0,0).
- Provide numerous problems for students to solve such as

  Michael has $30. During the summer, he charges $10 to mow neighbors' yards to earn money for his savings account. If he saves his money, how much money will he have after mowing 4 yards, 8 yards, and 12 yards? Create a graph to show the relationship between the number of yards he mowed and the amount of money he saved.

  Ask students to analyze and explain their graphs. Students can also create their own problems to solve, graph, and analyze.
- Provide problems that show "traveling distances" such as the one below. Ask questions such as "Which ordered pair represents the school? Explain a possible path from the school to the home." Have students create their own "traveling distance" problems.

- Focus on vocabulary for this standard because it plays an integral role in the understanding and learning of the coordinate plane system. Include the terms *coordinate system, coordinate plane, first quadrant, points, lines, axis/axes, x-axis, y-axis, horizontal, vertical, intersection of lines, origin, ordered pairs, coordinates, x-coordinate,* and *y-coordinate*.
- Ensure that students have opportunities to talk with the teacher and each other to make sense of what they are learning.

What the STUDENTS do:

- Use the first quadrant of a coordinate grid to represent real-world problems.
- Correctly use ordered pairs.

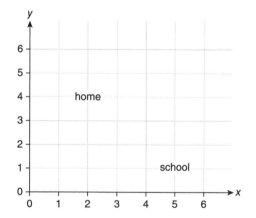

Addressing Student Misconceptions and Common Errors

Fifth graders may not realize how important the order is in plotting a coordinate point. A reminder of the order in ordered pairs may help. In labeling points, the *x*-coordinate is always given first, then the *y*-coordinate. Additional experiences for the students to plot the coordinates correctly may be necessary. Some students may not realize that a coordinate system differs from a grid system. In a coordinate system, the lines, not the area surrounding the lines, are labeled. Providing the opportunity to talk about this will help.

Geometry
5.G.B*

Cluster B

Classify two-dimensional figures into categories based on their properties.

STANDARD 3   **5.G.B.3:** Understand that attributes belonging to a category of two-dimensional figures also belong to all subcategories of that category. *For example, all rectangles have four right angles and squares are rectangles, so all squares have four right angles.*

STANDARD 4   **5.G.B.4:** Classify two-dimensional figures in a hierarchy based on properties.

*Additional cluster

Geometry 5.G.B

Cluster B: Classify two-dimensional figures into categories based on their properties.
Grade 5 Overview

In this cluster students will continue the study of polygons, rhombuses, rectangles, squares, triangles, and quadrilaterals, all previously learned in fourth grade. Fifth graders will also continue to learn about properties of sides and angles.

Standards for Mathematical Practice
SFMP 1. Make sense of problems and persevere in solving them.

Students will become problem solvers as they reason about shapes to create a graphic organizer to classify shapes.

SFMP 6. Attend to precision.

Students will use clear, specific language when discussing their reasoning about shapes.

SFMP 8. Look for and make use of structure.

Students will identify attributes to classify shapes and create a graphic organizer to help them make sense of the hierarchy of shapes.

Related Content Standards

3.G.A.1   4.G.A.1   4.G.A.2

Notes

STANDARD 3 (5.G.B.3)

Understand that attributes belonging to a category of two-dimensional figures also belong to all subcategories of that category. For example, all rectangles have four right angles and squares are rectangles, so all squares have four right angles.

What the TEACHER does:

- Focus on helping fifth graders reason about attributes (properties) of shapes. The properties fifth graders study include sides (parallel, perpendicular, congruent), angles (type, measurement, congruent), and symmetry (point and line).
- Provide experiences for students to discuss the property of shapes, including ideas from the following list:

  o A shape is a quadrilateral when it has exactly 4 sides and is a polygon. (To be a polygon the figure must be a closed plane figure with at least three straight sides.)
  o A square is always a rectangle because a square will always have 4 right angles like a rectangle.
  o A rectangle does not have to have 4 equal sides like a square. It can have 4 right angles without 4 equal sides. So, a rectangle is not always a square.
  o A square is always a rhombus because it has 4 equal sides like a rhombus and it is also a rectangle because it has 4 right angles like a rectangle.
  o A rhombus does not have to have right angles like a square. It can have 4 equal sides without having 4 right angles. Therefore a rhombus is not always a square.
  o A parallelogram can be a rectangle if it has 4 right angles. When investigating whether all quadrilaterals have right angles, students can give examples and non-examples.

- Be sure to help students understand that attributes belonging to a category of two-dimensional figures also belong to all subcategories of that category. For example, all rectangles have four right angles and squares are rectangles, so all squares have four right angles. Direct students to find quadrilaterals around the classroom and then classify them by their attributes. Have students create a list of what they found.
- Focus on vocabulary for this standard, including *attribute, category, subset/subcategory, properties, two-dimensional, polygon, rhombus, rectangle, square, triangle, quadrilateral, pentagon, hexagon, trapezoid, parallel, perpendicular, congruent angles, right angles, acute angles, obtuse angles, symmetry, line,* and *line segment.*

What the STUDENTS do:

- Explain their reasoning about the properties of shapes.
- Use vocabulary associated with the properties of shapes.

Addressing Student Misconceptions and Common Errors

Some students may think that when describing geometric shapes and placing them into subcategories, the last category is the only classification that can be used. As students are creating a chart with subcategories, have them talk about why attributes belonging to a category of two-dimensional figures also belong to *all* subcategories of that category.

Classify two-dimensional figures in a hierarchy based on properties.

What the TEACHER does:

- Lead discussions asking students not only to talk about the properties of polygons but also to reason about the attributes of shapes including triangles. The more ways students can classify and reason about shapes, the better they understand the properties of the shapes. To reason about the shapes, students can investigate things such as:

  o What are ways to classify triangles?
  o Why are trapezoids and kites not classified as parallelograms?
  o Which quadrilaterals have opposite angles congruent?
  o How many lines of symmetry does a regular polygon have?
  o Why is a square always a rectangle?
  o Why is a rectangle not always a square?

- Try a sorting activity. Display the names and pictures of the quadrilateral shapes on the board. Using index cards, ask students to draw one labeled shape on each card. Have students sort the shapes according to their attributes. Ask questions such as "How did you decide where to put each shape? Which shapes have similar attributes? Can a quadrilateral shape belong to more than one subset or subcategory of quadrilaterals? Why or why not?"

- Allow students to create a reference, diagram, or graphic organizer to help them make sense of the hierarchy of shapes, such as the following example.

polygon	a closed plane figure formed from line segments that meet only at their endpoints
quadrilateral	a four-sided polygon
rectangle	a quadrilateral with two pairs of congruent parallel sides and four right angles
rhombus	a parallelogram with all four sides equal in length
square	a parallelogram with four congruent sides and four right angles

What the STUDENTS do:

- Investigate properties of shapes. Sort and classify two-dimensional figures in a hierarchy based on properties.
- Use graphic organizers such as flow charts to compare and contrast the attributes of geometric shapes.

Addressing Student Misconceptions and Common Errors

Some students may not be able to just look at pictures of shapes and talk about their properties. To address this, some students may need to touch and turn the shapes to help determine the properties.

Geometry
Cluster A: Graph points on the coordinate plane to solve real-world and mathematical problems.

Standard: 5.G.A.1. *Use a pair of perpendicular number lines, called axes, to define a coordinate system, with the intersection of the lines (the origin) arranged to coincide with the 0 on each line and a given point in the plane located by using an ordered pair of numbers, called its coordinates. Understand that the first number indicates how far to travel from the origin in the direction of one axis, and the second number indicates how far to travel in the direction of the second axis, with the convention that the names of the two axes and the coordinates correspond (e.g.,* x-axis *and* x-coordinate, y-axis *and* y-coordinate*).*

Standards for Mathematical Practice:
SFMP 6. Attend to precision.
Students will use clear, specific directions, attending to precision as points are plotted on the coordinate plane.

Goal:
Students will create a shape using a coordinate plane and ordered pairs. Students will accurately plot ordered pairs where two lines intersect.

Planning:

Materials: Coordinate grid paper, pencil, paper for each student

Sample Activity:
- On a coordinate grid, have students create a shape using at least six ordered pairs connected with line segments. Ask students to make a list of the ordered pairs for their shape on a separate sheet of paper.
- Students should exchange the lists of coordinates with a classmate to reconstruct each other's shape via the written directions.
- Students should check their work with another classmate.

Questions/Prompts:

- Can students explain how to use an ordered pair to locate a point on the coordinate plane?
- Can students accurately plot ordered pairs where two lines intersect?
- Can students describe an ordered pair of numbers (4,5) using correct terminology, that is, *x*-axis, and so on?

Differentiating Instruction:

Struggling Students: Some students may not understand that the first number of the ordered pair (*x*-axis) indicates how far to move horizontally from the origin and must occur first. Listen to students explain what they are doing as they plot ordered pairs. Provide additional experiences to develop this skill.

Extension: Instead of creating a shape, allow each student to create a picture using ordered pairs on the coordinate plane. Have the students make a list of the ordered pairs for their picture on a separate sheet of paper. Place the directions, pencil, and coordinate grids in a learning station for students to work on for extended learning.

Geometry

Cluster A: Graph points on the coordinate plane to solve real-world and mathematical problems.

Standard:

Standards for Mathematical Practice:

Goal:

Planning:

Materials:

Sample Activity:

Questions/Prompts:

Differentiating Instruction:

Struggling Students:

Extension:

Geometry

Cluster B: Classify two-dimensional figures into categories based on their properties.

Standard:

Standards for Mathematical Practice:

Goal:

Planning:

Materials:

Sample Activity:

Questions/Prompts:

Differentiating Instruction:

Struggling Students:

Extension:

Reflection Questions: Geometry

1. Explain why students in grades 3–5 must have opportunities to talk with other students and their teachers to make sense of the geometry they are learning.

2. Discuss why it is critical for teachers to think and know about potential student misconceptions before a geometry lesson is taught.

3. Explain why solving real-world problems in geometry can motivate student learning.

4. Talk about why focusing on geometrical terminology and vocabulary is critical to student achievement on assessment tests.

Resources

Table 1 Addition and Subtraction Situations, Grades 3–5

Situation	Problem	Equation(s)
Add to—result unknown	Frank had 235 pennies. Mark gave him 156 more. How many pennies does Frank have?	**235 + 156 = p**
Add to—change unknown	Frank had 235 pennies. Mark gave him some more. Now Frank has 391 pennies. How many pennies did Mark give to Frank?	**235 + p = 391**
Add—start unknown	Frank had some pennies in his piggy bank. Mark gave him 156 more. Now Frank has 391 pennies. How many pennies did Frank have at the beginning?	**p + 156 = 391**
Take from—result unknown	Frank had 45 pennies. He spent 29 pennies on a package of jawbreakers. How many pennies does he have left?	**45 − 29 = p**
Take from—change unknown	Frank had 45 pennies. He spent some pennies on a pack of jawbreakers. Now Frank has 16 pennies. How much did he spend on the jawbreaker?	**45 − p = 16**
Take from—start unknown	Frank had some pennies in his bank. He spent 29 pennies on a package of jawbreakers. Now he has 16 pennies. How many pennies did Frank have in his bank?	**p − 29 = 16**
Put together take apart—total unknown	Anna has been saving coins. She has 348 pennies and 267 nickels. How many coins does she have?	**348 + 267 = p**
Put together take apart—addend unknown	Anna 615 coins in her piggy bank. She has 348 pennies and the rest are nickels. How many coins are nickels?	**615 = 348 + p**
Put together take apart—addends unknown	Anna has 11 coins. Some are pennies and some are nickels. How many pennies and how many nickels could Anna have?	**1 + 10 = 11** **2 + 9 = 11** **3 + 8 = 11** **4 + 7 = 11** **5 + 6 = 11** **6 + 5 = 11** **7 + 4 = 11** **8 + 3 = 11** **9 + 2 = 11** **10 + 1 = 11**

Table 1 (Continued)

Situation	Problem	Equation(s)
Compare— difference unknown How many more?	Marty used $2\frac{1}{3}$ feet of wrapping paper to wrap a present. Tony used $3\frac{2}{3}$ feet. How much more paper did Tony use?	$2\frac{1}{3} + p = 3\frac{2}{3}$ $3\frac{2}{3} - p = 2\frac{1}{3}$
Compare— difference unknown How many fewer?	Marty used $2\frac{1}{3}$ feet of wrapping paper to wrap a present. Tony used $3\frac{2}{3}$ feet. How much less paper did Marty use?	$2\frac{1}{3} + p = 3\frac{2}{3}$ $3\frac{2}{3} - p = 2\frac{1}{3}$
Compare— bigger unknown More version	Tony used $1\frac{1}{3}$ more feet of wrapping paper to wrap a present than Marty used. Marty used $2\frac{1}{3}$ feet. How much paper did Tony use?	$1\frac{1}{3} + 2\frac{1}{3} = t$ $2\frac{1}{3} + 1\frac{1}{3} = t$
Compare— bigger unknown Fewer version	Marty used $1\frac{1}{3}$ fewer feet of wrapping paper to wrap a present than Tony used. If Marty used $2\frac{1}{3}$ feet, how much paper did Tony use?	$1\frac{1}{3} + 2\frac{1}{3} = t$ $2\frac{1}{3} + 1\frac{1}{3} = t$
Compare— smaller unknown Fewer version	Marty used $1\frac{1}{3}$ fewer feet of wrapping paper to wrap a present than Tony used. If Tony used $3\frac{2}{3}$ feet, how much paper did Marty use?	$3\frac{2}{3} - 1\frac{1}{3} = m$ $m + 1\frac{1}{3} = 3\frac{2}{3}$
Compare— smaller unknown More version	Tony used $1\frac{1}{3}$ more feet of wrapping paper to wrap a present than Marty used. If Tony used $3\frac{2}{3}$ feet, how much paper did Marty use?	$3\frac{2}{3} - 1\frac{1}{3} = m$ $m + 1\frac{1}{3} = 3\frac{2}{3}$

Table 2 Multiplication and Division Situations, Grades 3–5

Situation	Known/Unknown Information	Sample Problem	Model	Equation
Equal Groups Multiplication *Introduce: Grade 3* *Extend: Grades 4–5*	**Known:** • Number of groups • Number of items in a group **Unknown:** • Total number of items	Four children want to play marbles. Each child needs 5 marbles. How many marbles so all 4 children can play?		4 × 5 = ___
Equal Groups Partitive division *Introduce: Grade 3* *Extend: Grades 4–5*	**Known:** • Total number of items • Number of groups **Unknown:** • Number of items in each group	There are 20 marbles in the jar. Four student want to play marbles. How many marbles will each child get?		4 × ___ = 20 20 ÷ 4 = ___
Equal Groups Measurement division *Introduce: Grade 3* *Extend: Grades 4–5*	**Known:** • Total number of items • Number of items in each group **Unknown:** • Number of groups	There are 20 marbles in the jar. Each child needs 5 marbles to play the game. How many children can play?		___ × 5 = 20 20 ÷ 5 = ___
Equal Groups *(Measurement situation)* Multiplication *Introduce: Grade 3* *Extend: Grades 4–5*	**Known:** • Number of groups • Number of items in a group **Unknown:** • Total number of items	I have 4 pieces of ribbon to make a bow. Each piece must be 5 inches long. How much ribbon will I need to make the bow?		4 × 5 = ___
Equal Groups *(Measurement situation)* Partitive division *Introduce: Grade 3* *Extend: Grades 4–5*	**Known:** • Total number of items • Number of groups **Unknown:** • Number of items in each group	I have 20 inches of ribbon. I need 4 pieces that are the same length to make a box. How long should each piece be?		4 × ___ = 20 20 ÷ 4 = ___

Table 2 (Continued)

Situation	Known/Unknown Information	Sample Problem	Model	Equation
Equal Groups *(Measurement situation)* Measurement division *Introduce: Grade 3 Extend: Grades 4–5*	**Known:** • Total number of items • Number of items in each group **Unknown:** • Number of groups	I have 20 inches of ribbon. I need some pieces that are 5 inches long to make a bow. How many pieces can I cut?	20 inches / 5 / 5 / 5 / 5 / 4 parts	____ × 5 = 20 20 ÷ 5 = ____
Arrays Multiplication *Introduce: Grade 3 Extend: Grades 4–5*	**Known:** • Number of rows • Number of items in a row **Unknown:** • Total number of items	My garden has 4 rows and 5 tomato plants in each row. How many tomato plants are in my garden?		4 × 5 = ____
Arrays Partitive division *Introduce: Grade 3 Extend: Grades 4–5*	**Known:** • Total number of items • Number of rows **Unknown:** • Number of items in a row	My garden has 20 tomato plants. There are 4 rows with the same number of plants in each row. How many plants are in each row?	row 20 plants 1, 2, 3, 4 (X array)	4 × ____ = 20 20 ÷ 4 = ____
Arrays Measurement division *Introduce: Grade 3 Extend: Grades 4–5*	**Known:** • Total number of items • Number items in each row **Unknown:** • Number of rows	My garden has 20 tomato plants. There are 5 plants in each row. How many rows are in my garden?	20 plants 5, 10, 15, 20 small (X array)	____ × 5 = 20 20 ÷ 5 = ____
Area *Introduce: Grade 3 Extend: Grades 4–5*	**Known:** • Dimensions of the rectangle **Unknown:** • Area of the rectangle	The length of my garden is 4 feet. The width is 5 feet. What is the area of my garden?	5 ft, 4 ft	4 × 5 = ____
Area *Introduce: Grade 3 Extend: Grades 4–5*	**Known:** • Area of the rectangle • One dimension **Unknown:** • The other dimension	The area of my garden is 20 feet. It is 4 feet long. How wide is my garden? Or . . . The area of my garden is 20 feet. It is 5 feet wide. How long is my garden?	4 ft, 20 sq. ft, ?	4 × ____ = 20 ____ × 5 = 20 20 ÷ 5 = ____ 20 ÷ 4 = ____

(Continued)

Table 2 (Continued)

Situation	Known/Unknown Information	Sample Problem	Model	Equation
Comparison Multiplication *Introduce: Grade 4* *Extend: Grade 5*	**Known:** • Smaller number of items • Multiplier **Unknown:** • The other number of items	Anna has 5 marbles. Ray has 4 times as many. How many marbles does Ray have?	OOOOO Anna OOOOO OOOOO OOOOO OOOOO]Ray Ray has 20 marbles.	4 × 5 = _____
Comparison Partitive division *Introduce: Grade 4* *Extend: Grade 5*	**Known:** • Larger number of items • Multiplier **Unknown:** • Smaller number of items	Ray has 20 marbles. That is 4 times as many as Anna. How many marbles does Anna have?	OOOOO OOOOO]Ray OOOOO OOOOO ●●●●● Anna has 5 marbles.	4 × _____ = 20 20 ÷ 4 = _____
Comparison Measurement division *Introduce: Grade 4* *Extend: Grade 5*	**Known:** • Larger number of items • Smaller number of items **Unknown:** • Multiplier	Ray has 20 marbles. Anna has 5 marbles. How many times as many marbles as Anna does Ray have?	OOOOO OOOOO ●●●●● OOOOO Ray has 4 times as many.	_____ × 5 = 20 20 ÷ 5 = _____
Comparison *(Measurement situation)* Multiplication *Introduce: Grade 4* *Extend: Grade 5*	**Known:** • Shorter length* • Multiplier **Unknown:** • Longer length* *adjust for other measurement situations	Bruce drove 5 miles. Bob drove 4 times as far. How far did Bob drive?	5 miles Bruce 5 5 5 5 Bob Bob drove 20 miles.	4 × 5 = _____
Comparison *(Measurement situation)* Partitive division *Introduce: Grade 4* *Extend: Grade 5*	**Known:** • Longer length • Multiplier **Unknown:** • Shorter length	Bob drove 20 miles. That is 4 times as far as Bruce drove. How far did Bruce drive?	20 miles Bob 5 Bruce Bruce drove 5 miles.	4 × _____ = 20 20 ÷ 4 = _____
Comparison *(Measurement situation)* Measurement division *Introduce: Grade 4* *Extend: Grade 5*	**Known:** • Longer length • Shorter length **Unknown:** • Multiplier	Bob drove 20 miles. Bruce drove 5 miles. How many times farther did Bob drive compared to Bruce?	20 miles Bob 5 5 5 5 Bob drove 4 times farther.	_____ × 5 = 20 20 ÷ 5 = _____

Table 3 Standards for Mathematical Practice

Standard for Mathematical Practice	What the Teacher Does	What the Students Do

1. Make sense of problems and persevere in solving them.	• Provides students with rich tasks that focus on and promote student understanding of an important mathematical concept.
	• Provides time for and facilitates the discussion of problem solutions using engaging questions.
	
	  ○ What are you trying to find out?
	  ○ Have you solved similar problems before?
	  ○ What is your plan for solving the problem?
	  ○ Can you explain how you solved the problem?
	  ○ Does your answer make sense?
	  ○ Can you use a different method to check your answer?
		• Actively engage in solving problems by working to understand the information that is in the problem and the question that is asked.
		• Choose appropriate manipulatives or drawings to help make sense of the actions in the problem.
		• Use a variety of strategies that make sense to solve the problem.
		• Ask themselves if their solution makes sense.

2. Reason abstractly and quantitatively.	• Provides a variety of concrete materials and encourage their use to help students develop mathematical ideas.
	• Gives students problem situations and encourages varied solution paths.
	• Helps students use mathematical reasoning by asking question such as
	
	  ○ Can you tell me what is happening here?
	  ○ How can you show what is happening in the problem using materials?
	  ○ Can you write a number sentence (equation) to match the story?
	  ○ What do the numbers in the number sentence mean?
		• Use various strategies, models, and drawings to think about the mathematics of a task or example.
		• Demonstrate mathematical understanding about the "numberness" of a given situation (quantitative reasoning).
		• Connect concrete examples with pictorial and symbolic representations as developmentally appropriate.

3. Construct viable arguments and critique the reasoning of others.	• Provides tasks that encourage students to construct mathematical arguments.
	• Expects students to explain their strategies and mathematical thinking to others.
	• Expects students to listen to the reasoning of others.
	• Helps students to compare strategies and methods by asking questions such as
	
	  ○ How can you prove that your answer is correct?
	  ○ What do you think about _____'s strategy?
	  ○ How is your method different than _____'s? How is it similar?
	  ○ What questions do you have for _____?
		• Explain their strategies and thinking orally or in writing using concrete models, drawings, actions, or numbers.
		• Use number sense to determine whether a solution is reasonable.
		• Listen to the thinking of others in the class.
		• Ask questions of one another and of the teacher to clarify their understanding.
		• Look for similarities among different ways to solve problems.

(Continued)

Resources **259**

Table 3 (Continued)

Standard for Mathematical Practice	What the Teacher Does	What the Students Do

4. **Model with mathematics.**	• Provides a variety of materials for students to use as they work to make sense of mathematical ideas and solve problems.
	• Uses real-world applications that are developmentally appropriate for students.
	• Uses the progression of developing conceptual understanding through the use of concrete models, pictorial models, and, when students are ready, symbolic representations.
	• Encourages students to use models as they create mathematical arguments and explain their thinking to others.
	• Ask students questions such as
	  ○ Can you show me how you solved this using a _____?
	  ○ Can you draw a picture or act out what is happening in the problem?
	  ○ Is this working or do you need to change your model?
		• Put the problem or situation in their own words.
		• Model the situation using concrete materials and an appropriate strategy (part-part-whole, bar model, place value chart, fraction bars).
		• Describe what they do with the models and how it relates to the problem situation.
		• Check to see whether an answer makes sense and change the model when necessary.

5. **Use appropriate tools strategically.**	• Encourages students to use models in constructing mathematical arguments. • Provides a variety of concrete materials and encourages their use to help students develop mathematical ideas. • Helps students to link concrete to pictorial to numerical representations as developmentally appropriate.	• Select materials that will help to develop mathematical understanding. • Begin to make the transition from concrete to pictorial representations when conceptual understanding is apparent. • Determine whether using mental computation, concrete models, or paper and pencil is the most efficient way to solve a problem or task.

6. **Attend to precision.**	• Supports students in developing an understanding of mathematical vocabulary by explicitly introducing terms and having them available for students to use (for example, by using a word wall).
	• Repeats a student's explanation using accurate vocabulary when necessary.
	• Supports students' precision by asking them the following questions:
	  ○ What does _____ mean?
	  ○ What labels could you use with your answer?
	  ○ What unit of measure would you use when you are measuring _____?
		• Communicate using grade-level-appropriate vocabulary.
		• Work to carefully formulate clear explanations.
		• State the meaning of symbols, calculate accurately and efficiently.
		• Choose appropriate units of measure.
		• Label accurately when measuring.

Table 3 (Continued)

Standard for Mathematical Practice	What the Teacher Does	What the Students Do
7. **Look for and make use of structure.**	<ul><li>Provides explicit situations in which students can use a strategy to develop understanding of a concept.</li><li>Supports student thinking by providing materials that are appropriate to the concept (for example, using tiles and area models in learning multiplication and division facts).</li><li>Asks questions that help students see the structure of the mathematics and make generalizations.<ul><li>What happens when you multiply a number by 0?</li><li>What happens when you multiply a number by a multiple of ten? Why?</li><li>Compare what happens when you divide 250 by 5 with when you divide 250 by 50. Find similar examples and predict the quotient.</li><li>How can you use what you know to explain why this works?</li><li>What patterns do you see?</li></ul></li></ul>	<ul><li>Look for patterns when developing conceptual understanding of place value, addition, subtraction, and other grade-level concepts.</li><li>Recognize patterns related to properties of addition and subtraction.</li><li>Identify efficient strategies to use in a variety of situations using concrete materials and then generalizing to any similar situation.</li><li>Develop conceptual understanding by working to determine why numbers work the way they do.</li></ul>
8. **Look for and express regularity in repeated reasoning.**	<ul><li>Provides a variety of examples that explicitly focus on patterns and repeated reasoning.</li><li>Asks students to fine-tune their mathematical arguments with questions such as<ul><li>What do you notice about the products of 3 × 5 and 5 × 3?</li><li>If you think about the value of the numbers, can you find an easier way to think about the problem?</li><li>How could this problem help you solve another problem?</li></ul></li></ul>	<ul><li>Notice repeated calculations and make generalizations.</li><li>Continually evaluate the reasonableness of their answers and their thinking.</li><li>Make generalizations by seeing patterns based on properties or models and use these generalizations to develop conceptual understanding.</li></ul>

Table 4 Effective Teaching Practices

Teaching Practice	Purpose	What the Teacher Does	What the Students Do

1. **Establish mathematics goals to focus learning.**	• Set the stage to guide instructional decisions.
	• Include expecting students to understand the purpose of a lesson beyond simply repeating the Standard.
		• Considers broad goals as well as the goals of the unit and the lesson including:
		  ○ What is to be learned?
		  ○ Why is the goal important?
		  ○ Where students need to go?
		  ○ How can learning be extended?
			• Make sense of the new concepts and skills, making connections to concepts learned in K–2.
			• Experience connections among the Standards and across domains.
			• Deepen their understanding and expect mathematics to make sense.

2. **Implement tasks that promote reasoning and problem solving.**	• Provide opportunities for students to engage in exploration and make sense of important mathematics.
	• Encourage students to use procedures in ways that are connected to understanding.
		• Chooses tasks that
		  ○ are built on current student understandings;
		  ○ have various entry points with multiple ways for the problems to be solved;
		  ○ are interesting to students.
			• Work to make sense out of the task and persevere in solving problems.
			• Use a variety of models and materials to make sense of the mathematics in the task.
			• Convince themselves and others the answer is reasonable.

3. **Use and connect mathematical representations.**	• Concrete representations lead students to developing conceptual understanding and later connect that understanding to procedural skills.	• Uses tasks that allow students to use a variety of representations. • Encourages the use of different representations, including concrete models, pictures, words, and numbers, that support students in explaining their thinking and reasoning.	• Use materials to make sense out of problem situations. • Connect representations to mathematical concepts and the structure of big ideas, including operational sense, place value with whole numbers, fractions, and decimals.
4. **Facilitate meaningful mathematical discourse.**	• Provide students with opportunities to share ideas, clarify their understanding, and develop convincing arguments. • Talking and sharing aloud advances the mathematical thinking of the whole class.	• Engages students in explaining their mathematical reasoning in small-group and classroom situations. • Facilitates discussions among students that supports making sense of a variety of strategies and approaches. • Scaffolds classroom discussions so that connections between representations and mathematical ideas take place.	• Explain their ideas and reasoning in small groups and with the entire class. • Listen to the reasoning of others. • Ask questions of others to make sense of their ideas.
5. **Pose purposeful questions.**	• Reveal students' current understanding of a concept. • Encourage students to explain, elaborate, and clarify thinking. • Make the learning of mathematics more visible and accessible for students.	• Asks questions that build on and extend student thinking. • Is intentional about the kinds of questions asked to make the mathematics more visible to students. • Uses wait time to provide students with time to think and examine their ideas.	• Think more deeply about the process of the mathematics rather than simply focusing on the answer. • Listen to and comment on the explanations of others in the class.

Table 4 (Continued)

Teaching Practice	Purpose	What the Teacher Does	What the Students Do
6. **Build procedural fluency from conceptual understanding.**	• Experiences with concrete materials allow students to make sense of important mathematics and flexibly choose from a variety of methods to solve problems.	• Provides opportunities for students to reason about mathematical ideas. • Expects students to explain why their strategies work. • Connects student methods to efficient procedures as appropriate.	• Understand and explain the procedures they are using and why they work. • Use a variety of strategies to solve problems and make sense of mathematical ideas. • Do not rely on shortcuts or tricks to do mathematics.
7. **Support productive struggle in learning mathematics.**	• Productive struggle is significant and essential to learning mathematics with understanding. • Allow students to grapple with ideas and relationships. • Giving young students ample time to work with and make sense out of new ideas is critical to their learning with understanding.	• Supports student struggle without showing and telling a procedure but rather focusing on the important mathematical ideas. • Asks questions that scaffold student thinking. • Builds questions and lessons on important student mistakes rather than focusing on the correct answer. • Recognizes the importance of effort as students work to make sense of new ideas.	• Stick to a task and recognize that struggle is part of making sense. • Ask questions that will help them to better understand the task. • Support each other with ideas rather than telling others the answer or how to solve a problem.
8. **Elicit and use evidence of student thinking.**	• Eliciting and using evidence of student thinking helps teachers assess learning progress and can be used to make instructional decisions during the lessons as well as help to prepare what will occur in the next lesson. • Formative assessment through student written and oral ideas are excellent artifacts to assess student thinking and understanding.	• Determines what to look for in gathering evidence of student learning. • Poses questions and answer student questions that provide information about student understanding, strategies, and reasoning. • Uses evidence to determine next steps of instruction.	• Accept that reasoning and understanding are as important as the answer to a problem. • Use mistakes and misconceptions to rethink their understanding. • Ask questions of the teacher and peers to clarify confusion or misunderstanding. • Self-assess and progress toward developing mathematical understanding.

Source: Adapted from *Principles to Actions*, National Council of Teachers of Mathematics (2014).

CCSS Where to Focus Grade 3 Mathematics

CCSS
WHERE TO FOCUS
GRADE 3
MATHEMATICS

MATH · 3 · F

MATHEMATICS · GRADE 3 · FOCUS

This document shows where students and teachers should spend the large majority of their time in order to meet the expectations of the Standards.

Not all content in a given grade is emphasized equally in the Standards. Some clusters require greater emphasis than others based on the depth of the ideas, the time that they take to master, and/or their importance to future mathematics or the demands of college and career readiness. More time in these areas is also necessary for students to meet the Standards for Mathematical Practice.

To say that some things have greater emphasis is not to say that anything in the Standards can safely be neglected in instruction. Neglecting material will leave gaps in student skill and understanding and may leave students unprepared for the challenges of a later grade.

Students should spend the large majority[1] of their time on the major work of the grade (■). Supporting work (□) and, where appropriate, additional work (○) can engage students in the major work of the grade.[2,3]

MAJOR, SUPPORTING, AND ADDITIONAL CLUSTERS FOR GRADE 3

Emphases are given at the cluster level. Refer to the Common Core State Standards for Mathematics for the specific standards that fall within each cluster.

Key: ■ Major Clusters   □ Supporting Clusters   ○ Additional Clusters

3.OA.A	■	Represent and solve problems involving multiplication and division.
3.OA.B	■	Understand properties of multiplication and the relationship between multiplication and division.
3.OA.C	■	Multiply and divide within 100.
3.OA.D	■	Solve problems involving the four operations, and identify and explain patterns in arithmetic.
3.NBT.A	○	Use place value understanding and properties of operations to perform multi-digit arithmetic.
3.NF.A	■	Develop understanding of fractions as numbers.
3.MD.A	■	Solve problems involving measurement and estimation of intervals of time, liquid volumes, and masses of objects.
3.MD.B	□	Represent and interpret data.
3.MD.C	■	Geometric measurement: understand concepts of area and relate area to multiplication and to addition.
3.MD.D	○	Geometric measurement: recognize perimeter as an attribute of plane figures and distinguish between linear and area measures.
3.G.A	□	Reason with shapes and their attributes.

HIGHLIGHTS OF MAJOR WORK IN GRADES K–8

K–2	Addition and subtraction – concepts, skills, and problem solving; place value
3–5	Multiplication and division of whole numbers and fractions – concepts, skills, and problem solving
6	Ratios and proportional relationships; early expressions and equations
7	Ratios and proportional relationships; arithmetic of rational numbers
8	Linear algebra and linear functions

REQUIRED FLUENCIES FOR GRADE 3

3.OA.C.7	Single-digit products and quotients (Products from memory by end of Grade 3)
3.NBT.A.2	Add/subtract within 1000

1 At least 65% and up to approximately 85% of class time, with Grades K–2 nearer the upper end of that range, should be devoted to the major work of the grade. For more information, see Criterion #1 of the K–8 Publishers' Criteria for the Common Core State Standards for Mathematics www.achievethecore.org/publisherscriteria.

2 Refer also to criterion #3 in the K–8 Publishers' Criteria for the Common Core State Standards for Mathematics www.achievethecore.org/publisherscriteria.

3 Note, the critical areas are a survey of what will be taught at each grade level; the major work is the subset of topics that deserve the large majority of instructional time during a given year to best prepare students for college and careers.

STUDENT ACHIEVEMENT PARTNERS

Find additional resources at achievethecore.org

Source: http://achievethecore.org

CCSS Where to Focus Grade 4 Mathematics

CCSS
WHERE TO FOCUS
GRADE 4
MATHEMATICS

MATH | **4** | **F**

MATHEMATICS | GRADE 4 | FOCUS

This document shows where students and teachers should spend the large majority of their time in order to meet the expectations of the Standards.

Not all content in a given grade is emphasized equally in the Standards. Some clusters require greater emphasis than others based on the depth of the ideas, the time that they take to master, and/or their importance to future mathematics or the demands of college and career readiness. More time in these areas is also necessary for students to meet the Standards for Mathematical Practice.

To say that some things have greater emphasis is not to say that anything in the Standards can safely be neglected in instruction. Neglecting material will leave gaps in student skill and understanding and may leave students unprepared for the challenges of a later grade.

Students should spend the large majority[1] of their time on the major work of the grade (■). Supporting work (☐) and, where appropriate, additional work (○) can engage students in the major work of the grade.[2, 3]

MAJOR, SUPPORTING, AND ADDITIONAL CLUSTERS FOR GRADE 4

Emphases are given at the cluster level. Refer to the Common Core State Standards for Mathematics for the specific standards that fall within each cluster.

Key: ■ Major Clusters ☐ Supporting Clusters ○ Additional Clusters

4.OA.A	■	Use the four operations with whole numbers to solve problems.
4.OA.B	☐	Gain familiarity with factors and multiples.
4.OA.C	○	Generate and analyze patterns.
4.NBT.A	■	Generalize place value understanding for multi-digit whole numbers.
4.NBT.B	■	Use place value understanding and properties of operations to perform multi-digit arithmetic.
4.NF.A	■	Extend understanding of fraction equivalence and ordering.
4.NF.B	■	Build fractions from unit fractions by applying and extending previous understandings of operations on whole numbers.
4.NF.C	■	Understand decimal notation for fractions, and compare decimal fractions.
4.MD.A	☐	Solve problems involving measurement and conversion of measurements from a larger unit to a smaller unit.
4.MD.B	☐	Represent and interpret data.
4.MD.C	○	Geometric measurement: understand concepts of angle and measure angles.
4.G.A	○	Draw and identify lines and angles, and classify shapes by properties of their lines and angles.

HIGHLIGHTS OF MAJOR WORK IN GRADES K–8

K–2	Addition and subtraction – concepts, skills, and problem solving; place value
3–5	Multiplication and division of whole numbers and fractions – concepts, skills, and problem solving
6	Ratios and proportional relationships; early expressions and equations
7	Ratios and proportional relationships; arithmetic of rational numbers
8	Linear algebra and linear functions

REQUIRED FLUENCIES FOR GRADE 4

4.NBT.B.4	Add/subtract within 1,000,000

STUDENT
ACHIEVEMENT
PARTNERS

Find additional resources at achievethecore.org

1 At least 65% and up to approximately 85% of class time, with Grades K–2 nearer the upper end of that range, should be devoted to the major work of the grade. For more information, see Criterion #1 of the K–8 Publishers' Criteria for the Common Core State Standards for Mathematics www.achievethecore.org/publisherscriteria.

2 Refer also to criterion #3 in the K–8 Publishers' Criteria for the Common Core State Standards for Mathematics www.achievethecore.org/publisherscriteria.

3 Note, the critical areas are a survey of what will be taught at each grade level; the major work is the subset of topics that deserve the large majority of instructional time during a given year to best prepare students for college and careers.

Source: http://achievethecore.org

Resources **265**

CCSS Where to Focus Grade 5 Mathematics

CCSS
WHERE TO FOCUS
GRADE 5
MATHEMATICS

MATH 5 F

MATHEMATICS   GRADE 5   FOCUS

This document shows where students and teachers should spend the large majority of their time in order to meet the expectations of the Standards.

Not all content in a given grade is emphasized equally in the Standards. Some clusters require greater emphasis than others based on the depth of the ideas, the time that they take to master, and/or their importance to future mathematics or the demands of college and career readiness. More time in these areas is also necessary for students to meet the Standards for Mathematical Practice.

To say that some things have greater emphasis is not to say that anything in the Standards can safely be neglected in instruction. Neglecting material will leave gaps in student skill and understanding and may leave students unprepared for the challenges of a later grade.

Students should spend the large majority[1] of their time on the major work of the grade ( ). Supporting work ( ) and, where appropriate, additional work ( ) can engage students in the major work of the grade.[2,3]

MAJOR, SUPPORTING, AND ADDITIONAL CLUSTERS FOR GRADE 5

Emphases are given at the cluster level. Refer to the Common Core State Standards for Mathematics for the specific standards that fall within each cluster.

Key: ■ Major Clusters   ☐ Supporting Clusters   ○ Additional Clusters

5.OA.A	○ Write and interpret numerical expressions.
5.OA.B	○ Analyze patterns and relationships.
5.NBT.A	■ Understand the place value system.
5.NBT.B	■ Perform operations with multi-digit whole numbers and with decimals to hundredths.
5.NF.A	■ Use equivalent fractions as a strategy to add and subtract fractions.
5.NF.B	■ Apply and extend previous understandings of multiplication and division to multiply and divide fractions.
5.MD.A	☐ Convert like measurement units within a given measurement system.
5.MD.B	☐ Represent and interpret data.
5.MD.C	■ Geometric measurement: understand concepts of volume and relate volume to multiplication and to addition.
5.G.A	○ Graph points on the coordinate plane to solve real-world and mathematical problems.
5.G.B	○ Classify two-dimensional figures into categories based on their properties.

HIGHLIGHTS OF MAJOR WORK IN GRADES K–8

K–2	Addition and subtraction – concepts, skills, and problem solving; place value
3–5	Multiplication and division of whole numbers and fractions – concepts, skills, and problem solving
6	Ratios and proportional relationships; early expressions and equations
7	Ratios and proportional relationships; arithmetic of rational numbers
8	Linear algebra and linear functions

REQUIRED FLUENCIES FOR GRADE 5

5.NBT.B.5	Multi-digit multiplication

STUDENT
ACHIEVEMENT
PARTNERS

Find additional resources at achievethecore.org

1 At least 65% and up to approximately 85% of class time, with Grades K–2 nearer the upper end of that range, should be devoted to the major work of the grade. For more information, see Criterion #1 of the K–8 Publishers' Criteria for the Common Core State Standards for Mathematics www.achievethecore.org/publisherscriteria.

2 Refer also to criterion #3 in the K–8 Publishers' Criteria for the Common Core State Standards for Mathematics www.achievethecore.org/publisherscriteria.

3 Note, the critical areas are a survey of what will be taught at each grade level; the major work is the subset of topics that deserve the large majority of instructional time during a given year to best prepare students for college and careers.

Source: http://achievethecore.org

Reproducibles

1	2	3	4	5	6	7	8	9	10
11	12	13	14	15	16	17	18	19	20
21	22	23	24	25	26	27	28	29	30
31	32	33	34	35	36	37	38	39	40
41	42	43	44	45	46	47	48	49	50
51	52	53	54	55	56	57	58	59	60
61	62	63	64	65	66	67	68	69	70
71	72	73	74	75	76	77	78	79	80
81	82	83	84	85	86	87	88	89	90
91	92	93	94	95	96	97	98	99	100

Reproducible 2. Place Value Chart to Hundreds

hundreds	tens	ones

1 cm Graph Paper

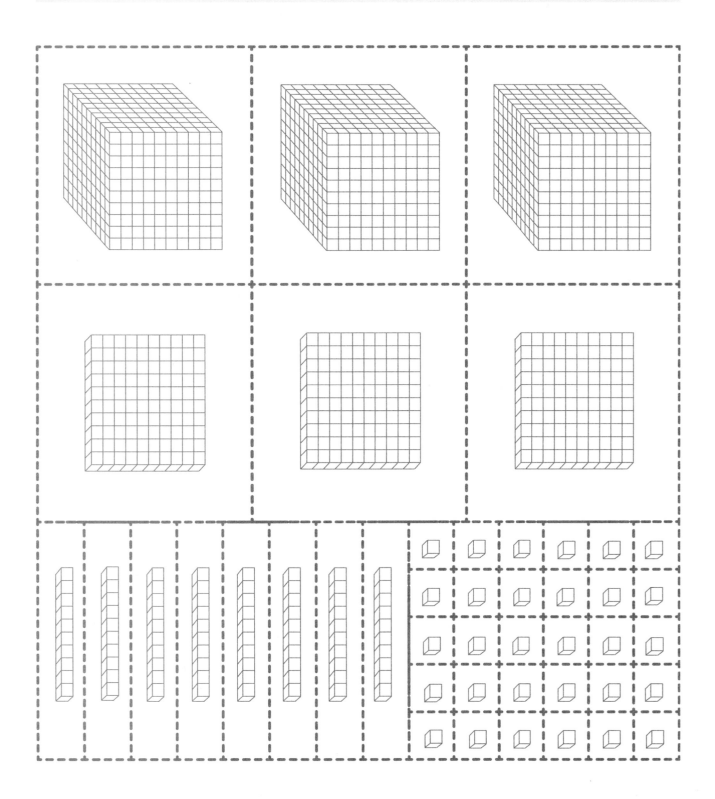

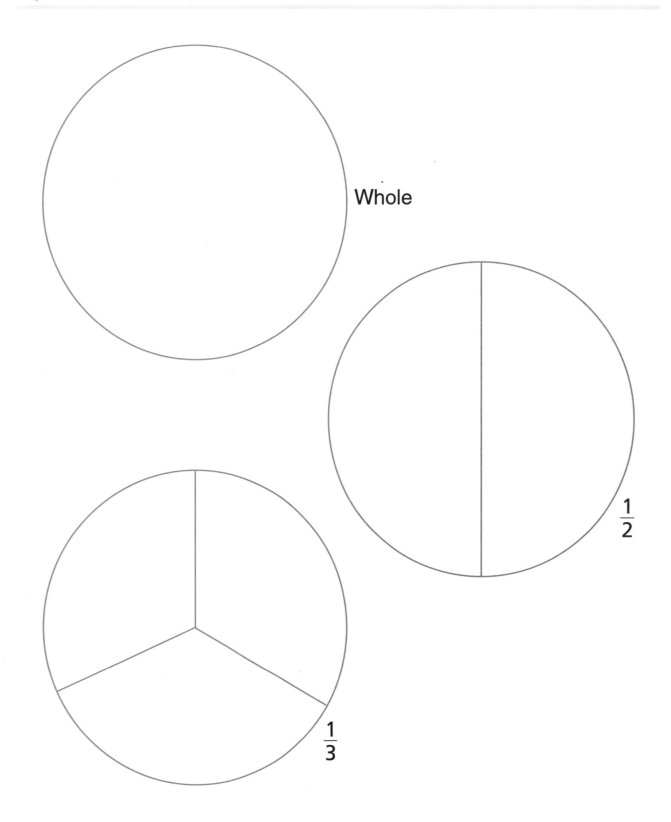

Whole

$\dfrac{1}{2}$

$\dfrac{1}{3}$

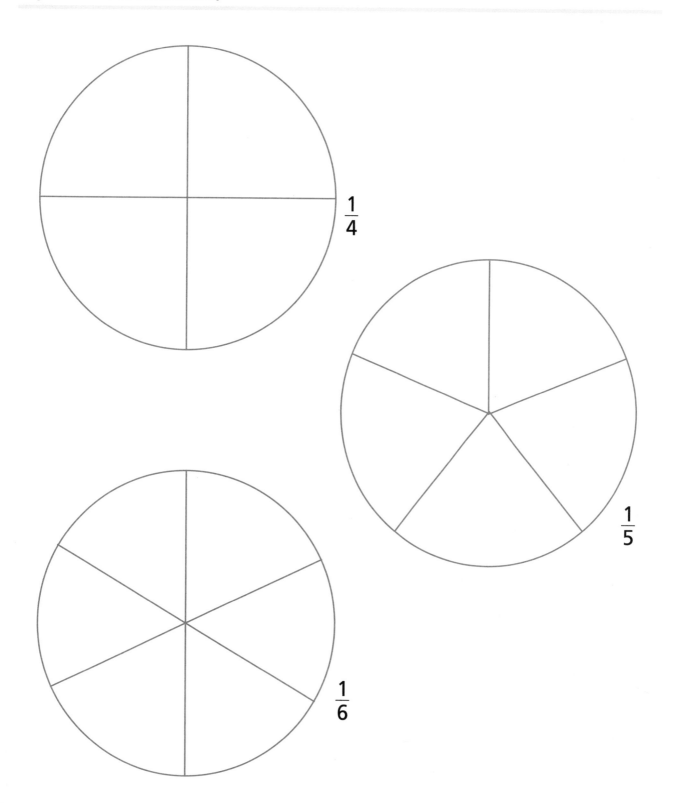

(Continued)

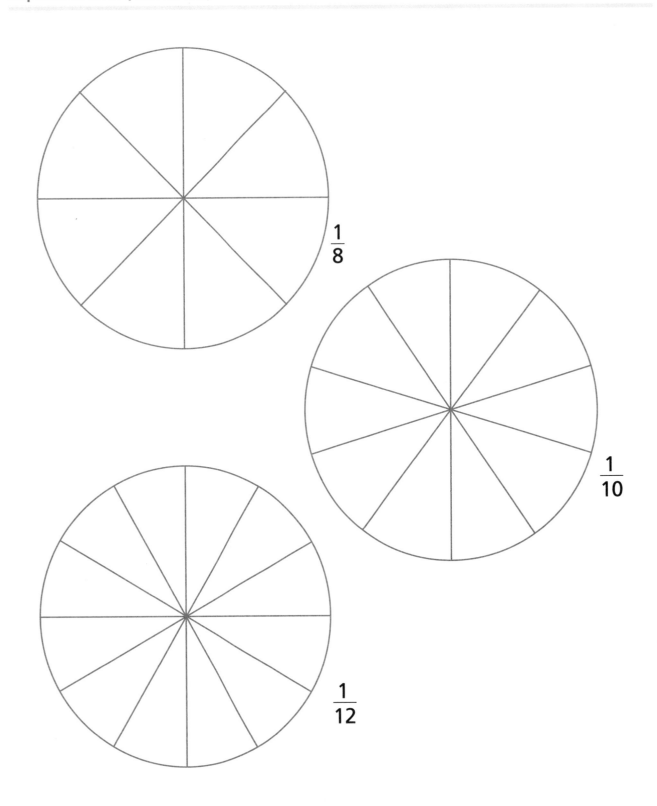

$\frac{1}{8}$

$\frac{1}{10}$

$\frac{1}{12}$

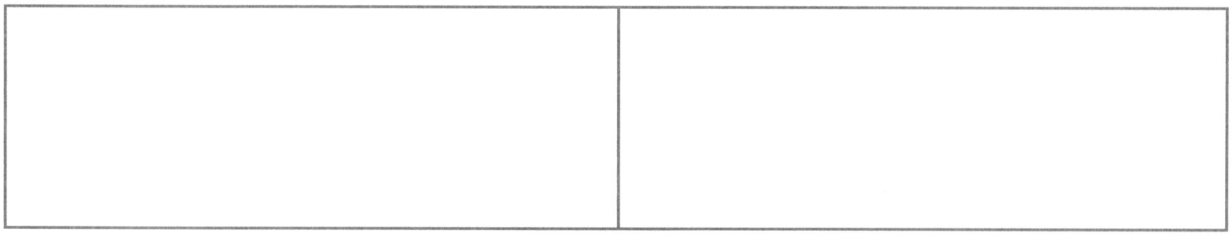

halves

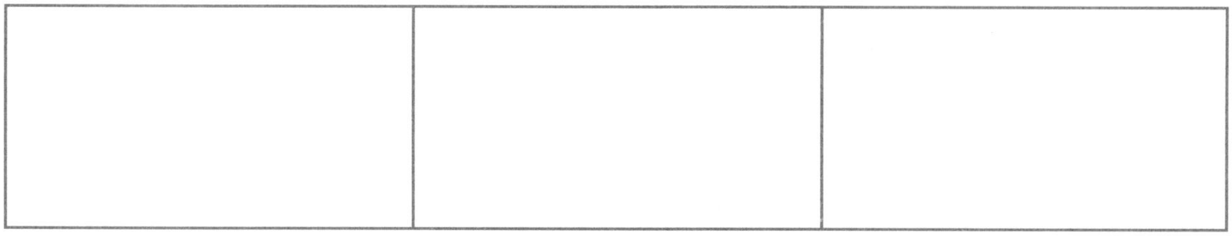

thirds

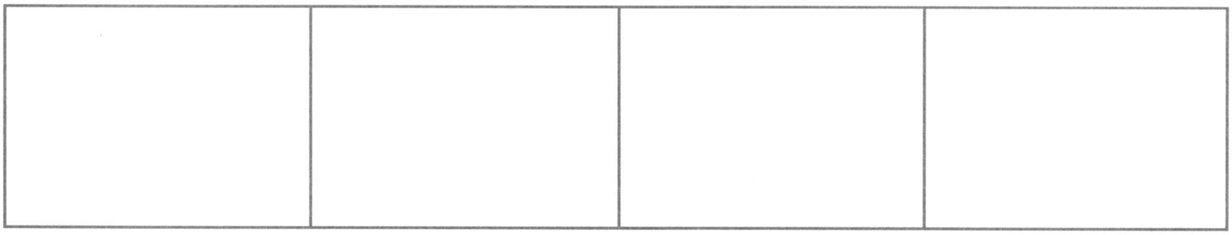

fourths

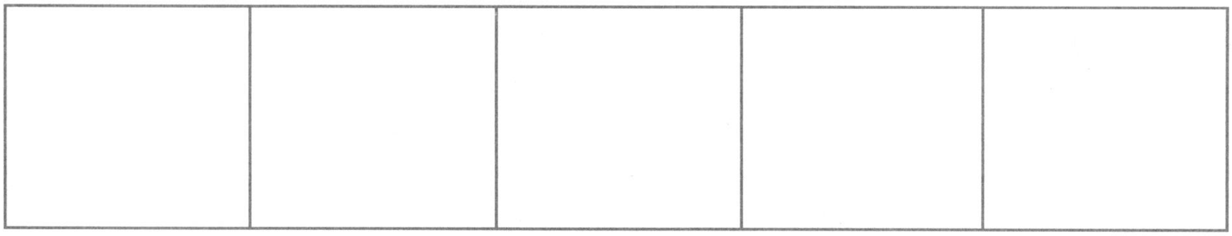

fifths

(Continued)

sixths

eighths

tenths

twelfths

Fraction Strips – Grade 3

One Whole

$\frac{1}{2}$	$\frac{1}{2}$

$\frac{1}{3}$	$\frac{1}{3}$	$\frac{1}{3}$

$\frac{1}{4}$	$\frac{1}{4}$	$\frac{1}{4}$	$\frac{1}{4}$

$\frac{1}{6}$	$\frac{1}{6}$	$\frac{1}{6}$	$\frac{1}{6}$	$\frac{1}{6}$	$\frac{1}{6}$

$\frac{1}{8}$	$\frac{1}{8}$	$\frac{1}{8}$	$\frac{1}{8}$	$\frac{1}{8}$	$\frac{1}{8}$	$\frac{1}{8}$	$\frac{1}{8}$

(Continued)

Fraction Strips – Grades 4 and 5

One Whole

$\dfrac{1}{2}$	$\dfrac{1}{2}$

$\dfrac{1}{3}$	$\dfrac{1}{3}$	$\dfrac{1}{3}$

$\dfrac{1}{4}$	$\dfrac{1}{4}$	$\dfrac{1}{4}$	$\dfrac{1}{4}$

$\dfrac{1}{6}$	$\dfrac{1}{6}$	$\dfrac{1}{6}$	$\dfrac{1}{6}$	$\dfrac{1}{6}$	$\dfrac{1}{6}$

$\dfrac{1}{8}$	$\dfrac{1}{8}$	$\dfrac{1}{8}$	$\dfrac{1}{8}$	$\dfrac{1}{8}$	$\dfrac{1}{8}$	$\dfrac{1}{8}$	$\dfrac{1}{8}$

$\dfrac{1}{10}$	$\dfrac{1}{10}$	$\dfrac{1}{10}$	$\dfrac{1}{10}$	$\dfrac{1}{10}$	$\dfrac{1}{10}$	$\dfrac{1}{10}$	$\dfrac{1}{10}$	$\dfrac{1}{10}$	$\dfrac{1}{10}$

$\dfrac{1}{12}$	$\dfrac{1}{12}$	$\dfrac{1}{12}$	$\dfrac{1}{12}$	$\dfrac{1}{12}$	$\dfrac{1}{12}$	$\dfrac{1}{12}$	$\dfrac{1}{12}$	$\dfrac{1}{12}$	$\dfrac{1}{12}$	$\dfrac{1}{12}$	$\dfrac{1}{12}$

Reproducible 8. Place Value Chart

ones	tenths	hundredths

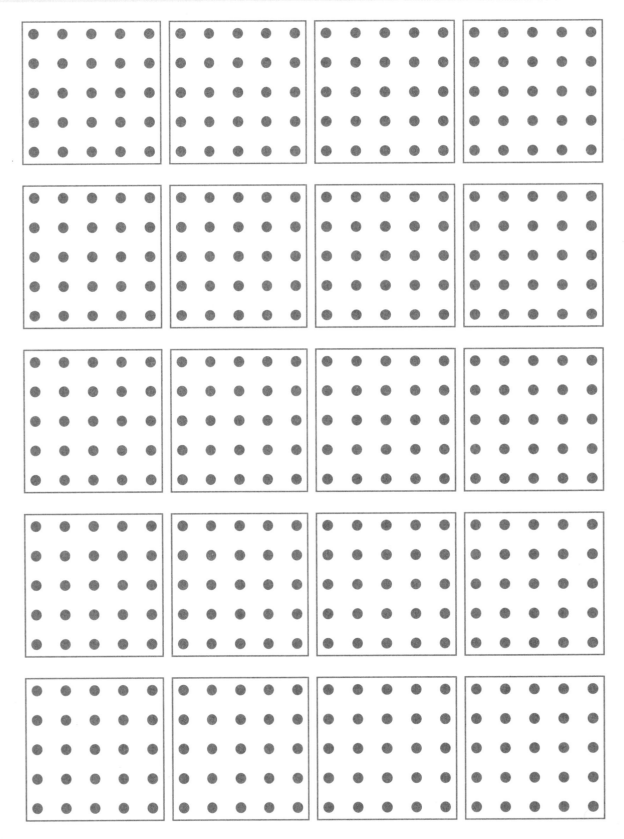

Reproducible 10. Dot Paper (Centimeter)

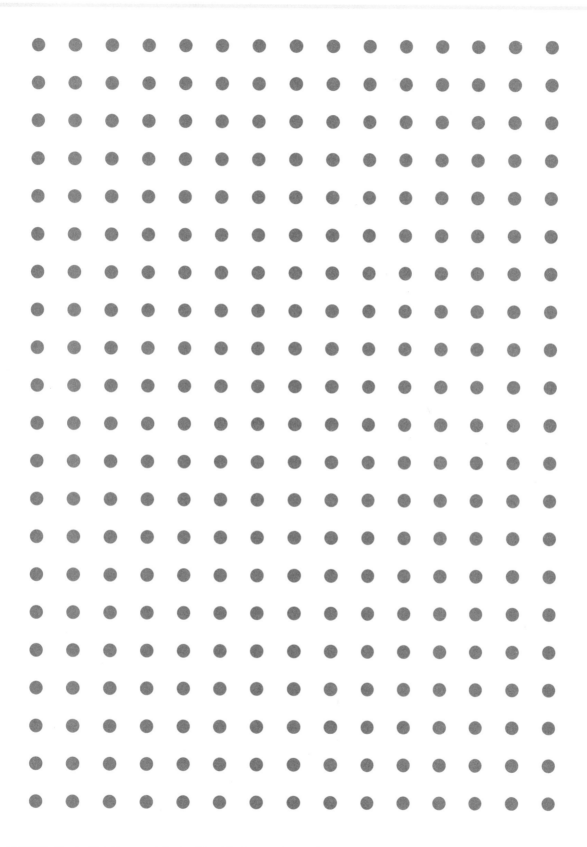

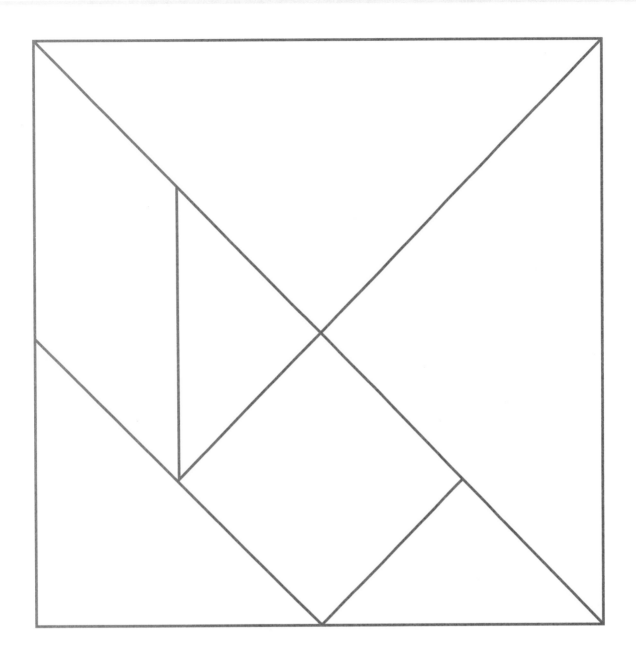

Additional Resources

Online

http://www.corestandards.org

A complete copy of the Common Core Standards and the Standards by grade level are available on this site. Other supporting resources, including background on the development of the Standards, videos, documents, FAQs, and much more.

http://ime.math.arizona.edu/progressions

The series of progressions documents written by leading researchers in the field summarizing the Standards progressions for specific CCSS domains.

http://illustrativemathematics.org

A variety of videos, tasks, and suggestions for professional development accessible to all teachers.

http://illuminations.nctm.org

A collection of high-quality tasks, lessons, and activities that align with the Common Core and include the Standards for Mathematical Practice.

http://www.pta.org/parents/content.cfm?ItemNumber=2583

The *Parents' Guides to Student Success* were developed by teachers, parents, and education experts in response to the Common Core Standards. Created for grades K–8, high school English language arts/literacy, and mathematics, the guides provide clear, consistent expectations for what students should be learning at each grade in order to be prepared for college and career.

http://www.achievethecore.org

Practical tools designed to help students and teachers see their hard work deliver results. *achievethecore.org* was created in the spirit of collaboration and includes planning materials, professional development resources, assessment information, and implementation support.

Books

Teaching Student-Centered Mathematics: Developmentally Appropriate Instruction for Grades 3–5; VadenWalle, Lovin, Karp, Bay-Williams (ISBN-13: 978-0132824873)

Putting Essential Understanding of Multiplication and Division into Practice in Grades 3–5; Lannin, Chval, Jones, Dougherty (ISBN 978-0-87353-715-5)

The Common Core Mathematics Standards: Transforming Practice Through Team Leadership; Balka, Harbin Miles, Hull (ISBN-13: 978-1452226224)

Implementing the Common Core State Standards Through Mathematical Problem Solving: Grades 3–5; Curcio, Foote, Ernest, Mukhopadhyay (ISBN 978-0-87353-724-7)

Uncomplicating Fractions to Meet Common Core Standards in Math, K–7; Marion Small (ISBN 978-0-80775-485-6)

About the Authors

Linda M. Gojak is the immediate past president of the National Council of Teachers of Mathematics. At Hawken School in Gates Mills, Ohio, Linda chaired the mathematics department and taught grades 4–8 mathematics. As the director of the Center for Mathematics and Science Education, Teaching, and Technology (CMSETT) at John Carroll University, she spent 16 years planning and facilitating professional development for K–12 mathematics teachers. Linda has been actively involved in professional organizations, including the Mathematical Sciences Education Board, the Conference Board of the Mathematical Sciences, the Council of Presidential Awardees in Mathematics, and the MathCounts Board of Directors. She has served as president of the National Council of Supervisors of Mathematics and president of the Ohio Council of Teachers of Mathematics. Among her recognitions are the Presidential Award for Excellence in Mathematics and Science Teaching and the Christofferson-Fawcett Award for lifetime contribution to mathematics education.

Ruth Harbin Miles coaches rural, suburban, and inner-city school mathematics teachers. Her professional experiences include coordinating the K–12 Mathematics Teaching and Learning Program for the Olathe, Kansas, public schools for more than 25 years; teaching mathematics methods courses at Virginia's Mary Baldwin College; and serving on the board of directors for the National Council of Teachers of Mathematics, the National Council of Supervisors of Mathematic, and both the Virginia Council of Teachers of Mathematics and the Kansas Association of Teachers of Mathematics. Ruth is a coauthor of five Corwin books, including *A Guide to Mathematics Coaching*, *A Guide to Mathematics Leadership*, *Visible Thinking in the K–8 Mathematics Classroom*, *The Common Core Mathematics Standards*, and *Realizing Rigor in the Mathematics Classroom*. As co-owner of Happy Mountain Learning, Ruth specializes in developing teachers' content knowledge and strategies for engaging students to achieve high standards in mathematics.

CORWIN

A SAGE Company

Helping educators make the greatest impact

CORWIN HAS ONE MISSION: to enhance education through intentional professional learning.

We build long-term relationships with our authors, educators, clients, and associations who partner with us to develop and continuously improve the best evidence-based practices that establish and support lifelong learning.

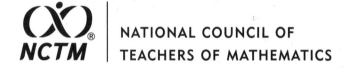

NATIONAL COUNCIL OF TEACHERS OF MATHEMATICS

The National Council of Teachers of Mathematics is the public voice of mathematics education, supporting teachers to ensure equitable mathematics learning of the highest quality for all students through vision, leadership, professional development, and research.